The Law Commission
Consultation Paper No 194

and

The Scottish Law Commission
Discussion Paper No 143

LEVEL CROSSINGS

A Joint Consultation Paper

ISBN: 9780118404914

Printed in the UK for The Stationery Office Limited
on behalf of the Controller of Her Majesty's Stationery Office

ID P002378640 07/10

Printed on paper containing 75% recycled fibre content minimum.

THE LAW COMMISSION AND THE SCOTTISH LAW COMMISSION – HOW WE CONSULT

About the Law Commissions

The Law Commission and the Scottish Law Commission were set up by section 1 of the Law Commissions Act 1965 for the purpose of promoting the reform of the law.

The Law Commissioners are: The Right Honourable Lord Justice Munby (*Chairman*), Professor Elizabeth Cooke, Mr David Hertzell, Professor Jeremy Horder and Frances Patterson QC.

The Chief Executive of the Law Commission is Mr Mark Ormerod CB and its offices are at Steel House, 11 Tothill Street, London SW1H 9LJ

The Scottish Law Commissioners are: The Honourable Lord Drummond Young (*Chairman*), Laura J Dunlop QC, Professor George L Gretton, Patrick Layden QC TD and Professor Hector L MacQueen.

The Chief Executive of the Scottish Law Commission is Malcolm McMillan and its offices are at 140 Causewayside, Edinburgh EH9 1PR.

Topic of this consultation

This consultation paper reviews the law relating to level crossings and makes proposals for its reform.

Scope of this consultation

The purpose of this consultation is to generate responses to our provisional proposals and consultation questions with a view to developing recommendations for reform of the law.

Geographical scope

The contents of this consultation paper refer to the law of England and Wales and the law of Scotland.

Impact assessment

An impact assessment is available to download from our websites: www.lawcom.gov.uk and www.scotlawcom.gov.uk

Duration of the consultation

We invite responses before 30 November 2010.

How to respond

Send your responses either –

By email to: levelcrossings@lawcommission.gsi.gov.uk

By post to: Sarah Young, Law Commission, Steel House, 11 Tothill Street, London SW1H 9LJ

Tel: 020 3334 0279 / Fax: 020 3334 0201

If you send your comments by post, it would be helpful if, whenever possible, you could send them to us electronically as well (for example, on CD or by email to the above address, in any commonly used format).

After the consultation

In the light of the responses we receive, we will decide our final recommendations and we will present them to Parliament.

Code of Practice

We are a signatory to the Government's Code of Practice on Consultation and carry out our consultations in accordance with the Code criteria (set out on the next page).

Freedom of information

We will treat all responses as public documents in accordance with the Freedom of Information Act 2000 and we may attribute comments and include a list of all respondents' names in any final report we publish. If you wish to submit a confidential response, you should contact us before sending the response. PLEASE NOTE – We will disregard automatic confidentiality statements generated by an IT system. Responses will also be shared with the Department for Transport and the Office of Rail Regulation.

Availability of this consultation paper

You can view/download it free of charge on our website at: **http://www.lawcom.gov.uk/docs/cp194.pdf**.

CODE OF PRACTICE ON CONSULTATION

○ **THE SEVEN CONSULTATION CRITERIA**

Criterion 1: **When to consult**

Formal consultation should take place at a stage when there is scope to influence the policy outcome.

Criterion 2: **Duration of consultation exercise**

Consultations should normally last for at least 12 weeks with consideration given to longer timescales where feasible and sensible

Criterion 3: **Clarity and scope of impact**

Consultation documents should be clear about the consultation process, what is being proposed, the scope to influence and the expected costs and benefits of the proposals.

Criterion 4: **Accessibility of consultation exercises**

Consultation exercises should be designed to be accessible to, and clearly targeted at, those people the exercise is intended to reach.

Criterion 5: **The burden of consultation**

Keeping the burden of consultation to a minimum is essential if consultations are to be effective and if consultees' buy-in to the process is to be obtained.

Criterion 6: **Responsiveness of consultation exercises**

Consultation responses should be analysed carefully and clear feedback should be provided to participants following the consultation.

Criterion 7: **Capacity to consult**

Officials running consultations should seek guidance in how to run an effective consultation exercise and share what they have learned from the experience.

○ **CONSULTATION CO-ORDINATOR**

The Law Commission's Consultation Co-ordinator is Phil Hodgson.

○ You are invited to send comments to the Consultation Co-ordinator about the extent to which the criteria have been observed and any ways of improving the consultation process.

○ **Contact:** Phil Hodgson, Consultation Co-ordinator, Law Commission, Steel House, 11 Tothill Street, London SW1H 9LJ – Email: phil.hodgson@lawcommission.gsi.gov.uk

Full details of the Government's Code of Practice on Consultation are available on the BIS website at http://www.bis.gov.uk/policies/better-regulation/consultation-guidance.

THE LAW COMMISSION

LEVEL CROSSINGS: CONSULTATION PAPER

CONTENTS

TABLE OF PHOTOGRAPHS

A number of photographs are included in this consultation paper, as set out below.

When properly used, a modern level crossing is very safe.

The automatic half-barrier level crossing (AHB) at Dilston near Corbridge on the Newcastle to Carlisle line: note the flashing lights and the car correctly stopped at the white "stop" line.

Photographer: Ian Britton.

PART 1
INTRODUCTION

1.1 A level crossing is a place where a railway is crossed by another type of way on the same level. There are between 7,500 and 8,000 level crossings in Great Britain.[1] Level crossings represent the largest single risk of catastrophic train accident on Britain's railways, albeit such accidents are rare.[2] In physical terms, a level crossing is a comparatively simple thing. Legally, it is much more complicated.

1.2 The legislation governing level crossings is complex and antiquated, much of it dating back to the nineteenth century when the main railways were constructed. The provisions relevant to level crossings are difficult to access. This arises partly because they are spread across legislation relating to a number of different subject areas – railways, highways/roads, health and safety, planning and criminal law. Furthermore, the provisions are contained in a combination of public general Acts, private Acts, bye-laws, and subordinate legislation in the form of Orders and Regulations, many of which have been amended heavily in recent years.[3] Some of the Acts have been partially repealed and some of their provisions have become spent or obsolete, causing confusion as to which provisions still apply and which are redundant. Many of the Acts of the Victorian era contain terminology that is no longer in use such as "turnpike roads" and "statute labour roads". Such terminology is unhelpful when trying to interpret the law in a modern context. There has been no attempt at consolidating the legislation in this area.

1.3 More specifically, under the current system, the procedure for making generic changes to the protective measures at level crossings is cumbersome and expensive, and the relationship between the various safety regulation systems is far from clear.[4] In addition, the procedures for closure of level crossings are complicated and time-consuming. There are economically-unhelpful procedural obstacles to the closure of crossings, and the allocation of costs involved in closing a crossing does not always reflect the respective benefits to the parties concerned.[5] Furthermore, although there exists a huge swathe of criminal offences relevant to level crossings, the existing criminal law has not, for the most

---

[1] This includes an estimated 1,000-1,500 level crossings on heritage railways. For details of the number of public and private level crossings on the mainline railway network, see below.

[2] See http://www.networkrail.co.uk/aspx/4817.aspx (last visited 27 June 2010). Please see Part 13 for detailed statistics on level crossing risk, fatalities and serious injuries.

[3] While public general Acts and subordinate legislation are available electronically, for example on legal databases, the private Acts relating to the railways are not currently available electronically. This raises issues in relation to accessibility. For example, a private Act of 1949 creates an offence of trespass on the railways and yet it is not readily available either in its original or amended form.

[4] This is considered in detail in Part 5.

[5] This is considered in detail in Part 7, particularly in relation to the economic model for level crossings: Alternatives to Level Crossings Assessment Tool or "AXIAT".

1

part, been explicitly designed to address misconduct at level crossings.[6]

1.4 This project examines the legal framework concerning level crossings with a view to its modernisation and simplification. The aim is to make recommendations which will reform the framework so that it is more coherent, accessible and up-to-date, allowing for better regulation and the reduction of risk.

1.5 This consultation paper has therefore been prepared with the following key aims in mind:

(1) establishment of an accessible legislative framework governing level crossings;

(2) clarification of the relationship between the legal regime relating specifically to level crossings and other legal regimes, in particular the general duties under the Health and Safety at Work etc Act 1974;

(3) maintenance of a workable system for the regulation of safety at level crossings;

(4) preservation of a proper balance between the interests of road and railway users;

(5) clarification of issues in relation to the nature of rights of access to private level crossings, and the creation and extinguishment of such rights;

(6) review of current arrangements for considering the potential impact of proposed developments on level crossings before planning decisions are reached;

(7) formulation of a comprehensive legal framework for closure and, where appropriate, replacement of level crossings, providing all interested parties with an adequate opportunity to put forward their views before a decision is reached;

(8) review of the existing criminal offences that can apply in relation to level crossings; and

(9) development of a legal framework for level crossings which would be adaptable to alternative institutional or regulatory structures relating to the railways.

BACKGROUND TO THE PROJECT

1.6 In response to the Law Commission's consultation on its Tenth Programme of Law Reform, the Department for Transport suggested a project to review the legislation relating to level crossings. The suggestion stemmed from concerns by the Office of Rail Regulation (ORR) as the railway safety and economic regulator that the legislation concerning level crossings was in need of review.

1.7 ORR's concerns were shared by others with an interest in level crossings. Before

---

[6] This is considered in detail in Part 13.

the Department for Transport put forward the suggestion to the Law Commission, ORR undertook a consultation exercise with key stakeholders, who strongly supported the proposal for a review of the legislation. Many considered that the legislation was unclear, outdated, difficult to access and hard to understand. The overwhelming view was that a review should seek to consolidate, simplify and modernise the existing legislation.

1.8   In the spring of 2008, the Law Commission and the Scottish Law Commission discussed the proposal and agreed that, for two reasons, any project on level crossings would need to be undertaken jointly by both Commissions. First, much of the legislation governing level crossings applies throughout Great Britain. Second, the mainline railway network serves Scotland as well as England and Wales. The Law Commission also discussed the scope of the project with the Northern Ireland Law Commission and it was agreed that the project should not extend to Northern Ireland but that the Northern Ireland Law Commission should be kept informed of progress. The Commissions agreed therefore that in terms of geographical scope the project should relate to England and Wales, and Scotland. Following these discussions, the Law Commission included a project on level crossings in its Tenth Programme of Law Reform on the basis that it would be undertaken jointly with the Scottish Law Commission.[7] It is also referred to in the Scottish Law Commission's Eighth Programme of Law Reform.[8]

1.9   Early in the project, the Commissions realised that the project teams would require assistance from industry-led stakeholders with expertise in relation to the regulation and operation of level crossings. With that in mind, an advisory group was established to assist the project teams. Initially the group comprised representatives of the Department for Transport and other government departments, bodies involved in the safety regulation of the railways, such as ORR, the Rail Safety and Standards Board (RSSB), and other groups with an interest in level crossings, including the Heritage Railway Association and the National Farmers' Union. An initial meeting was held in July 2008 to outline the scope of the project, discuss the main issues and invite assistance from members.

1.10   In January 2009, ORR hosted a seminar on level crossings to encourage discussion of the problems and how they might be resolved. Following the success of the seminar, the Commissions decided to expand the advisory group to include other interested bodies which had been represented at the seminar, such as the Ramblers Association and the Scottish Rights of Way and Access Society (Scotways) who are concerned about rights of way and access to the countryside.[9] A further meeting of the advisory group and a separate meeting with key stakeholders took place in December 2009 when we discussed possible proposals for reform.

---

[7]   Tenth Programme of Law Reform (2008) Law Com No 311. The Programme, which was published on 11 June 2008, outlines the Law Commission's main law reform projects covering the 3 years from 1 April 2008 until 1 April 2011.

[8]   Eighth Programme of Law Reform (2010) Scot Law Com No 220. The Programme outlines the Commission's main law reform projects covering the 5 years from January 2010 until the end of December 2014.

[9]   A list of members of the advisory group is available on our websites: www.lawcom.gov.uk and www.scotlawcom.gov.uk.

1.11 In addition, the teams have had meetings with ORR, the Department for Transport, Network Rail, RSSB, the Ramblers Association, Scottish Natural Heritage, Scotways and Transport Scotland, to discuss different aspects of the project. We are very grateful to our advisory group and key stakeholders. The feedback from these meetings has helped us to formulate the provisional proposals and questions for consultees set out in this consultation paper.

Responding to this consultation paper

1.12 In this paper we ask a number of questions and make a number of provisional proposals for reform of the law relating to level crossings. In doing so, we emphasise that the proposals represent our initial view about how the law might be reformed. We will be reviewing these proposals on the basis of the responses to this consultation paper. We welcome responses from all interested parties. Responses will be shared with the Department for Transport and ORR. Details of how to respond can be found on the inside front page of this consultation paper.

1.13 The next stage will be to produce and submit a report to the Lord Chancellor and also to the Scottish Ministers. Taking into account the responses we receive to this consultation paper, the report will contain our final recommendations with the reasons for them. A draft Bill, giving effect to our final recommendations, will also be included. At this point, an analysis of consultation responses will be published on our websites.[10]

HISTORICAL CONTEXT

Historical development: railways

1.14 The railways developed at a time of industrial growth when entrepreneurs benefited from investing in what was an increasingly popular mode of transport. The early railways were constructed and maintained by private companies, normally on the basis of Acts of Parliament known as "special Acts".[11] Although statutory powers were not (and are not) necessary in law to construct or operate a railway, and some railways were (and are) constructed and operated without statutory authority, statutory powers were usually obtained in order to confer on the railway the benefits of incorporation and limited liability, powers of compulsory purchase of land and immunity from liability for public nuisance. In addition, the special Acts would contain provisions imposing responsibilities on the company in relation to matters such as the fencing of the line and building and maintaining bridges and level crossings. Many special Acts were passed during the nineteenth century when railways were being established throughout the country.

1.15 The promotion of private legislation, including railway special Acts, became a major part of Parliamentary business.[12] In order to ease the burden on Parliament, a number of public Acts were passed in an attempt to regulate the

---

[10] www.lawcom.gov.uk and www.scotlawcom.gov.uk.

[11] An example of a special Act is available on our websites: www.lawcom.gov.uk and www.scotlawcom.gov.uk.

[12] According to the Chronological Table of Local Legislation (1996), vol 1, p vii, there were some 26,000 local Acts passed between 1797 and 1973, a time period that encompasses the vast majority of special Acts. We estimate that somewhere between a quarter and a third of all local legislation related to railways.

contents of private legislation. In relation to railways, such Acts were passed in the form of the Railways Clauses Consolidation Act 1845, Railways Clauses Consolidation (Scotland) Act 1845 and Railways Clauses Act 1863. The 1845 Acts provided model clauses which would automatically be deemed to be included in a special Act, unless the special Act expressly excluded or varied them. The 1863 Act worked the other way round – the model clauses could be expressly incorporated, but if the special Act was silent they were not included. It appears that after the 1845 Acts, the promoters of special Acts tended to include the clauses expressly, although that was strictly unnecessary. The clauses Acts, and in particular the 1845 Acts, are important in relation to the development of level crossings.

1.16   The nineteenth century also marked the beginning of public regulation of the railway network. A series of Acts, from the Railway Regulation Acts 1840 and 1842 to the Regulation of Railways Acts 1868, 1871, 1873 and 1889,[13] demonstrate the statutory development of railway regulation during the 1800s. The 1840 Act, for example, provided for the first railway inspectors (known as HM Railway Inspectorate - HMRI) who were responsible for overseeing safety on the railways.

1.17   During the First World War, the Government took temporary control of the railways. After the War, the Government thought it necessary to intervene in the organisation of the railway industry. This led to the passing of the Railways Act 1921 which reorganised the individual private railway companies into four companies (often referred to as the "Big Four"). During the Second World War, the Government again took temporary control of the railways. Following the War, the general election of 1945 brought to power a government committed to nationalisation, and in 1947 the Transport Act nationalised the railways. However, by 1960, concern was growing about the economic viability of the railways. The 1963 report by Dr R Beeching, *The Reshaping of British Railways,*[14] triggered the biggest changes to the railway network since its creation.[15] The report concluded that a large number of stations and railway lines should be closed in order to achieve a more efficient and financially viable railway network. Roads were to be provided as an alternative for many of the railway lines that were closed.

1.18   In the early 1990s, privatisation was seen as a way of tackling falling revenue and

[13]   All of the Regulation of Railways Act 1871 has been repealed, as have most of the 1873 and 1889 Acts. The 1889 Act is an interesting example of how speedy law reform could be in the high Victorian era. It was the response to a catastrophic accident which occurred at Armagh on 12 June 1889 causing unprecedented loss of life. Six days later, on 18 June 1889, the President of the Board of Trade told the House of Commons that if the Inspector's Report on the accident came to a certain conclusion he would introduce legislation (*Hansard*, (HC), 18 June 1889, vol 337, col 119). The Inspector, Maj-Gen C S Hutchinson, in his report on the accident dated 8 July 1889 did indeed come to that conclusion. The Bill was introduced into the House of Commons and given its first reading on 30 July 1889 (*Hansard* (HC), 30 July 1889, vol 338, col 1792) and a second reading on 2 August 1889 (*Hansard* (HC), 2 August 1889, vol 339, col 229). It had passed all its Parliamentary stages by 28 August 1889 (*Hansard* (HC), 28 August 1889, vol 340, col 818) and received Royal Assent on 30 August 1889.

[14]   British Railways Board, *The Reshaping of British Railways, Part 1 Report* (1963). Available at: http://www.railwaysarchive.co.uk/documents/BRB_Beech001a.pdf (last visited 27 June 2010).

[15]   Christian Wolmar, *Fire and Steam – How the Railways Transformed Britain* (2008) p 283.

making the railways more efficient and competitive.[16] However, the mechanics of privatisation were inevitably difficult. It was seen as undesirable simply to privatise the existing railways as a single private sector monopoly. Rejecting the creation of integrated regional railway companies, the Government opted to separate ownership of the track and stations from the running of train services.

1.19   As regards regulation of the railways, the Railways Act 1993 established the Rail Regulator with powers of enforcement and investigation but not *safety* regulation. Subsequently the Transport Act 2000 set up another body - the Strategic Rail Authority (SRA) - primarily to promote the use of the railways.

1.20   On 1 April 1994, a single company, Railtrack plc, took over the management of the national railway infrastructure (track, signalling, stations, tunnels, bridges, level crossings, depots and certain other assets) from the British Railways Board.[17] Train operating companies (TOCS) and freight operating companies (FOCS) took over running the services.

1.21   However, in October 2001 the Government placed Railtrack plc into railway administration.[18] In October 2002, the share capital of Railtrack plc was acquired by a new company, Network Rail Holdco Ltd – a wholly-owned subsidiary of Network Rail Limited. Railtrack plc was later renamed Network Rail Infrastructure Limited and was registered as a private company. Network Rail Infrastructure Limited became responsible for the management of the mainline railway infrastructure. However, Network Rail Infrastructure Limited is not responsible for the entire railway network; some parts of it are owned by heritage railway companies and commercial organisations.

1.22   Following a series of fatal rail accidents at Ladbroke Grove, Hatfield, Potters Bar and Southall, the Government introduced a number of reforms to the system for regulating the railways and several new railway bodies were created. The Railway and Transport Safety Act 2003 established the Rail Accident Investigation Branch (RAIB),[19] and abolished the role of Rail Regulator, transferring its functions to the newly established Office of Rail Regulation (ORR).[20] The Railways Act 2005 also transferred certain functions to ORR, the

---

[16]   The privatisation of the railways came at a late stage in the programme of de-nationalisation implemented by successive governments from 1979: the Department of Transport's White Paper, New Opportunities for the Railways: The Privatisation of British Rail, was published in 1992 - (1992) Cm 2012.

[17]   The British Railways Board was established by the Transport Act 1962. By the end of 1997 it had been divested of all its functions relating to railway operation. The remaining functions of the British Railways Board are now discharged by BRB (Residuary) Ltd.

[18]   Railway administration is a special form of insolvency designed for use by railway companies. It was created by the Railways Act 1993 and the new procedure was used for the first time when Railtrack plc was placed into administration. The purpose of railway administration is to allow for the continuation of the operations of the railway network pending its transfer to a new entity.

[19]   Railway and Transport Safety Act 2003, s 3.

[20]   Railway and Transport Safety Act 2003, s 16.

Department for Transport and Scottish Ministers.[21] Although the functions initially transferred to ORR did not include the regulation of railway safety, the Department for Transport proposed the transfer of responsibility for railway safety (including level crossings) from the Health and Safety Commission/Health and Safety Executive (HSC/HSE) to ORR.[22] This recommendation was implemented by the 2005 Act,[23] read together with the Health and Safety (Enforcing Authority for Railways and Other Guided Transport Systems) Regulations 2006[24] and the Memorandum of Understanding between the HSE and ORR.[25]

1.23   A consequence of transferring the HSC/HSE's railway safety functions to ORR was that HM Railway Inspectorate (HMRI) was also transferred from the HSE to ORR. In May 2009, the body known as "HM Railway Inspectorate" ceased to exist when a new Railway Safety Directorate was created within ORR. HMRI now forms part of that Directorate, although the individual inspectors are known as HM Inspectors of Railways.[26]

1.24   Accordingly, under the current arrangements the various responsibilities for railway safety and investigation of accidents are divided between ORR, including the Railway Safety Directorate which is part of ORR, and the RAIB.[27] A detailed explanation of the roles and responsibilities of these bodies is provided in the glossary in Appendix C. The current regime regulating health and safety at level crossings is described further in Part 5.

Historical development: level crossings

1.25   From the early days of the railways, gates and gatekeepers provided a means of protection at public level crossings. By the end of the 1830s it was clear that general rules were needed to bring about standardisation in relation to safety and to speed up the process of private legislation for individual railway lines. The Highway Act 1835 introduced safety requirements where railways crossed "public carriage roads" on the level. The Highway (Railway Crossings) Act 1839 extended the requirements of the 1835 Act so as to include turnpike roads and also highways in Scotland. The 1835 Act was the first Act to regulate level crossings. It required that gates be provided and "good and proper persons" to operate them. Section 1 of the 1839 Act provided for gates across turnpike roads and gatekeepers to open and shut them. The 1839 Act also gave rise to the

---

[21]   The Railways Act 2005, s 1 and sch 1 transferred the Strategic Rail Authority's consumer protection functions to ORR, while its strategic and financial functions were passed to the Department for Transport and Scottish Ministers. The 2005 Act, s 5 also transferred certain functions to Scottish Ministers in relation to railways in Scotland.

[22]   Department for Transport, The Future of Rail (2004) Cm 6233.

[23]   Railways Act 2005, s 2 and sch 3.

[24]   The Health and Safety (Enforcing Authority for Railways and Other Guided Transport Systems) Regulations 2006, SI 2006 No 557.

[25]   Available at: http://www.hse.gov.uk/aboutus/howwework/framework/mou/orrmou.pdf (last visited 27 June 2010).

[26]   Inspectors are referred to formally as HM Inspectors of Railways as stated in their warrants. Corporately, they are now referred to as ORR inspectors within the Railway Safety Directorate.

[27]   The Railways (Accident Investigation and Reporting) Regulations 2005, SI 2005 No 1992, sets out the roles and responsibilities of the RAIB and ORR.

question of the relative priority of road and rail traffic at level crossings. Many of the special Acts provided that gates should be kept shut across the railway.[28] However, as trains became faster and more frequent, the practice of closing the gates across the railway line was found to cause delays. The problem was remedied by the Railway Regulation Act 1842 which provided for gates to be kept closed across roads instead of across the railway.

A traditional level crossing on a heritage railway: Blue Anchor station on the West Somerset Railway.

Photographer: Adrian Copley. This work is licensed under a Creative Commons Licence: http://creativecommons.org/licenses/by-nc/3.0/.

1.26 By the start of the twentieth century, the railway network was more or less complete and the number of level crossings in existence was sufficient to accommodate the amount of road traffic. However, by the early 1950s there was an increasing awareness of the need to modernise the system of gated level crossings. It had become clear that safety was no longer the only consideration. The cost of employing gatekeepers had risen dramatically and it was proving difficult to find reliable people to be gatekeepers. Moreover, the operation of gated level crossings often led to substantial delays for road users. The Ministry of Transport concluded that the solution lay in taking advantage of modern technological developments.[29]

1.27 The British Transport Commission Act 1957 provided the necessary legislative basis for automatic lifting barriers without attendants. Section 66(2) of the 1957

---

[28] Stanley Hall and Peter van der Mark, *Level Crossings* (2008) p 7.

[29] *Level Crossing Protection – A report by officers of the Ministry of Transport and Civil Aviation and of the British Transport Commission* (1957) (the "McMullen Report") appendix 1. Available at: http://www.railwaysarchive.co.uk/documents/MoT_LevelCrossing1957.pdf (last visited 27 June 2010).

Act[30] provided that an order could require the Commission to provide:

> …such barriers, lights, traffic signs and automatic or other devices and appliances and may lay down such other conditions and requirements to be observed by the Commission in relation to such level crossing and the use and operation thereof as shall in the opinion of the Minister be necessary or desirable for the protection safety and convenience of the public…

1.28 The 1957 Act thus sought to promote the interests of both safety *and* convenience in relation to level crossings. Section 124 of the Transport Act 1968[31] and later the Level Crossings Act 1983 recognised these complimentary interests. This balance between safety on the one hand and convenience on the other is something which we aim to replicate in our proposals for reform.

1.29 There followed a modernisation plan during the 1960s and 1970s which resulted in changes to many crossings. Traditional wooden gates were replaced by full-width, lightweight metal barriers, initially controlled from signal boxes, but more recently, remotely operated with CCTV. Automatic half-barriers (AHBs) were installed at some level crossings,[32] and locally monitored automatic open crossings (AOCLs)[33] and remotely monitored automatic open crossings (AOCRs)[34] were also introduced. At the same time, many railway lines were closed. The overall result was a reduction in the number of level crossings and the modernisation of many of those which remained.[35]

1.30 The introduction of AHBs in the early 1960s, and subsequently of AOCLs and AOCRs, "represented a major shift in the philosophy of railway safety".[36] The nineteenth century safety regime for level crossings, with its requirement that the railway provide both gates and gatekeepers, meant that control of level crossings over public roads was vested exclusively in the railway operator. Safety at level crossings over public roads was therefore the sole responsibility of the railway operator, and was thus subject to high standards which were monitored and regulated by the Railway Inspectorate. Moreover, level crossings were often integrated with the railway signalling system. At the same time, the railway's operational and safety requirements were given priority. The effect of this was that, although level crossings on public roads were very safe, their operation

---

[30] Section 66 of the 1957 Act was repealed by the Level Crossings Regulations 1997, SI 1997 No 487, reg 2.

[31] Section 124 of the Transport Act 1968 gave the Minister of Transport power to make an order to require the British Railways Board to provide, maintain and operate "…such lifting or other barriers, lights, signs or other devices or appliances" at any level crossing across any road other than a public carriage road as the Minister considered "necessary or desirable for the protection and convenience of the public".

[32] See page x, after the Table of Photographs at the start of this consultation paper, for a photograph of an automatic half barrier crossing.

[33] See pages 22 and 25 for photographs of locally monitored automatic open crossings.

[34] See page 15 for a photograph of a remotely monitored automatic open crossing.

[35] *First Report of the Working Party to the National Level Crossings Safety Group* (September 2006) p 3. Thus in 1953 there were 4,505 level crossings on public roads, but by 1967 there were 2,425, and by 1979 there were 1,960.

[36] Stanley Hall and Peter van der Mark, *Level Crossings* (2008) p 35.

often led to substantial delays for road users. However, the introduction of AHBs, AOCLs and AOCRs meant that the operational and safety requirements of the railway ceased to have priority, regard now being had to cost and, as the 1957 and 1968 Acts made clear, also to the "convenience" of road users. Furthermore, the technical changes brought about by the automation of level crossings shifted more responsibility onto the road user for avoiding collisions.[37]

1.31 The situation was very different for level crossings over *private* roads, footpaths or bridleways. Here, the gates were neither manned nor integrated with the railway signalling system. Unless an order under section 124 of the Transport Act 1968 Act had been made, responsibility for ensuring that it was safe to cross rested with the road, footpath or bridleway user. The only safety devices at private level crossings, apart from an unlocked gate, were warning signs on the road or path and whistle boards on the railway reminding train drivers to sound the train's whistle (or nowadays blow the horn) when approaching the crossing.

The modern regulatory regime

1.32 Prior to the Health and Safety at Work etc Act 1974 (HSWA 1974), which makes general provision relating to safety in the workplace, safety provision for the railways including track and level crossings was governed primarily by railway-specific provisions.[38]

1.33 HSWA 1974 introduced a new general system to protect health and safety, both of workers and others affected by undertakings. The Act combined a set of general duties with a power to make detailed regulations for specific industries. A set of pre-existing industry-specific Acts and regulations were also brought into the system of enforcement introduced by the Act. The intention was that these provisions would be progressively replaced by regulations under the Act.

1.34 While the general duties under HSWA 1974 applied to railway employers, the railway specific legislation, unlike that governing other industries, was not initially caught by the Act's enforcement regime. This meant that legislation like the Highway (Railway Crossings) Act 1839, the Railway Regulation Act 1842 and the Regulation of Railways Act 1868 remained outside the scope of HSWA 1974 and operated in parallel with it. This changed following the coming into force of section 117 of the Railways Act 1993, when these provisions were deemed to be part of the 1974 Act system for enforcement purposes.

1.35 As a result of section 117 of the 1993 Act, the HSC/HSE had jurisdiction over the monitoring and enforcement of railway-specific safety legislation under the 1974 Act. In addition to the Acts mentioned above, this included orders under section 66 of the British Transport Commission Act 1957, section 124 of the Transport

---

[37] For example, AHBs, AOCLs and AOCRs are not integrated or interlocked with the railway signalling system and are operated automatically by the passing train. There is therefore nothing to prevent a train running under "clear" signals and colliding with a vehicle which is on the level crossing, something which was impossible on a traditional level crossing where the gates were interlocked with the signalling.

[38] For example, the Highway (Railway Crossings) Act 1839 and the Regulation of Railways Acts 1868, 1871, 1873 and 1889.

Act 1968[39] and section 1 of the Level Crossings Act 1983.

1.36   The Level Crossings Act 1983 introduced specific provision which enabled the Secretary of State to make orders ("level crossings orders") specifying new or updated protective arrangements at individual, mainly public, level crossings. As a result of section 117 of the Railways Act 1993, individual level crossing orders under the 1983 Act became directly enforceable by HSC/HSE, though their powers were devolved to HM Railway Inspectorate (now the Railway Safety Directorate of ORR).

1.37   The Transport and Works Act 1992[40] introduced provisions governing the use and protection of private level crossings, namely those crossing roads to which the public does not, as a matter of fact, have access. The Secretary of State was given the power under section 52 of the Act to make Regulations concerning the type of traffic signs to be used at such crossings, as the type of signs was not covered by road traffic legislation. This power was exercised in the Private Crossings (Signs and Barriers) Regulations 1996[41] which specify the signs to be used at private level crossings.

The manually controlled (full) barrier level crossing (MCB) operated by the signalman in the adjacent signal box at Foxton station on the Hitchin to Cambridge line: note the flashing lights.
Credit: Rail Accident Investigation Branch.

---

[39]   Section 124 of the Transport Act 1968 was repealed by the Transport and Works Act 1992 (as regards England and Wales) and by the Level Crossings Regulations 1997, SI 1997 No 487, as regards Scotland.

[40]   Part 1 of the 1992 Act (which introduced the order-making procedure for authorising railway works) in effect applies to England and Wales only. However, most of the remaining provisions of the 1992 Act, including those relating to private crossings, apply to Scotland as well as to England and Wales.

[41]   The Private Crossings (Signs and Barriers) Regulations 2006, SI 1996 No 1786.

SCOPE OF THE PROJECT

1.38 This section first considers what a railway is and explains the definition we have chosen to use in this consultation paper. Then we consider the definition of a level crossing and the various ways in which level crossings can be classified.

What is a railway?

1.39 There are several legal definitions of railway. The definition that comes closest to a general one is that to be found in section 67(1) of the Transport and Works Act 1992 and (in identical terms) in section 23 of the Transport and Works (Scotland) Act 2007:

> "Railway" means a system of transport employing parallel rails which—
>
> (a) provide support and guidance for vehicles carried on flanged wheels; and
>
> (b) form a track which is either of a gauge of at least 350 millimetres or crosses a carriageway (whether or not on the same level),
>
> but does not include a tramway.

This definition includes those railways sometimes described as "light railways".[42]

1.40 The definition of "railway" in the 1992 and 2007 Acts excludes tramways. "Tramway" is defined in section 67(1) of the 1992 Act and section 23 of the 2007 Act,[43] the essential element in the definition for present purposes being that a tramway is something "laid mainly or wholly along a street or in any other place to which the public has access".

1.41 We are inclined to think, however, that these merely *legal* definitions should not be determinative in the context of a project relating to level crossings and that what is more important is the *physical* or *functional* aspect of a railway. There are, after all, what most people would think of as railways in the popular sense of the word which run along the public highway.[44] And many modern metro, tramway and light railway systems have two types of tracks:[45]

---

[42] There does not appear to be a statutory definition of the term "light railway"; there is no such definition in the Light Railways Act 1896 as amended by the Light Railways Act 1912. Some guidance as to the typical characteristics of such a railway can, however, be found in section 28 of the Regulation of Railways Act 1868. This imposed certain restrictions as to speed and weight that were to be taken to apply in order that a railway be classed as "light". In simple terms a light railway may be said to mean a railway which operates with lighter equipment and in most cases lower speeds than other types of railway. There may therefore be some overlap between light railways and tramways. The 1896 Act has been repealed as regards England and Wales and now applies to Scotland only. However, section 22 of the Transport and Works (Scotland) Act 2007 provides that no further orders can be made by Scottish Ministers under the Light Railways Act 1896.

[43] A similar definition is used in the Health and Safety (Enforcing Authority for Railways and Other Guided Transport Systems) Regulations 2006, SI 2006 No 557.

[44] Examples are the Weymouth Harbour branch (still in place though currently not used) and the new Welsh Highland Railway extension through the streets of Porthmadog.

[45] For example, in Croydon.

(1)   those tracks, often in central areas, which run alongside other traffic on roads to which the public has access; and

(2)   those tracks, often in more outlying areas, which are segregated from the road, running separately from any other traffic and sometimes alongside railway lines.

1.42   In England and Wales, the former are referred to as "street tramways" and the latter as "tramroads".[46] These terms do not appear to be used in Scotland, although in practice such categories of tramway exist.

1.43   We tend to the view that, for the purposes of this project, the important distinction is not between "railways", "light railways", "tramways" or "tramroads" but between those systems (or parts of systems) where the tracks are segregated from the public and other traffic and those systems (or parts of systems) where the tracks run alongside other traffic on roads to which the public has access. We propose therefore that only the former should fall within the scope of the project and that the latter should not. We also limit "railways" in this project to those where the gauge is over the statutory minimum of 350mm (approximately 13 ¾").

1.44   **We would welcome the views of consultees on whether, for the purposes of our proposals, "railway" should be defined as a transport system where the tracks are segregated from other traffic.**

1.45   There are of course tramways or parts of tramways (such as in Croydon and the proposed Edinburgh system) where the tracks run along a road to which the public has access which is itself crossed by another road to which the public has access. On our approach, such systems will not fall within the scope of this project. We suggest there is good reason why they should not, for such intersections are not at present regulated by the kind of barriers and lights one finds at level crossings but (if at all) by ordinary traffic lights.

A taxonomy of railways

1.46   Thus defined, railways can be categorised in various ways in their physical or functional aspects. For present purposes it is relevant to bear in mind that:

(1)   the railway may be standard gauge (4'8½" or 1,435 mm) or narrow gauge (for example, 15" or 381mm, 1'11⅝" or 600 mm, or 2'5⅞" or 760 mm);

(2)   the railway may be single track, double track, quadruple track or occasionally even more;

(3)   the railway line may carry only a sporadic and infrequent freight service, a service of no more than three or four trains a day each way, or a frequent service of three, four, or more trains an hour each way; and

---

[46]   Transport and Works (Model Clauses for Railways and Tramways) Order 2006, sch 2, part 1, SI 2006 No 1954. This Order was made under the Transport and Works Act 1992 and applies in England and Wales only.

(4)   the railway may be part of the national rail network operated by Network Rail, or part of the Transport for London network (formerly London Underground), or part of a Metro tramway or light railway system, or a private industrial, dock or military system,[47] or a privately owned "heritage railway"[48] open to the public, or even a privately owned "hobby" railway which is not open to the public.

What is a level crossing?

1.47   A level crossing is a place where a railway (as we have defined that term) is crossed by another type of way on the same level. We exclude from the scope of this project crossings on the level, sometimes called flat crossings, where a railway is crossed by another railway on the level.[49] Such crossings are functionally entirely different from level crossings, being under the exclusive control of the railways involved and protected by the ordinary railway signalling systems.

A taxonomy of level crossings

1.48   There are several ways in which level crossings can be classified. For present purposes it is relevant to consider them first by reference to their physical features, then by reference to users of level crossings, and then by reference to the legal nature of level crossings.

Physical features

1.49   At one extreme, a level crossing may be no more than a footpath or bridleway crossing a railway, existing as a line on a map with no physical manifestation of any sort between the gates or stiles that separate the railway from the adjoining land and where the pedestrian or rider has to walk across the ballast. At the other extreme, a level crossing may be a full-width macadamised road crossing the railway. There are many variants in between, varying as to both the width of the "way" and the materials from which it is constructed. The level crossing may or may not be protected by gates or barriers or by warning signs, lights or bells.

---

[47] For example, the Bicester Military Railway.

[48] "Heritage" railways preserve traditional operating and signalling systems. For such railways, the preservation and operation of traditional level crossings is therefore important.

[49] For example, the flat crossing at Newark where the Nottingham to Lincoln line crosses the East Coast Main Line and the new flat crossing at Porthmadog where the narrow gauge Welsh Highland Railway crosses the standard gauge Cambrian line.

The level crossing in a busy urban setting: the manually controlled (full) barrier level crossing operated remotely by a signalman and monitored by CCTV (MCB-CCTV) at Lincoln High Street.

Photographer: Chris McKenna.

1.50   Within the rail industry, crossings are categorised according to whether or not they have equipment to protect users. Crossings can be categorised as "active" or "passive". "Active" crossings (also called "protected") are those at which the user is given warning of the approach of a train by equipment provided at the crossing. This type of crossing can be full-barrier, half-barrier, without any barriers, automatic or manual, with local or remote control.

1.51   "Passive" crossings are those at which generally there is no warning of an approaching train and the user must determine if it is safe to cross. However, in some cases whistle boards are installed near crossings requiring train drivers to sound the horn or blow the whistle to warn pedestrians and others of an approaching train. Passive crossings may be open crossings (with no road traffic signs and no barriers or gates) or user-worked crossings or footpath and bridleway crossings where the user has to be satisfied that it is safe to cross. User-worked and pedestrian or bridleway crossings usually have gates (originally installed to prevent access by animals to the track). At some passive crossings telephones may be provided to enable the user to seek permission from the railway operator before using the crossing.

1.52   In 2009, there were 3,950 public level crossings in use on the mainline network, comprising 1,747 on public vehicular roads, 2,073 on public footpaths, and 130 on public bridleways. 2,114 public level crossings had special protection measures, such as whistle boards and miniature warning lights, to indicate that a train was approaching; 1836 crossings had no special protection.

1.53   There were 2,642 private level crossings in use on the mainline network in 2009,

15

of which 2,383 were on private vehicular roads, 248 were on private footpaths, and 11 were on private bridleways. 228 private level crossings had special protection measures and 2,414 had no special protection.[50]

1.54 A total of 71 level crossings, both public and private, were closed in 2009.

Users of level crossings

1.55 By definition, the users of every level crossing fall into two classes: those using the railway and those using the non-railway way.

1.56 In general it is motorists and pedestrians, rather than train crew and passengers, who are most likely to be killed or physically injured as a result of a collision at a level crossing. But a train derailment or a collision between a train and an unusually heavy vehicle[51] can result in multiple fatalities to a train's passengers and crew.

1.57 It also needs to be borne in mind that the drivers of modern trains, placed in driving cabs at the front, are particularly vulnerable. A number of train drivers have been killed in collisions at level crossings even where there were no passenger fatalities. Furthermore, train drivers and others can suffer serious psychological or psychiatric injury after witnessing an accident at a level crossing.

1.58 So far as users of the non-railway way are concerned, it is important to bear in mind that there are many types of user and that the different types of level crossing may in the nature of things need to accommodate different types of use. Thus it is necessary to distinguish between the different needs of, for example, motorists, pedestrians, cyclists, horse-riders, those with animals (which may be a pet dog or a herd of cattle), those with large or unusual vehicles or loads, and those with smaller equipment (for instance, push-chairs, shopping trolleys, mobility equipment).

1.59 It is also important to bear in mind the needs of disabled people and those with special or unusual mobility difficulties, for example, elderly people (who may move more slowly than younger people or who may have physical difficulties in using steps or an un-metalled crossing) or those whose vision or hearing is impaired. We discuss disability and accessibility in Part 3.

Legal rights

1.60 More central for the purposes of this project is the system of classification based upon the legal nature of the crossing. Distinctions can be drawn between those crossings over which there is a public right of way, those over which there is a private right of way and those over which there is no right of way at all.

---

[50] Network Rail's level crossings census (2009). These figures do not include heritage railways. The total number of level crossings is estimated in paragraph 1.1 above at 7,500-8,000 to include an estimated 1,000-1,500 level crossings on heritage railways.

[51] As at Hixon in January 1968.

"The largest single risk of catastrophic train accident on Britain's railways" – the aftermath of the collision in 1968 between an express train and a heavy road vehicle on the automatic half-barrier level crossing (AHB) at Hixon in Staffordshire.

Credit: Mirrorpix.

PUBLIC LEVEL CROSSINGS

1.61   These occur where the railway is crossed on the level by a way over which a public right of way or public right of passage exists. The right may be a right to pass on foot (a footpath), a right to pass on horseback (a bridleway) or a right to pass with vehicles.

PRIVATE LEVEL CROSSINGS

1.62   Level crossings over which there are private rights of way are customarily categorised as being either "accommodation" or "occupation" crossings.

1.63   Accommodation crossings came into existence where the building of the railway bisected a piece of land in single ownership. This made access to each parcel of land a problem for the landowner. The railway company established by the special Act authorising the construction of the railway was required by statute to create sufficient crossings to enable an owner or occupier of land – often a farmer and/or his or her tenants – to access the land on either side of the railway line.[52]

1.64   As regards occupation crossings, though the meaning here is more obscure, it can be said that such a crossing is one over an occupation road. However, that does not help a great deal, for although the term "occupation road" appears in early statutes in relation to England and Wales, it is not a legal term of art and the term appears altogether absent from Scottish use. Perhaps the best one can say is that an occupation crossing occurred where the railway crossed a private road or way which served a farm, hamlet or village. We think that normally the private road or way would have a pre-existing right of way over it. However, it may be that a crossing could properly be described as an occupation crossing where there had been, before the railway bisected the road or way, no right of way separate from the owner's interest. There would, of course, be a right of way of some sort across the crossing in this situation, once the railway was built.

1.65   Some of these "accommodation" and "occupation" rights can be seen as implied solely from operation of the special Act which may have incorporated the relevant model clauses. We think that such rights are best described as "statutory rights of way" and therefore such level crossings should be categorised as "statutory rights of way crossings". These rights of way were not created by the special Acts as public rights of way but were intended for the use of the adjacent landowner. However, we discuss in Parts 11 and 12 whether such rights may become public rights of way by operation of the law of prescription.

1.66   In other cases there was a new easement or servitude, reserved in the conveyance of the land to the railway company at the time of construction of the railway. In the first case, where the easement or servitude was a new one, it might have been created as a result of the need to accommodate the landowner under the special Act, but nevertheless its legal effect relied on the fact that it was reserved as an easement or servitude. Therefore, although created for

---

[52]   The obligation to provide a crossing was imposed by the Railways Clauses Consolidation Act 1845, s 68 or in relation to Scotland, the Railways Clauses Consolidation (Scotland) Act 1845, s 60, insofar as these provisions had not been excluded or varied by the relevant special Act.

accommodation purposes, it is *not* merely a statutory right of way. Alternatively, a crossing might have been created as a result of the fact that there was a pre-existing private right of way before the construction of the railway. In this case, the crossing was necessary to *preserve* the pre-existing right. In both cases the right of way across the railway should be considered an easement or servitude right of way. We therefore suggest that such crossings should be termed "easement or servitude crossings".

1.67 It seems more appropriate, therefore, to use a taxonomy for private level crossings based on the legal nature of the right of way across the railway, if such a right of way exists. We therefore classify private level crossings according to the rights which exist over them, as follows:

(1) those crossings over which there is a statutory right of way ("statutory rights of way crossings"); and

(2) those crossings over which there is an easement or servitude ("easement or servitude crossings").

1.68 Under this taxonomy both categories can be seen as *accommodating* those whose land or private rights of way have been interfered with as a result of the creation of the railway.

1.69 Consequently, though frequently used in railway literature, the terms "accommodation crossing" and "occupation crossing" do not seem helpful in classifying level crossings. Accommodation crossings might be either statutory rights of way crossings or easement or servitude crossings, so the term is not useful as a legal category. We suggest that "occupation crossing" is both insufficiently precise to stand as a legal category and in any event is subsumed in easement or servitude crossings.

1.70 As we mention above, the Level Crossings Act 1983 introduced a power to make orders for the protection of individual, mainly public level crossings. However, in relation to England and Wales, the 1983 Act applies rather differently than in Scotland. As a result of the definition of "road" in section 1(11), the 1983 Act applies to level crossings in England and Wales to which the public has legitimate access as a matter of fact. We are concerned with such crossings in this project. However, the definition of "road" in relation to Scotland is narrower and as a result the 1983 Act does not apply in the same way. This is considered in more detail in Part 5.

LEVEL CROSSINGS AT WHICH DIFFERENT RIGHTS OF WAY CO-EXIST OR EXIST IN CLOSE PROXIMITY

1.71 In many instances two different types of crossing co-exist at the same place, for example, where there is a private road and an adjacent public footpath which are crossed by the railway line. These are treated in law as two separate crossings, one private and the other public. There may also be a situation in which a single way crossed by a railway is simultaneously public and private. For example, a railway may be crossed on the level by a way over which the public has a right of way on foot only, though the local farmer may have a vehicular right over the same way entitling him to cross by foot or, for example, by tractor.

1.72   It follows from the fact that in such cases there are two separate legal rights that the public right could be extinguished whilst the private right remained; conversely, the private right could be extinguished whilst the public right remained. This would apply regardless of whether the scope of the public and private rights was different, as in the above example, or whether they were identical. It is possible for a public right of passage on foot and a private right of passage on foot to co-exist. In such a case, either could be extinguished whilst the other remained intact.

1.73   Similarly, in relation to private level crossings, there could be circumstances in which both an easement or servitude and a statutory right of way co-exist over the same crossing. For example, if there was an express grant of an easement or servitude over a pre-existing statutory right of way, or if an easement or servitude has arisen by prescription.

1.74   We consider these issues in more detail in Parts 11 and 12.

LEVEL CROSSINGS WITH NO RIGHT OF WAY

1.75   Usually the way which crosses the railway is either a public or a private right of way (or in some cases both). However, we must also consider the situation where there is use of a level crossing even though there is no *right* of way over the way. This may arise, for example, where the railway operator provides a crossing over the railway, often at a station, for the use of railway employees carrying out works (sometimes called "barrow crossings"). It seems unlikely that the public will commonly have lawful access to such crossings. However, although track/railway owners are under no legal obligation to permit the public to use such crossings, they may allow or tolerate their use.[53] In England and Wales, these crossings fall within the scope of the Level Crossings Act 1983 and therefore they are covered by our proposals.[54]

1.76   Accordingly, we take the view that the project should cover the following types of crossing:

   (1)   public crossings where the railway is crossed by a footpath, a bridleway, and/or a road/highway;

   (2)   private statutory rights of way crossings;

   (3)   private easement or servitude crossings; and

   (4)   in England and Wales, track/railway owner crossings in cases where the public has legitimate access over them as a matter of fact.

1.77   However, we would welcome consultees' views on the scope of the project in respect of the types of crossing covered.

---

[53]   Thus in Scotland, under a pilot programme in 2003 Network Rail allowed members of the public to use 20 private crossings which had been for the use of authorised users only.

[54]   As mentioned above, the position in Scotland is different and is discussed further in Part 5.

STRUCTURE OF THE CONSULTATION PAPER

1.78 In Part 2 we discuss how devolution both as regards Scotland and Wales affects responsibilities for railways, roads and safety. We also discuss relevant differences in the law as between England and Wales, and Scotland. In Part 3, we consider disability and accessibility issues.

1.79 Part 4 looks at how level crossings were, and are, created. Part 5 sets out the current system for regulating safety at level crossings. In Part 6, we turn to the legal mechanisms for closing level crossings. Part 7 considers the case for reform. Part 8 contains our proposals and questions for consultees on possible reform as regards the regulation of safety and closure of level crossings.

1.80 One of the features of this project has been the very broad range of law that is engaged when considering level crossings. Parts 9 and 10 deal with relevant aspects of planning law in England and Wales, and Scotland respectively. Parts 11 and 12 deal with rights of way in England and Wales, and in Scotland respectively, while Part 13 deals with criminal offences. Finally, Part 14 considers issues relating to signs and the Highway Code. We provide a summary of our provisional proposals and consultation questions in Part 15, while a number of appendices provide additional relevant information. Further appendices are to be found on our websites.[55]

1.81 Colour photographs have been included throughout this consultation paper to illustrate the various types of level crossing to which we refer and their surroundings. Alternatives to colour photographs were considered, but none of these adequately communicated the points raised in this consultation paper – for instance, it became clear that only colour photographs could effectively display the warning lights, signs and barriers at level crossings.

1.82 We have published an assessment of the economic impact of the changes proposed in this consultation paper, which can be found on our websites.

1.83 **We welcome consultees' views on the economic impact of the proposed reforms.**

LEGISLATIVE COMPETENCE

1.84 The division in terms of the Scotland Act 1998 between those matters that fall within the legislative competence of the Scottish Parliament and those matters that are reserved to the UK Parliament is of potential significance in relation to the implementation of the Bill giving effect to the recommendations arising from the project. Insofar as the Bill annexed to our subsequent report will cover matters which fall within the legislative competence of the Scottish Parliament, it would be for the Scottish Parliament to decide whether to grant a legislative consent motion giving its consent to the inclusion of those matters in a Bill for introduction in the UK Parliament. Alternatively the Scottish Parliament might wish to legislate itself on such matters as regards Scotland. We discuss devolution issues further in Part 2.

1.85 Furthermore, any legislation we eventually recommend would, of course, need to comply with the European Convention on Human Rights.

[55] www.lawcom.gov.uk and www.scotlawcom.gov.uk.

PART 2
SCOTLAND AND WALES: DEVOLUTION AND OTHER ISSUES

INTRODUCTION

2.1 This Part considers the current devolution settlements in Scotland and Wales. It also outlines those areas in which Scots law differs from that in England and Wales and which need to be taken into account when considering our policy approach to reform.

The automatic open (ungated) locally monitored level crossing (AOCL) at Garve station on the Inverness to Kyle of Lochalsh line seen from the hillside.
Photographer: John Furnevel.

SCOTLAND

2.2 The project needs to take account of differences in both public and private law as between England and Wales, and Scotland. From a public law perspective, much of the legislation relating to railways and to level crossings applies similar provisions throughout Great Britain. However, differences in relation to highways/roads law, planning law, criminal law and statutory rights of access to land as between England and Wales, and Scotland, must be considered. From a private law perspective, the most important differences arise in relation to property law.

2.3 First, we discuss the matters reserved to the United Kingdom Parliament in terms of Schedule 5 to the Scotland Act 1998 which are of potential relevance to the level crossings project. Secondly, we identify relevant areas in which Scots law differs from that in England and Wales, and areas in which the Scottish Ministers have separate though broadly equivalent powers to those of the Secretary of State.

Background to the reserved/non-reserved divide

Legislative competence

2.4 Whilst section 28(1) of the Scotland Act 1998 confers a general power on the Scottish Parliament to enact legislation, this is qualified by section 29, which reserves certain matters to the United Kingdom Parliament. Section 29(2) defines what is referred to as the "legislative competence" of the Scottish Parliament with reference to a number of grounds on which a provision in an Act of the Scottish Parliament is *outside* that competence. According to section 29(2)(b), one such ground is that the matter is reserved to the United Kingdom Parliament. Matters that are so reserved are specified in Schedule 5 to the 1998 Act. Section 29(3) of the 1998 Act provides that:

> For the purposes of this section, the question whether a provision of an Act of the Scottish Parliament relates to a reserved matter is to be determined, subject to subsection (4), by reference to the purpose of the provision, having regard (among other things) to its effect in all the circumstances.

2.5 Any matter that is not expressly reserved in terms of Schedule 5 falls within the legislative competence of the Scottish Parliament, subject to the possible application of any of the other restrictions set out in section 29(2), as read with Schedule 4.[1]

Executive competence

2.6 Just as section 28 of the 1998 Act confers general legislative powers upon the Scottish Parliament, so section 53 of the 1998 Act transfers to the Scottish Ministers all the powers of Ministers of the Crown. Apart from the implementation of Community obligations, where there is concurrent power, other functions of Ministers of the Crown are transferred to Scottish Ministers, in so far as they are exercisable within "devolved competence". The result is that, following devolution, these powers cannot be exercised by Ministers of the Crown. Section 54 of the 1998 Act explains what is meant by "devolved competence". Whether the power of a Minister is to make subordinate legislation, or to carry out some other executive action, section 54 provides that the Minister cannot make that legislation, or carry out that executive action, if it would be outside the legislative competence of the Scottish Parliament to pass legislation to that effect. Accordingly, the test for ministerial competence is the same as the test for legislative competence. This is relevant to the making of level crossing orders under section 1 of the Level Crossings Act 1983, as discussed later in the consultation paper.

---

[1] Scotland Act 1998, s 29(2) says that a provision of an Act of the Scottish Parliament is also outside the legislative competence of the Scottish Parliament if it is, for example, incompatible with the European Convention on Human Rights or in breach of the restrictions in sch 4. Sch 4 lists certain enactments that may not be modified by an Act of the Scottish Parliament or subordinate legislation made in exercise of a power conferred by such an Act. These enactments are referred to as "protected" enactments. The law relating to reserved matters is similarly protected from modification by virtue of that schedule. The question of the legislative competence of the Scottish Parliament (in the context of a road traffic offence) was considered in the case of *Martin v HM Advocate* 2010 [UKSC] 10.

Relevant reservations

2.7 As noted above, Schedule 5 to the Scotland Act 1998 reserves certain matters to the United Kingdom Parliament. Part 1 of the Schedule provides for various general reservations, whilst Part 2 provides for specific reservations. Some of the matters in Part 2 are described by reference to subject areas (for example, emergency powers and extradition). Other matters are described by reference to the subject matter of specific legislation. Some of the legislation which is of relevance to level crossings falls within the scope of the specific reservations, which we now turn to consider.

Road transport

2.8 The law relating to the regulation of traffic using the road (for example through traffic signs, temporary road closures and provision and prosecution of road traffic offences) is largely reserved. Section E1 of Schedule 5 to the Scotland Act 1998 provides for the reservation of Part V of the Road Traffic Regulation Act 1984 (dealing with traffic signs), the Road Traffic Act 1988 and the Road Traffic Offenders Act 1988. However, what may be referred to as "substantive" roads law (for example, the creation, maintenance and stopping-up of roads and the provision of temporary roads) falls largely within the legislative competence of the Scottish Parliament.

Health and safety

2.9 Section H2 of Schedule 5 to the Scotland Act 1998 provides for the reservation of the subject matter of Part 1 of the Health and Safety at Work etc Act 1974 (HSWA 1974). This reservation falls under the general head of employment. The reservation is relevant to railways generally and in particular to level crossings in two respects.

2.10 First, sections 2, 3 and 4 of HSWA 1974 provide a general legislative framework with regard to health and safety that applies in relation to level crossings.

2.11 Secondly, section 117 of the Railways Act 1993 deems the Level Crossings Act 1983 to be an "existing statutory provision" for the purposes of Part 1 of HSWA 1974. On that basis it would seem that all aspects of the operation of the 1983 Act must be said to fall within the health and safety reservation, notwithstanding the fact that, in terms of the 1983 Act, level crossing orders may cover matters of convenience as well as safety. This view seems to be supported by the fact that the 1983 Act is described in section 117(1) of the 1993 Act as relating to "the proper construction *and safe operation* of certain transport systems". This would tend to suggest that protection of safety has to be the primary purpose of any level crossing order. This is borne out by the wording of section 1(1) of the Level Crossings Act 1983 which gives the Secretary of State power to make level crossing orders "...for the protection of those using the level crossing". Accordingly, the power to make level crossing orders in the 1983 Act continues to rest with the Secretary of State (as was the case prior to devolution).

The automatic open (ungated) locally monitored level crossing (AOCL) at Strathcarron station on the Inverness to Kyle of Lochalsh line: note the flashing lights.

Photographer: John Furnevel.

Rail transport

2.12 Rail transport is largely a reserved matter under section E2 of Schedule 5 to the Scotland Act 1998. In particular the reservation encompasses the "provision and regulation of railway services". The reservation is subject to a number of specific exceptions, one of which is the "promotion and construction of railways which start, end and remain in Scotland". This exception does not extend to the regulation of any railway so constructed.

2.13 In any event, if it is accepted that the power to make level crossing orders falls within the health and safety reservation (because all such orders deal primarily with safety) there is no need to consider the provision and regulation of railway services reservation.

Criminal law and procedure

2.14 Criminal law in Scotland is a matter that falls largely within the legislative competence of the Scottish Parliament. However, section 29(4) of the Scotland Act 1998 provides that a provision of an Act of the Scottish Parliament which would not otherwise relate to reserved matters, but which makes modifications to Scots criminal law as it applies to reserved matters, is normally to be treated as applying to reserved matters.

2.15 In terms of procedure, in Scotland the decision as to whether to bring a prosecution for failure to meet the terms of an improvement notice under HSWA 1974 requiring compliance with a level crossings order is taken by the Procurator Fiscal. By contrast, in England and Wales the decision as to whether to bring such a prosecution is taken by the Office of Rail Regulation.

Executive devolution

2.16 In Part 8 we propose a new system of orders dealing with closure of level crossings. The new system would give rise to a potential constitutional difficulty as regards the respective powers of the Secretary of State and the Scottish Ministers. We propose a transfer of certain functions to the Scottish Ministers by means of executive devolution so as to address this difficulty. This transfer would be limited to administrative functions and would not alter the legislative competence of the Scottish Parliament. We discuss our proposal for executive devolution in more detail in Part 8.

Areas in which Scots law differs from that of England and Wales

Planning law

2.17 Town and country planning matters fall within the legislative competence of the Scottish Parliament.[2] Whilst the law in relation to town and country planning is broadly similar in Scotland, England and Wales, the law is contained in separate statutes and there are certain differences that may be of potential relevance in the level crossings context. At present, the Town and Country Planning (Scotland) Act 1997 makes provision for planning *agreements,* whereas in England and Wales the Town and Country Planning Act 1990 makes provision for planning *obligations.* However, a new section 75 is to be substituted into the Town and Country Planning (Scotland) Act 1997 by section 23 of the Planning etc (Scotland) Act 2006, making provision for planning obligations broadly equivalent to that applying to England and Wales. Section 23 also inserts a new section 75A, providing for the modification or discharge of planning obligations.[3]

2.18 A more significant divergence between the planning law of Scotland and that of England and Wales arises with the introduction of the Community Infrastructure Levy in England and Wales through regulations made under section 205 of the Planning Act 2008.[4] The First Minister made a statement in August 2008 to the effect that there was no intention to introduce an equivalent levy in Scotland. Planning law is discussed in detail in Parts 9 and 10.

Highways/roads law

2.19 As noted above, the substantive law relating to roads in Scotland is, for the most part, a matter within the legislative competence of the Scottish Parliament. For the purposes of the project, the main relevant legislation as regards Scotland is the Roads (Scotland) Act 1984, while in England and Wales it is the Highways Act 1980.

2.20 There is no Scottish equivalent to sections 118A and 119A of the Highways Act 1980, making specific provision respectively for the stopping up and diversion of footpaths and bridleways which cross railways on the level. Similarly, there is no equivalent to section 255 of the 1980 Act, providing for distribution of costs

---

[2] There are no reservations in relation to town and country planning under sch 5 to the 1998 Act.

[3] Section 23 has not yet been commenced but as we mention in Part 10 the Scottish Government has issued a consultation paper on implementation of section 23 of the 2006 Act. The consultation period is due to finish at the end of July 2010.

[4] Community Infrastructure Levy Regulations 2010, SI 2010 No 948.

between the railway operator and the highways authority where a level crossing is to be replaced by a bridge. These provisions are discussed in Part 6. A further important difference between the law of the two jurisdictions in the context of level crossings arises from the different definitions of "road" which apply in the Level Crossings Act 1983 (discussed further in Part 5). The 1983 Act gives the Secretary of State the power to make orders "in relation to any place where a railway crosses a road on the level." In relation to England and Wales, a "road" is defined as "any highway or other road to which the public has access." In relation to Scotland, "road" has the same meaning as in section 151(1) of the Roads (Scotland) Act 1984:

> "Road" means, subject to subsection (3) below, any way (other than a waterway) over which there is a public right of passage (by whatever means and whether subject to a toll or not) and includes the road's verge, and any bridge (whether permanent or temporary) over which, or tunnel through which, the road passes; and any reference to a road includes a part thereof.

2.21 The key distinguishing factor between the definitions is the absence in the Scottish definition of any reference to "any other road to which the public has access." We discuss this in detail in Part 5 where we refer to the case of *Hamilton v Dumfries and Galloway Council*[5] in which the court held that a right of passage amounted to a right of way. The effect of this decision is that in relation to Scotland, only crossings where there is a public right of way can be subject to an order under the Level Crossings Act 1983; crossings over ways to which access is taken by the tolerance, permission, or acquiescence of the person entitled to control the use of the way are not governed by the 1983 Act.

Access rights under the Land Reform (Scotland) Act 2003

2.22 The Land Reform (Scotland) Act 2003 confers a right to be on land for certain specified purposes and a general right to cross land, providing that those rights are exercised responsibly. These rights are much wider in scope than the access rights applying to England and Wales, under Part 1 of the Countryside and Rights of Way Act 2000. However, the question arises as to whether or not access rights under the 2003 Act apply to private level crossings. These issues are discussed further in Part 12.

Issues of relevance to private law

2.23 Differences in the nature and methods of constituting and extinguishing easements, in relation to England and Wales, and servitudes in Scotland must be taken into account. Moreover, differences in the law of prescription as between the two jurisdictions are also of significance. These affect both the creation and extinction of rights of way over level crossings by means of prescription.

2.24 In addition, case law would seem to suggest that there might be a divergence between the jurisdictions in relation to the effect upon the continued exercise of rights over private level crossings where two pieces of land bisected by a railway

---

[5] 2009 SC 277.

cease to be owned by the same person.[6] These issues are considered in more detail in Parts 11 and 12.

Areas in which Scottish Ministers have separate functions

2.25   In relation to some areas, the Scottish Ministers have separate, though broadly similar functions to those of the Secretary of State.

Railway finance

2.26   The Scottish Ministers have certain functions under Schedule 4A to the Railways Act 1993 in relation to railway finance. In the context of level crossings, the most significant function is possibly that relating to the preparation of the High Level Output Specification (HLOS) and the Statement of Funds Available (SoFA). We discuss aspects of railway finance in Part 7 in connection with the need for reform of the procedures relating to the closure of level crossings.

Transport and works

2.27   The Scottish Ministers also have the power to make orders under the Transport and Works (Scotland) Act 2007,[7] in connection with the construction and operation of railways which start, end and remain in Scotland. The powers under the 2007 Act are broadly equivalent to the powers exercisable by the Secretary of State and/or Welsh Ministers under the Transport and Works Act 1992 to make transport and works orders in relation to England and Wales.

WALES

2.28   The National Assembly for Wales was established by the Government of Wales Act 1998. The Act created a form of what was described as "executive" devolution. This allowed for the transfer to the National Assembly for Wales of functions exercised in relation to England by Secretaries of State. While the 1998 Act set out the broad areas in which such powers were to be transferred, the actual legal transfer of the powers was effected by a series of "transfer of functions" orders made subsequently under the Act. The Government of Wales Act 2006 changed the basis of devolution to Wales. First, it made provision for the incremental transfer to the National Assembly for Wales of legislative powers. It did so by delineating broad "fields" (largely the same as the areas of executive devolution under the 1998 Act), within which "matters" would be added in order to give the National Assembly power to make a new form of legislation called "measures". One such "field" relates to highways and transport. However, it has not as yet been populated with any matters. More importantly for our purposes, the 1998 Act put into statutory form a division between the legislative National Assembly and the executive "Welsh Assembly Government" (thereby giving legal effect to a division the Assembly had striven to create in practice from an earlier date). Broadly, the executive functions previously transferred to the National Assembly were transferred by the 2006 Act to the Welsh Assembly Government.

---

[6]   In relation to England and Wales the relevant authority is *Midland Railway Company v Gribble* [1895] 2 Ch 827; in relation to Scotland the relevant authority is *Robertson v Network Rail Infrastructure Limited*, Inverness Sheriff Court 28 May 2007 (unreported) http://www.scotcourts.gov.uk/opinions/A161_06.html (last visited 27 June 2010).

[7]   Such orders are referred to as "TAW/S orders".

The implications of the Welsh devolution settlement for the level crossings project are discussed further below.

2.29 There are matters about which the National Assembly for Wales has competence to legislate under the Government of Wales Act 2006. There are also areas where the Welsh Ministers have taken over certain statutory functions that in England are performed by the Secretary of State. The law of England and Wales is one body of law and whilst there are certain differences which reflect the devolution settlement and which will be outlined where relevant, there are no major areas of difference which affect our policy. This is in contrast to the position in relation to Scots law, which is separate and, in certain areas such as land law, very different to that in England and Wales.

A public road crosses a railway at an open (ungated) level crossing at Cwm Cloch near Beddgelert on the recently reconstructed narrow gauge Welsh Highland Railway: note the bilingual warning signs but the absence of flashing lights.

Photographer: Rowland Turner.

Legislative competence of the National Assembly for Wales

2.30 As mentioned above, the National Assembly for Wales has competence to make laws, known as assembly measures, which relate to matters outlined in Part 1 of Schedule 5 to the Government of Wales Act 2006. The United Kingdom Parliament retains the power to legislate on any matter, but a Memorandum of Understanding[8] between the United Kingdom Government and the Welsh Ministers (and also the Scottish Ministers and Northern Ireland Executive Committee) means that the United Kingdom Government will seek the consent of

---

[8] Devolution: Memorandum of Understanding and Supplementary Agreements (2001) CM 5240, available at http://www.justice.gov.uk/guidance/mou.htm (last visited 27 June 2010).

the relevant devolved administration before seeking to legislate on matters within devolved competence.[9] Schedule 5 to the 2006 Act outlines 20 general fields of legislative competence which are then populated with specific matters. Of relevance to our policy are field 10: highways and transport, and field 18: town and country planning. It is intended that the legislative competence of the National Assembly for Wales will be extended incrementally, and matters added to the general fields.[10]

Field 10: highways and transport

2.31 The only matters currently within field 10 (and upon which the National Assembly for Wales may therefore legislate) relate to roads and road traffic matters.

Field 18: Town and country planning

2.32 The Planning Act 2008 recently added matters to field 18, giving the National Assembly for Wales increased legislative competence in relation to town and country planning (referred to below and in Part 9 as spatial planning). The matters relate, first, to development plans in Wales, including the relationship between regional (Wales-wide) and local plans, but excluding plans in relation to development consent under the Planning Act 2008. Secondly, the matters relate to the provision for and in connection with the review by local planning authorities of matters which may be expected to affect development of the authorities' areas or the planning of such development. The National Assembly for Wales has not yet legislated in this area.

Functions transferred from the Secretary of State to Welsh Ministers

Highways

2.33 Functions under the Highways Act 1980 are devolved under article 2 and Schedule 1 to the National Assembly for Wales (Transfer of Functions) Order 1999[11] and paragraph 30 of Schedule 11 to the Government of Wales Act 2006. The division between local authority responsibility for local roads and central government responsibility for trunk roads and special roads is the same as that in England. The Highways Agency does not operate in Wales and responsibility lies directly with the Welsh Ministers. In practice, maintenance of the trunk road network in Wales is carried out by local authorities under delegation arrangements made with the Welsh Ministers under section 6 of the Highways Act 1980.

2.34 However, very few public road level crossings lie on highways that are the responsibility of the Secretary of State/Welsh Ministers. Of more importance for the project is the responsibility for confirming and extending the life of stopping up/diversion orders. Almost all the stopping up and diversion powers available give this role to the Secretary of State/Welsh Ministers, including sections 118A and 119A of the Highways Act 1980 relating specifically to level crossings. Any

---

[9] See Ministry of Justice, *Devolution Guidance Note 9 Post Devolution Primary Legislation Affecting Wales* (2007) p 1.

[10] Ministry of Justice, *Devolution Guidance Note 9 Post Devolution Primary Legislation Affecting Wales* (2007) p 4.

[11] National Assembly for Wales (Transfer of Functions) Order 1999, SI 1999 No 672.

proposals which build on or include these provisions, or which propose a system of appeal or confirmation of orders of the local highways authority would have to bear in mind that the relevant body for the appeal/confirmation in Wales would be the Welsh Ministers rather than the Secretary of State.

Spatial planning

2.35 Spatial planning functions under the Town and Country Planning Act 1990 are devolved to the Welsh Ministers, who are responsible for the Wales Spatial Plan which provides an overarching policy for sustainable development within Wales. Planning policy is set out in the Welsh Assembly document *Planning Policy Wales* (2002), which is supplemented by ministerial interim planning policy statements. The Welsh Ministers have the equivalent of the "call-in" power of the Secretary of State in England,[12] where the application in question raises issues of more than local importance. The Planning Act 2008 introduced further devolution in relation to spatial planning, giving powers to the Welsh Ministers in relation to plans for development and land use.

2.36 Local planning authorities also have certain powers in relation to the stopping up of highways. For example, section 257 of the Town and Country Planning Act 1990 allows for the stopping up or diversion of footpaths, bridleways and restricted byways by a local planning authority where stopping up or diversion is necessary to carry out works authorised under planning permission. This is a corollary of the power to grant planning permission for such a development. In England if there are objections it is the Secretary of State who ultimately decides whether the highway should be stopped up; in Wales it is now the Welsh Ministers.

Transport planning

2.37 As with spatial planning, local and regional transport planning has been devolved and for Wales, it is now the responsibility of the Welsh Ministers.

2.38 There are some differences relating to local transport plans between the system which operates in England and that in Wales. These are minor, but are worth noting in terms of consultation requirements and the potential need for guidance under any proposals. Under section 109(2C) of the Transport Act 2000,[13] local authorities in England must consult with the operators of any "network or station, or of any railway services, in their area"[14] in relation to the drawing up of local transport plans as required under section 108 of that Act. Section 109 does not apply to Wales. Instead sections 109A, 109B and 109C require that transport plans be submitted to the Welsh Ministers. The Welsh Ministers may only approve the transport plans where they are "consistent" with the Wales Transport Strategy[15] and are "adequate" for its implementation.[16]

---

[12] Town and Country Planning Act 1990, s 77.

[13] Transport Act 2000, s 109(2C) was inserted by the Local Transport Act 2008, s 9(4) with effect as regards England from 9 February 2009 (by virtue of SI 2009 No 107).

[14] Transport Act 2000, s 109(2C).

[15] Transport Act 2000, s 109A(4)(a).

[16] Transport Act 2000, s 109A(4)(b).

2.39 Sections 113A and 113B of the Transport Act 2000[17] give the Welsh Ministers the power to make an order allowing local authorities to produce a local transport plan for only part of their area, or for two or more authorities to produce one plan for an area comprising all or part of their respective areas. The Regional Transport Planning (Wales) Order 2006[18] was made in exercise of this power, permitting local transport plans to be made on a regional rather than individual local authority basis. The order also groups Welsh local authorities into four groups, each of which is to prepare a single plan. It appears, therefore, that transport planning in Wales is moving to a regional, rather than local basis.

Transport and works orders

2.40 Responsibilities under the Transport and Works Act 1992 are also devolved. Where a proposed project is to take place entirely within Wales, an application under the 1992 Act is decided by the Welsh Ministers. Where proposed works are to take place both in England and Wales, the Secretary of State will take the decision, but is required to secure the agreement of the Welsh Ministers prior to making an order. If an order were merely for an individual level crossing this cross-border element is unlikely to come into play. However, in relation to level crossings closed or replaced as part of a larger scheme (which is the more common scenario) this may be of relevance. For the purposes of any future reforms, the devolved nature of the current authorisation regime will need to be taken into account.

Railway finance

2.41 Since 1 April 2006 the Welsh Ministers have had responsibility for rail franchising within Wales. In practice this means the Wales and Borders Rail Franchise which is operated by Arriva Trains Wales. This contract was concluded in 2003 and runs for 15 years.

2.42 Network Rail remains responsible for the maintenance and upgrade of the mainline railway infrastructure in Wales as in the rest of Great Britain, but not for heritage or commercial railways. Whilst the Welsh Ministers work in partnership with Network Rail on projects, they have no responsibility for infrastructure themselves, nor do they have a direct input into the funding streams available for Network Rail infrastructure improvements. We discuss railway finance further in Part 7.

Executive devolution

2.43 As we mention above, in Part 8 we propose a new system of orders dealing with closure of level crossings. In this connection, a similar difficulty arises as regards Wales to that in Scotland in relation to the respective powers of the Secretary of State and the Welsh Ministers. We therefore propose a transfer of certain functions to the Welsh Ministers by means of executive devolution so as to address this difficulty. The transfer would apply to administrative functions only and would not confer any legislative competence of the National Assembly for Wales. We discuss this matter in more detail in Part 8

---

[17] Inserted by the Transport (Wales) Act 2006.

[18] SI 2006 No 2993.

PART 3
DISABILITY AND ACCESSIBILITY

INTRODUCTION

3.1 Accessibility at level crossings is crucial to a safe and efficient road and rail transport system. However, on occasions people face difficulties when trying to cross level crossings. This may be due in part to issues with the design of the level crossing itself. Problems may also arise where a level crossing has been or is to be replaced by a bridge or an underpass which does not fully accommodate the needs of all those using it.

3.2 It is important to recognise that, as well as disabled persons, other groups of users may have additional needs, for example, people with children in push-chairs, elderly people, cyclists or horse riders. They may also experience difficulties using level crossings or bridges or underpasses which replace them.

3.3 During the course of our research we have been made aware of a number of issues which concern accessibility of level crossings, particularly for disabled persons. We understand that a particular difficulty can arise with public footpath crossings which have "kissing gates". In one case, questions arose about the obligations on the railway operator to ensure that the crossing was suitable for use by disabled persons. Such gates can be very difficult or even impossible for wheelchair users and other disabled persons to operate. Similar difficulties can arise at such crossings for elderly people and people with prams, push-chairs or bicycles.

ACCESSIBILITY AND THE ASSESSMENT OF SAFETY/CONVENIENCE OF LEVEL CROSSINGS

3.4 In determining what protective arrangements are to be put in place at a level crossing, it is necessary to consider both the safety and convenience of road and rail users. This assessment has to take into account the extent to which proposed protective arrangements would make a level crossing more or less accessible for users who may have particular accessibility needs. In other words, accessibility is part of the equation in balancing safety and convenience when deciding on appropriate protective arrangements at level crossings.

ACCESSIBILITY OF LEVEL CROSSINGS: DISABLED USERS

Equality Act 2010[1]

3.5 At present the Disability Discrimination Act 1995 provides protection in certain circumstances against discrimination on grounds of disability. However, it should be noted that the Equality Act 2010 contains provisions to repeal and replace the

---

[1] The 2010 Act has only partially been commenced. Section 216(3) of the 2010 Act provides that most of the provisions of the Act are to come into force on a day prescribed by commencement order. The Government Equalities Office had been working to a timetable whereby the core provisions of the 2010 Act were to come into force in October 2010. That timetable has since been withdrawn and is under review by the Coalition Government. However, at the time of writing, the Government Equalities Office is continuing to work on the basis of the previously announced timetable.

provisions of the 1995 Act. The purpose of the 2010 Act is to harmonise and consolidate the legislation in the UK relating to discrimination. It is not intended to make any fundamental changes to the law insofar as it relates to the disability discrimination provisions relevant to level crossings. However, the 2010 Act does make a small number of changes which may be relevant, and these are noted throughout this Part. The Equality Act 2010 also contains a new, streamlined general "public sector equality duty"[2] which will, when the Act comes fully into force, replace the current separate disability, gender, and race equality duties.[3]

3.6 Since the Equality Act 2010 is not yet fully in force, it is appropriate to consider the current provisions of the Disability Discrimination Act 1995 which are relevant to disability issues at level crossings.

Disability Discrimination Act 1995

3.7 The Disability Discrimination Act 1995 makes it unlawful to discriminate against people with disabilities[4] in relation to employment, the provision of goods and services, education and transport. For the purposes of level crossings, the relevant provisions are found in Part III. That Part prohibits discrimination by providers of services and public authorities in connection with the provision of goods, facilities and services to the public.

3.8 Section 19 provides that it is unlawful for a provider of services to the public to discriminate against a person with a disability in the provision of services.

3.9 Section 21B of the 1995 Act[5] provides that it is unlawful for a public authority to discriminate against a person who has a disability in carrying out its functions. There is also a general duty on public authorities under section 49A of the 1995 Act.[6] Under that section, public authorities must have due regard, in exercising their functions, to certain factors including the need to "(a) …eliminate discrimination that is unlawful under [the] Act" and "(d) …take steps to take account of disabled persons' disabilities, even where that involves treating disabled persons more favourably than other persons".

The distinction between "providers of services" and "public authorities"

3.10 Section 19(2) of the 1995 Act contains a broad definition of "provider of services", which includes any person who is concerned with the provision of services to the public or to a section of the public, regardless of whether the service is provided

---

[2] Equality Act 2010, s 149.

[3] In the case of disability, the Disability Discrimination Act 1995, s 49A provides that public authorities must have due regard to the need to promote equality of opportunity, take account of disabilities, encourage participation by disabled persons in public life, and encourage a positive attitude towards disabled persons, as well as the need to eliminate discrimination and harassment.

[4] Section 1(1) of the 1995 Act defines "disability" as "a physical or mental impairment which has a substantial and long-term adverse effect on [one's] ability to carry out normal day-to-day activities".

[5] Section 21B was inserted into the 1995 Act by section 2 of the Disability Discrimination Act 2005.

[6] Section 49A was inserted into the 1995 Act by section 3 of the Disability Discrimination Act 2005.

with or without payment.

3.11 The provision of services referred to in the definition of "provider of services" includes the provision of any goods or facilities, and an example of services to which the Act applies is "access to and use of any place which members of the public are permitted to enter".[7] It appears from this that in terms of the test in the 1995 Act, level crossings to which the public has legitimate access can be regarded as "services" and therefore they come within the scope of the Act. However, in order for the duties under the Act to apply, there needs to be either a provider of services or a public authority which is responsible for operating the "place" concerned.

3.12 In terms of section 21B(2) of the 1995 Act, "public authority" is also defined broadly to include any person whose functions are of a public nature. There are some exclusions but none of these is relevant to level crossings.[8]

3.13 Therefore, when determining the duties of a particular body under Part III of the 1995 Act, one must first consider whether it provides services to the public or exercises functions of a public nature.

3.14 The duties placed on public authorities and providers of services are broadly similar. Both must treat disabled persons equally to other members of the public and both are under a duty to make reasonable adjustments to make physical features (for example, a level crossing) more user-friendly and accessible for disabled persons.

3.15 For the purposes of level crossings, it is clear that the Secretary of State for Transport, the Department for Transport, highway/roads authorities, and the Office of Rail Regulation (ORR) are all public authorities as defined by the 1995 Act. Equally, it seems clear that operators of heritage railways and private railways such as those in docks or harbours are "providers of services" in respect of level crossings over which the public has lawful access. We come to this view on the basis of the discussion above of the definition of "provider of services" and in particular the meaning of "services". However, the distinction between providers of services and public authorities is less clear-cut when applied to Network Rail. Does Network Rail provide a service to the public or does it exercise functions of a public nature?

---

[7] Disability Discrimination Act 1995, s 19(3)(a).

[8] Disability Discrimination Act 1995, s 21B(3).

3.16　In *Cameron and others v Network Rail Infrastructure Ltd (formerly Railtrack plc),*[9] Turner J concluded that Railtrack was not a public authority for the purposes of section 6(3) of the Human Rights Act 1998.[10] In doing so, Turner J attempted to identify a *combination* of factors relevant to a determination of public authority status. These factors included the extent to which Railtrack was democratically accountable to central or local government, whether Railtrack pursued commercial objectives, whether it was publicly funded, and whether Railtrack was obliged to conduct its operations in a manner subservient to the public interest.[11]

3.17　Similarly in *YL v Birmingham City Council,*[12] Lord Bingham provided a list of factors which he considered were relevant to determining whether a function is of a public nature. Applying these factors to Network Rail, it becomes clear that the arguments can run both ways and that a determination of public status ultimately depends upon very fine factual distinctions.

(1) THE NATURE OF THE FUNCTION

3.18　Network Rail's function is to provide a safe, reliable and efficient railway by maintaining the rail infrastructure, which includes the tracks, signals, tunnels, level crossings, and some stations.

3.19　In *Cameron*, the claimants argued that Railtrack was a public body because it performed functions previously carried out by central government through the former British Railways Board and was the vehicle selected to perform the function of ensuring safety on the railway network. However, as Turner J held, although previous governments have taken control of the railways through nationalisation, the business of running a railway is not intrinsically an activity of government.

(2) THE ROLE AND RESPONSIBILITY OF THE STATE

3.20　Network Rail does receive some public funding.[13] However, it is not entirely funded or regulated by government, nor is it democratically accountable to government. Neither is its board of directors under government influence or control. Therefore, the role and responsibility of the State in respect of Network Rail is arguably minimal.

---

[9]　*Cameron and others v Network Rail Infrastructure Ltd (formerly Railtrack plc)* [2006] EWHC 1133 (QB), [2007] 1 WLR 163. The case concerned Railtrack plc but by the time of the judgment Railtrack had been taken over and was subsequently renamed Network Rail Infrastructure Limited which was registered as a private limited company.

[10]　While *Cameron* concerned the Human Rights Act 1998, we note that the definition of a "public authority" in section 6(3) of the 1998 Act is in similar terms to the definition of "public authority" in the Disability Discrimination Act 1995", namely: "any person certain of whose functions are functions of a public nature".

[11]　*Cameron and others v Network Rail Infrastructure Ltd (formerly Railtrack plc)* [2006] EWHC 1133 (QB), [2007] 1 WLR 163 at [29].

[12]　[2007] UKHL 27; [2008] 1 AC 95 at [6]-[11].

[13]　Network Rail receives network grants from the Government and it benefits from direct and specific governmental support in the form of a financial indemnity from the Secretary of State for Transport. See http://www.networkrail.co.uk/aspx/717.aspx (last visited 27 June 2010) and http://www.networkrail.co.uk/aspx/1385.aspx (last visited 27 June 2010).

(3) THE NATURE AND EXTENT OF ANY STATUTORY POWER OR DUTY

3.21 Network Rail was given a mandate by the Government to improve the safety, reliability and efficiency of the railway. As part of Network Rail's network licence granted by the Government, duties are imposed on Network Rail in relation to the operation, maintenance, renewal and development of the network. However, Turner J in *Cameron* held that:

> ...the fact that [Railtrack] held an operating licence does not satisfy the test: all infrastructure, train and station operators are required by the same statutory provisions to hold a licence issued by the Secretary of State for Transport. This feature cannot be decisive, yet in conjunction with other features it could be a factor to be taken into account.

(4) THE EXTENT OF STATE REGULATION

3.22 As mentioned above, Network Rail is not regulated by and is not democratically accountable to government. Rather, it is regulated by ORR, an independent safety and economic regulator for the railways.

(5) THE EXTENT OF THE STATE'S INVOLVEMENT IN PAYMENT

3.23 Again, as stated above, Network Rail does receive some public funding. However, its main sources of revenue are from track access charges and the lease of stations and depots. Track access charges amount to approximately 90% of Network Rail's income and come from the operators of passenger services, freight operators, and open access passenger services (such as Eurostar and excursion trains).[14]

(6) THE EXTENT OF THE RISK TO INDIVIDUALS' CONVENTION RIGHTS

3.24 It could be argued that Article 2 (the right to life) and Article 8 (the right to private and/or family life) of the European Convention on Human Rights are relevant in respect of Network Rail. However, it is likely that a successful ECHR claim against Network Rail (if considered a public authority) would be very fact-specific.[15]

---

[14] House of Commons Library Standard Note SN/BT/2129, *Railways: Network Rail* (4 February 2010) p 2.

[15] For example, although Article 8 imposes positive obligations on the State to secure respect for private and/or family life, these obligations only arise when there is a direct and immediate link between the measures sought and the applicant's private and/or family life. Article 8 would therefore only apply where the lack of access to a public level crossing affects the applicant's life in such a way as to interfere with his or her right to personal development and his or her right to establish and develop relationships with other human beings and the outside world: *Botta v Italy* (1998) 26 EHRR 241 (App No 21439/93); *Zehnalová and Zehnal v Czech Republic* App No 38621/97.

3.25 Although it is important to outline the legal problem, it is not necessary to express a decided view on the status of Network Rail. Our proposals in respect of level crossings must be capable of applying not only in the present, but also in the future, when the various railway actors may have changed. Whether the courts ultimately decide that Network Rail is a private provider of services or a public authority for the purposes of the Disability Discrimination Act 1995, Network Rail is subject to duties under the 1995 Act in relation to the level crossings that it provides to the public.

Duties on both "providers of services" and "public authorities"

3.26 Providers of services and public authorities are under two main duties:

(1) a duty to treat disabled persons equally to other members of the public; and

(2) a duty to make reasonable adjustments.[16]

3.27 These two duties are linked: in fulfilling the duty to make adjustments, providers of services and public authorities will be fulfilling their duty to treat disabled persons equally. "No dogs" policies and a refusal to permit access to disabled persons with assistance dogs is an example of disability-related discrimination. This discrimination can be resolved through the duty to make adjustments, to which we now turn.

3.28 Sections 21 and 21E[17] of the 1995 Act set out the duty on providers of services and public authorities respectively to make reasonable adjustments. This duty can be broken down into three further discrete duties:

(1) a duty to change practices, policies, and procedures;

(2) a duty to overcome a physical feature; and

(3) a duty to provide auxiliary aids and services.

3.29 It should be stressed that the Equality Act 2010 contains provisions to bring into line the threshold at which service providers are under a duty to make reasonable adjustments with the threshold for employers in the 1995 Act; that is, service providers will be under a duty to make adjustments when a provision, criterion or practice puts a disabled person at a "substantial disadvantage".[18] In contrast, the current threshold under the Disability Discrimination Act 1995 is a "practice, policy or procedure which makes it *impossible or unreasonably difficult* for disabled persons to make use of a service which he provides".[19] It remains to be seen whether this will have a substantial impact on the actions required by service providers in practice.

---

[16] Disability Discrimination Act 1995, ss 21 and 21E.

[17] Section 21E was inserted into the 1995 Act by section 2 of the Disability Discrimination Act 2005.

[18] Equality Act 2010, s 20. It should be noted that section 20, along with most of the provisions of the 2010 Act, has not yet been brought into force.

[19] Disability Discrimination Act 1995, s 21(1).

THE DUTY TO CHANGE PRACTICES, POLICIES, AND PROCEDURES

3.30 If a provider of services or a public authority has a practice, policy or procedure which:

  (1) in the case of providers of services, makes it impossible or unreasonably difficult ("substantial disadvantage" under the 2010 Act) for disabled persons to make use of a service provided to other members of the public, or

  (2) in the case of public authorities, makes it impossible or unreasonably difficult ("substantial disadvantage" under the 2010 Act) for disabled persons to receive any benefit or makes it unreasonably adverse for disabled persons to experience any detriment,

  it is under a duty to take reasonable steps to change that practice, policy or procedure so that it no longer has that effect.[20]

3.31 If, for example, Network Rail were to adopt a policy of placing signs at level crossings at a minimum height of six feet, this would make it impossible or unreasonably difficult ("substantial disadvantage" under the 2010 Act) for wheelchair users to read signs, thereby compromising their safe use of level crossings. In these circumstances, the policy would have to be changed so that it would no longer have that adverse effect.

THE DUTY TO OVERCOME A PHYSICAL FEATURE

3.32 If a physical feature makes it impossible or unreasonably difficult ("substantial disadvantage" under the 2010 Act) for disabled persons to make use of a service provided to other members of the public or to receive any benefit, or makes it unreasonably adverse for disabled persons to experience a detriment, providers of services and public authorities are under a duty to take reasonable steps to:

  (1) remove the feature;

  (2) alter it so that it no longer has that effect;

  (3) provide a reasonable means of avoiding the feature; or

  (4) provide or adopt a reasonable alternative method of making the service in question available to disabled persons or of carrying out the function in question.[21]

3.33 The expression "physical feature" in sections 21(2) and 21E(3) has a very broad meaning which includes:

  (1) any feature arising from the design or construction of a building on the premises occupied by the service provider or public authority;

---

[20] Disability Discrimination Act 1995, ss 21(1) and 21E(2).

[21] Disability Discrimination Act 1995, s 21(2) (for providers of services) and s 21E(4) (for public authorities).

(2)   any feature on those premises of any approach to, exit from, or access to such a building;

(3)   any fixtures, fittings, furnishings, furniture, equipment, or materials in or on such premises; and

(4)   any other physical element or quality of land contained in the premises occupied by the service provider or public authority.[22]

3.34   The code of practice for Part III of the 1995 Act also provides a non-exhaustive list of physical features which includes steps, stairways, kerbs, exterior surfaces and paving, gates, lighting, floor coverings, and signs.[23]

3.35   An adverse "physical feature" could be the uneven and inconsistent surface of a level crossing or its replacement. This physical feature might adversely affect wheelchair users because an uneven surface can make it impossible or unreasonably difficult ("substantial disadvantage" under the 2010 Act) for such persons to cross. In these circumstances, the uneven surface would have to be removed, altered, reasonably avoided, or a reasonable alternative method of crossing would need to be provided.

THE DUTY TO PROVIDE AUXILIARY AIDS AND SERVICES

3.36   Providers of services and public authorities are under a duty to take reasonable steps to provide an auxiliary aid or service if it would enable or facilitate disabled persons to make use of a service or to receive a benefit provided to other members of the public, or if it would reduce "the extent to which it is adverse for disabled persons to experience being subjected to a detriment".[24]

3.37   An example of an "auxiliary aid" in the context of level crossings would be the provision of a warning sound intended for visually impaired people when a train is approaching. Although a visually impaired person may still be able to make use of a level crossing without a warning sound, the threshold at which the duty to provide an auxiliary aid or service is triggered is lower than that provided for "practices, policies, and procedures" and "physical features". It is only necessary that an auxiliary aid or service would either enable or facilitate disabled persons, even when such a service is not impossible or unreasonably difficult ("substantial disadvantage" under the 2010 Act) for disabled persons to make use of.

APPLYING THESE DUTIES TO LEVEL CROSSINGS

3.38   In the case of *Keith Roads v Central Trains Limited*,[25] Sedley LJ held:

---

[22]   Disability Discrimination (Service Providers and Public Authorities Carrying Out Functions) Regulations 2005, SI 2005 No 2901, reg 9.

[23]   Disability Rights Commission, *Code of Practice, Rights of Access: services to the public, public authority functions, private clubs and premises* (2006) para 7.45.

[24]   Disability Discrimination Act 1995, ss 21(4) and 21E(6) and (7).

[25]   [2004] EWCA Civ 1541. We note that the case was raised against Central Trains Ltd, a train operating company, rather than against Railtrack plc as the operator of the railway infrastructure. We can only speculate on what the outcome of the case might have been had it been raised against Railtrack plc.

Where there is only one practicable solution, it may have to be treated as reasonable even if it is demeaning or onerous for disabled persons to use it. If on the other hand there is a range of solutions, the fact that one of them, if it stood alone, would satisfy section 21(2)(d) may not be enough to afford a defence. This is because the policy of the Act...is...to provide access to a service as close as it is reasonably possible to get to the standard normally offered to the public at large. While, therefore, the Act does not require the court to make nice choices between comparably reasonable solutions, it makes comparison inescapable where a proffered solution is said not to be reasonable precisely because a better one, in terms of practicality or of the legislative policy, is available.[26]

3.39 In the context of level crossings, therefore, when a provider of services or a public authority provides a level crossing to the public, it must ensure, so far as it is reasonable, that disabled persons are accommodated in the same way as other members of the public. In the case of the closure of a level crossing and its replacement with a bridge, for example, this also must be suitable to accommodate the needs of disabled persons. In accommodating these needs, regard must be had to the duties under sections 21 and 21E (the duty to make reasonable adjustments, as outlined above). If a range of solutions is available to a provider of services or a public authority, it must choose the solution which best succeeds in treating disabled persons equally to other members of the public. Only in this way can a provider of services or a public authority discharge its duties under the 1995 Act.

Proposed European Union Equal Treatment Directive[27]

3.40 In 2008, the European Commission proposed a Directive implementing the principle of equal treatment of persons irrespective of religion or belief, disability, age or sexual orientation, outside of the employment context. This Directive has not yet been approved and further discussions will be taking place in the European Parliament and in the Council of Europe. However, it is worth considering the proposed Directive because it could have implications for UK disability discrimination law.

3.41 "Disability" is not explicitly defined in the proposed Directive, but the European Parliament has stated that, in order to guarantee compliance with the principle of equal treatment in relation to persons with disabilities, "disability" is to be understood in light of the UN Convention on the Rights of Persons with Disabilities[28] which states:

---

[26] As above, at [13].

[27] *Proposal for a Council Directive on implementing the principle of equal treatment between persons irrespective of religion or belief, disability, age or sexual orientation* CNS/2008/0140.

[28] The Convention was adopted on 13 December 2006. The text of the Convention is available at: http://www.un.org/disabilities/convention/conventionfull.shtml (last visited 27 June 2010).

Persons with disabilities include those who have long-term physical, mental, intellectual or sensory impairments which in interaction with various barriers may hinder their full and effective participation in society on an equal basis with others.[29]

3.42   The definitions of "disability" used in both the proposed Directive and the Convention are considerably broader than the definition in the Disability Discrimination Act 1995.[30] Only physical and mental impairments are specifically included under the 1995 Act, and these impairments must not only be long-term but also "substantial". In addition, the definition under the 1995 Act looks to the effect of the impairment on a disabled person's "ability to carry out normal day-to-day activities". This is narrower than the wording of the definition in the proposed Directive, and UN Convention.

3.43   Article 3 of the proposed Directive states that:

> Discrimination based on religion or belief, disability, age or sexual orientation is prohibited by both the public and private sector in…access to and supply of goods and services which are available to the public…

3.44   The European Parliament has stated that "access" should include buildings open to the public, modes of transport, and other public spaces and facilities.[31] Publicly accessible level crossings therefore would fall within the scope of the proposed Directive.

3.45   Article 4 of the proposed Directive states that the measures necessary to enable disabled persons to have effective non-discriminatory access to and supply of goods and services otherwise available to the public must be provided by taking measures of "reasonable accommodation". This is very similar to the Disability Discrimination Act 1995 duty to make adjustments. However, the proposed Directive's duty to take measures of reasonable accommodation is limited if taking such measures would impose a disproportionate burden or require a fundamental alteration; that is, if it would alter the goods and services or the nature of the trade, profession or business, to such an extent that the provider of the goods or services is effectively providing a completely different kind of goods or services.[32] Similar qualifications to the duty to make reasonable adjustments apply under the Disability Discrimination Act 1995 to providers of services,[33] but

---

[29] UN Convention on the Rights of Persons with Disabilities 2006, Article 1.

[30] The definition in section 6 of the Equality Act 2010 is the same as that in the 1995 Act.

[31] *European Parliament legislative resolution of 2 April 2009 on the proposal for a Council directive on implementing the principle of equal treatment between persons irrespective of religion or belief, disability, age or sexual orientation*, amendment 97. Available at http://www.europarl.europa.eu/sides/getDoc.do?type=TA&language=EN&reference=P6-TA-2009-0211 (last visited 27 June 2010).

[32] As above, amendment 22.

[33] Disability Discrimination Act 1995, s 21(6)-(7).

they do not apply to public authorities.[34]

3.46   If the proposed Directive were to be accepted, it would need to be transposed (implemented) into UK law in order to give effect to the requirements of the Directive. It seems that on the basis of the terms of the proposed Directive, amendments would probably be necessary to either the Disability Discrimination Act 1995 or the Equality Act 2010, among other things, to expand the definition of "disability".

ACCESSIBILITY OF LEVEL CROSSINGS: OTHER USERS

3.47   The discussion above has focused on the needs of disabled persons when using level crossings. However, accessibility at level crossings can also be an issue for people who are not disabled, for example elderly people, people with children in push-chairs, horse riders, and cyclists, all of whom may face difficulties in using level crossings.

CONCLUDING REMARKS

3.48   It is with a view to addressing these issues that the Rail Safety and Standards Board (RSSB) is currently undertaking a research project looking at ways of improving safety and accessibility at level crossings for disabled pedestrians.[35] The project is considering practical ways in which in the future the design of level crossings can provide specific facilities for disabled pedestrians with a view to improving accessibility.

3.49   Whilst it is appropriate for disability and accessibility issues to be raised in this consultation paper, it seems likely that any changes that may be needed might focus on practical matters that are outside the scope of a law reform project. The RSSB project is a suitable vehicle for the discussion of such issues and consultees who have views on specific issues may wish to share those views with the RSSB.

3.50   **Nevertheless, we would welcome any comments that consultees may have on disability and accessibility issues in respect of level crossings.**

---

[34]   The Equality Act 2010 does not replicate the qualifications to the duty to make reasonable adjustments under the Disability Discrimination Act 1995. Rather, the duty hinges on whether the adjustment is reasonable – if it is not, then there is no need to make the adjustment. The 2010 Act provides that an adjustment is not reasonable if it would fundamentally alter the nature of the service: Equality Act 2010, sch 2, para 2(7).

[35]   RSSB Research Project T650, available at: http://www.rssb.co.uk/RESEARCH/Lists/DispForm.aspx?ID=125 (last visited 27 June 2010).

PART 4
CREATION OF LEVEL CROSSINGS

INTRODUCTION

4.1 In this Part we discuss the means by which level crossings come into existence as a matter of law.

4.2 As mentioned in Part 1, nearly all existing level crossings were created under private legislation in the form of special Acts as part of the construction of the railways during the nineteenth century. The modern system for authorising railways is contained in recent transport and works legislation. The creation of rights of way over the railway is discussed in Parts 11 and 12.

THE OLD SYSTEM: SPECIAL ACTS

4.3 Special Acts which authorised the construction of railways would generally:

(1) establish a company to build the railway;

(2) allow for the compulsory acquisition of land if this was found by the railway company to be necessary;

(3) allow for the construction of the railway and various ancillary works;

(4) impose continuing obligations on the railway company, which could include the maintenance of level crossings; and

(5) provide a mechanism for the resolution of disputes, frequently by recourse to Justices of the Peace in England and Wales, or a Sheriff in Scotland.

4.4 The early development of railways has been described as "haphazard",[1] with a large proliferation of small railway companies and consequently a large number of special Acts. For instance, in 1844, some 50 new lines were authorised.[2] Owing to the volume of special Acts and the resulting Parliamentary burden, Parliament enacted the Railways Clauses Consolidation Act 1845 and the Railways Clauses Consolidation (Scotland) Act 1845. These Acts provided standard clauses that were deemed to be incorporated into new special Acts unless they were expressly excluded or contrary provision was made, thereby making the Parliamentary process simpler and more efficient. The later Railways Clauses Act 1863 worked the other way round, requiring express incorporation of the model clauses into special Acts.

4.5 The main provision authorising the construction of level crossings on public highways for England and Wales is contained in section 46 of the Railways Clauses Consolidation Act 1845 (and in similar terms in section 39 of the

---

[1] Rev W Awdry in C Awdry, *Encyclopaedia of British Railway Companies* (1990) p 7. This is one of the Rev Awdry's less well known works.

[2] F Clifford, *A History of Private Bill Legislation* (1968) vol 1, p 87 (Originally published, 1885).

Railways Clauses Consolidation (Scotland) Act 1845):

> If the line of the railway cross any turnpike road or public highway, then ... either such road shall be carried over the railway, or the railway shall be carried over such road, by means of a bridge...: Provided always, that, with the consent of two or more justices ... it shall be lawful for the company to carry the railway across any highway, other than a public carriage road, on the level.[3]

4.6   The construction of private crossings is covered by section 68 of the Railways Clauses Consolidation Act 1845 as regards England and Wales and by section 60 of the Railways Clauses Consolidation Act (Scotland) 1845 as regards Scotland. Both sections make general provision listing a number of "works" that the company must provide for the "accommodation of the owners and occupiers of lands adjoining the railway". These are:

> Such and so many convenient gates, bridges, arches, culverts, and passages, over, under, or by the sides of or leading to or from the railway, as shall be necessary for the purpose of making good any interruptions caused by the railway to the use of the lands through which the railway shall be made...

4.7   Under section 73 of the Railways Clauses Consolidation Act 1845 and section 65 of the Railways Clauses Consolidation (Scotland) Act 1845, the railway company could not be required to put in place further accommodation works after the expiry of the period prescribed in the special Act, or after five years if no period was prescribed. As we discuss in Parts 11 and 12, the Acts themselves were silent as to the rights of way that were implied by the creation of a level crossing under these clauses. But it was possible for easements (in England and Wales) or servitudes (in Scotland) to be expressly reserved in the conveyance that transferred the relevant land to the railway company. As mentioned in Part 1, the term "accommodation crossing" is often used for a private crossing constructed at the same time as the railway, although the term is not itself used in the 1845 Acts and we do not use the term in this consultation paper.

4.8   A vast number of special Acts were passed for the authorisation of railways, and many are still in force today. The Acts were drafted by the promoting company's legal advisers or Parliamentary agents and the drafting was not usually in accordance with the style of drafting adopted nowadays.

4.9   The practice of using special Acts continued through the late nineteenth century and throughout most of the twentieth century. By the 1990s, the volume of new private legislation being promoted was much less than during the Victorian era. Nevertheless, by that time Parliament had become dissatisfied with the system of authorising the construction of railways and other works by means of private legislation. Members of Parliament were also critical of the disproportionate amount of Parliamentary time that was being taken to debate proposals that were often purely of local significance. It was against this background that legislation

---

[3]   The text is from the English and Welsh 1845 Act. Under the equivalent provision applying to Scotland the construction of a level crossing requires the consent of the Sheriff or two or more Justices. See section 39 of the Railways Clauses Consolidation (Scotland) Act 1845.

was passed to introduce a new system for the authorisation of railways by means of orders that would not in most cases take up Parliamentary time.[4]

THE MODERN SYSTEM: THE TRANSPORT AND WORKS ACT 1992 AND TRANSPORT AND WORKS (SCOTLAND) ACT 2007

4.10   The Transport and Works Act 1992 introduced a new order-making procedure. While the 1992 Act applies to Scotland as well as to England and Wales, the new procedure set out in Part 1 of the 1992 Act applies *in practice* to England and Wales only. At the time of the passing of the 1992 Act, Scotland had its own system for the promotion of private legislation in the UK Parliament[5] and it was considered that that system should remain in place. However, in 2007 the Scottish Parliament enacted similar order-making powers to those in Part 1 of the 1992 Act, in the Transport and Works (Scotland) Act 2007. The intention behind both Transport and Works Acts was to provide a modern system for authorising works and to remove the need to have recourse to private Acts of either the UK Parliament or Scottish Parliament.

4.11   The 1992 and 2007 Acts apply to certain types of works including "railways".[6] Although use of the order-making procedures under the Acts is not compulsory, where an infrastructure project requires compulsory purchase powers or the creation or extinguishment of rights over land, the transport and works procedure is usually adopted.[7] Both major and minor projects may be subject to a transport and works order, although in practice the process tends to be used for large scale schemes. In addition, a wide range of matters may potentially be covered by a transport and works order. A non-exhaustive list of such matters is set out in Schedule 1 to both Acts and includes:

> The construction, alteration, repair, maintenance, demolition and removal of railways, tramways, trolley vehicle systems and other transport systems within section 1(1) of this Act, waterways, roads, watercourses, buildings and other structures.

4.12   Applications for orders under the 1992 Act for works wholly within England are dealt with by the Secretary of State, while applications for works wholly within Wales are decided by the Welsh Assembly Government. Where proposed works would take place both in England and Wales, the Secretary of State will take the decision, but is required to secure the agreement of the Welsh Assembly Government prior to making an order. Applications for orders under the 2007 Act are dealt with by Scottish Ministers.

4.13   The procedure for applying for an order under the 1992 and 2007 Acts is set out in the Transport and Works (Applications and Objections Procedure) (England and Wales) Rules 2006 and the Transport and Works (Scotland) Act 2007

---

[4]   See Private Bill Procedure, Report of the Joint Committee (1987-88), HL 97 and HC 625, and Private Bills and New procedures: a consultation document (1990) Cm 1110.

[5]   Private Legislation Procedure (Scotland) Act 1936.

[6]   Transport and Works Act 1992, s 1 and sch 1, para 1; 2007 Act, s 1 and sch 1, para 1.

[7]   Transport and Works Act 1992, sch 2; Transport and Works (Scotland) Act 2007, sch 1.

(Applications and Objections Procedure) Rules 2007.[8] The Rules provide for appropriate publicity to be given to the proposals, and set out a timetable for the making of objections to the proposals. If there are no objections, the Secretary of State/Welsh Assembly Government or in Scotland, the Scottish Ministers, can proceed to determine the application.

4.14   If objections are received, the Secretary of State or Scottish Ministers may consider the objections by means of:

(1)   a public local inquiry; or

(2)   a hearing; or

(3)   an exchange of written representations between the parties.[9]

4.15   An inquiry or hearing must be held if a "statutory objector" informs the Secretary of State or the Scottish Ministers that they wish their objection to be referred to an inquiry or hearing. Statutory objectors include the local authorities for the areas in which the works would be carried out and people whose land would be compulsorily purchased.[10] In Scotland, Network Rail Infrastructure Limited is specifically mentioned as a statutory objector, in cases where any works authorised by the proposed order would affect the construction or operation of a railway.[11]

4.16   After considering objections, the Secretary of State or Scottish Ministers may refuse to make an order, or may make the order with or without modifications to the draft order submitted by the applicant.[12]

4.17   Section 9 of the Transport and Works Act 1992 in relation to England and Wales requires schemes that the Secretary of State considers to be of national significance to be referred to the UK Parliament for approval. The parliamentary procedure under section 9 gives both Houses of Parliament the opportunity to consider and decide whether to endorse the proposal in principle. If both Houses of Parliament approve the proposal it will go forward to a public inquiry. Section 13 of the Transport and Works (Scotland) Act 2007 makes similar provision for approval by the Scottish Parliament.

[8]   SI 2006 No 1466 and SSI 2007 No 570.

[9]   See Department for Transport, A Guide to Transport and Works Act Procedures (2006) and Scottish Government, Guide to Transport and Works (Scotland) Act 2007 (2007).

[10]   Transport and Works (Applications and Objections Procedure) (England and Wales) Rules 2006, r 9, 12, 14, 15, and 23; Transport and Works Act 1992, s 11(4).

[11]   Transport and Works (Scotland) Act 2007, s 9(4)(e).

[12]   Transport and Works Act 1992, s 13; Transport and Works (Scotland) Act 2007, s 11.

4.18 It will be seen that the 1992 and 2007 Acts provide a thorough process, designed to test the desirability of the schemes promoted under them. There have now been a number of years of experience of the 1992 Act, including a comprehensive review leading to substantial revisions of the procedural advice in 2006.[13] The result has been an attempt to ensure that the procedures are flexible and proportionate to the wide range of matters which may be the subject of an application under the 1992 Act. For example, the procedural requirements, application fee and likely timescales for determining applications are much less for a simple order transferring assets from one party to another, or an order authorising a short extension to a heritage railway, than for a major scheme like a new tramway or the West Coast Main Line upgrade.[14]

4.19 Nevertheless, we consider that in the context of level crossings, the procedure is still at least potentially expensive and time-consuming. Indeed, in practice the procedure may be more onerous than the Acts alone or Rules would suggest. Comprehensive guidance on the use of the procedure makes clear, for instance, that full consultation should have taken place with interested parties before an application for an order is made. Also the Secretary of State or Scottish Ministers must, among other things, be satisfied that the scheme is reasonably capable of attracting funding and that the environmental statement required by the Rules is full and robust.[15]

4.20 Under the Department for Transport guidance, promoters of railway schemes in England and Wales using the procedure under the Transport and Works Act 1992 are advised to consult appropriate bodies including the Office of Rail Regulation (ORR) before applying for an order. In relation to level crossings, the guidance says that ORR should be consulted "at an early stage to ascertain whether they consider that there are exceptional circumstances which would justify providing a level crossing as opposed to a bridge or tunnel".[16]

4.21 ORR takes the view that other than in exceptional circumstances, there should be no new level crossings on any railway.[17] It would appear, therefore, that although it is possible to authorise a new level crossing over a new railway, promoters may have a considerable task to justify the use of a level crossing, rather than a bridge or an underpass.

THE MODERN SYSTEM: PRIVATE AND HYBRID LEGISLATION

4.22 It is still possible for railway development to be authorised by either the United Kingdom Parliament or the Scottish Parliament by means of private legislation. However, private legislation is in practice now unlikely where a transport and

---

[13] Department for Transport, Guide to Transport and Works Act Procedures (2006).

[14] Only one order has been made so far in Scotland using the powers under the 2007 Act: The Network Rail (Waverley Steps) Order 2010, SSI 2010 No 188.

[15] Department for Transport, A Guide to Transport and Works Act Procedures (2006) and Scottish Government, Guide to Transport and Works (Scotland) Act 2007 (2007).

[16] Department for Transport, A Guide to Transport and Works Act Procedures (2006). The Guide to Transport and Works (Scotland) Act 2007, Scottish Government does not appear to cover this point.

[17] ORR policy on level crossings is available at http://www.rail-reg.gov.uk/upload/pdf/319.pdf (last visited 27 June 2010).

works order could be made.[18]

4.23 Where the Government is promoting major works, it may do so by means of a hybrid Bill in the United Kingdom Parliament.[19] A hybrid Bill is a public Bill, but one that treats private rights within the same class differentially (as would a private Bill, promoted by a private party):

> Hybrid bills are public bills which are considered to affect specific private or local interests, in a manner different from the private or local interests of other persons or bodies of the same category, so as to attract the provisions of the standing orders applicable to private business.[20]

4.24 A hybrid Bill may be necessary where the scheme requires a range of powers which are not available under the Transport and Works Acts or where a mix of public and private powers is involved. It may also be desirable to use the hybrid Bill procedure so as to enable a greater degree of Parliamentary debate than would be possible in relation to a transport and works order, even where such an order relates to a scheme of national significance in which case a certain amount of Parliamentary scrutiny is involved.[21]

THE MODERN SYSTEM: POWERS UNDER TOWN AND COUNTRY PLANNING LEGISLATION

4.25 Where a transport and works order is used, the Secretary of State or Scottish Ministers may deem planning permission to have been granted in respect of the proposed works.[22] In addition, Network Rail is deemed to have planning permission to undertake certain developments on its own operational land, without having to submit an application to the local planning authority for planning permission.[23] In the case of minor developments – for example, constructing a new private footpath crossing – it seems that no particular authorisation or planning consents would be required.

---

[18] In Scotland private legislation has been used in recent years to authorise new railways for example the Waverley Railway (Scotland) Act 2006, the Stirling-Alloa-Kincardine Railway and Linked Improvements Act 2004 and the Airdrie-Bathgate Railway and Linked Improvements Act 2007. These Acts were passed using the private legislation procedure before the Transport and Works (Scotland) Act 2007 and the new system of orders came into force.

[19] Hybrid Bills may also be passed by the Scottish Parliament to authorise the construction or alteration of works or to authorise the compulsory acquisition or use of any land or buildings.

[20] Sir William McKay KCB, *Erskine May, Parliamentary Practice* (23rd ed 2004) p 566.

[21] Transport and Works Act 1992, s 9.

[22] Town and Country Planning Act 1990, s 90(2A); Town and Country Planning (Scotland) Act 1997, s 57(2A).

[23] Town and Country Planning (General Permitted Development) Order 1995, SI 1995 No 418, art 3 and sch 2, part 17, class A (development by railway undertakers) as regards England and Wales; Town and Country Planning (General Permitted Development) (Scotland) Order 1992, SI 1992 No 223, art 3, sch 1, part 13, class 34 (development by railway undertakers).

4.26 In relation to England, the Planning Act 2008[24] is intended to cover at least some of the kinds of major works which are currently authorised under the Transport and Works Act 1992. As outlined above, the 1992 Act makes specific provision for schemes of national significance. Such a scheme would appear likely to be a "nationally significant infrastructure project" under the Planning Act 2008 and also the subject of a National Planning Statement. The 2008 Act asserts its primacy over the 1992 Act – if a scheme requires development consent under the Planning Act 2008 it may not be authorised under the 1992 Act.[25] Where a scheme is wholly within Wales, or straddles the border between England and Wales, the procedure under the Transport and Works Act 1992 will remain relevant. The Planning Act 2008[26] does not prevent the possibility of a hybrid Bill for railway schemes.

NEW LEVEL CROSSINGS ON EXISTING RAILWAY LINES

4.27 One further situation requires some consideration: how would a new level crossing be created over an existing line? We should preface this discussion by noting that it is not apparent to us that there is a substantial demand for new level crossings on existing lines. It is, however, possible that such a development would be desirable in exceptional circumstances. One such exceptional circumstance might be if a "new" level crossing was required to replace a nearby level crossing, where closure was justified on the grounds of safety or convenience, but the expenditure on a replacement bridge or underpass could not be justified.[27] Another situation might be where it is desired to bring back into use a level crossing which was previously closed.[28]

4.28 It may be that no special legal difficulties would arise if the building of a new crossing was uncontentious. A railway operator may be able to build the crossing without recourse to compulsory purchase powers, and to grant a private or public right of way,[29] over the railway.

4.29 If compulsory purchase powers were needed, it would be possible to use the transport and works order procedure (there might be other circumstances in which this would be the desirable course), but the procedure may be seen as overly expensive and time-consuming for individual level crossings.

CONCLUSION

4.30 It seems to us that on the whole the modern system as outlined above is appropriate and works well. However, **we would welcome the views of**

---

[24] There is currently no equivalent legislation in Scotland.

[25] Planning Act 2008, s 33(2)(c).

[26] The Planning Act 2008 is discussed in relation to Wales in Parts 2 and 9.

[27] The diversion of level crossings is discussed in more detail in Part 6 in connection with section 119A of the Highways Act 1980 in relation to England and Wales.

[28] A situation like this arose in the case of *Robertson v Network Rail Infrastructure Ltd* Inverness Sheriff Court, 28th May 2007 http://www.scotcourts.gov.uk/opinions/A161_06.html (last visited 27 June 2010) unreported.

[29] But note the possible limitations on the ability of a railway operator to grant a right of way across the railway discussed in Parts 11 and 12.

consultees on the current system of creating level crossings.

4.31 The one possible exception is in relation to the creation of new level crossings on existing railway lines. We consider the desirability of a new procedure for creating level crossings in Part 8.

PART 5
THE CURRENT REGULATION OF LEVEL CROSSINGS

INTRODUCTION

5.1 In this Part we consider the current provisions regulating safety at level crossings. We consider first the railway-specific regulatory provisions, then the general safety regime provided for by the Health and Safety at Work etc Act 1974 (HSWA 1974). Finally, we consider the relationship between level crossing-specific provisions and the general safety regime.

RAILWAY-SPECIFIC SAFETY PROVISIONS

5.2 The early railway-specific safety provisions can be found in a mixture of public general Acts[1] and special (private) Acts which established the railways. The Railways Clauses Consolidation Act 1845 and the Railways Clauses Consolidation (Scotland) Act 1845[2] provided model clauses (often dealing with safety matters) which were deemed to be incorporated into special Acts unless specifically excluded or varied. The Railways Clauses Act 1863 also provided model clauses which applied to special Acts if the clauses were expressly included in the Acts.

5.3 The early legislation required the railway companies to provide "good and sufficient gates" across the road on either side of the railway and to employ people to open them. It also required railway companies to provide gates or stiles for bridleway and footpath crossings.[3] A model clause prevented trains being shunted across level crossings or left to stand on them.[4] The Road and Rail Traffic Act 1933 gave the Secretary of State power to direct that gates on any level crossing over a public road should be kept closed across the railway rather than across the road.

5.4 Another relevant provision which remains in force is section 123 of the Transport Act 1968. That section gives highway authorities and local authorities in England and Wales, and roads authorities in Scotland, the power to contribute to expenses incurred by a railway owner in providing barriers, or other devices, for the protection or convenience of the public at or near any level crossing.

Level Crossings Act 1983

5.5 The main purpose of the 1983 Act was to provide a simpler way of making changes to the safety arrangements at level crossings. The 1983 Act was required because at that time changes to safety arrangements at such crossings

---

[1] For example, the Highways Act 1835 and the Highway (Railway Crossings) Act 1839.

[2] The Railways Clauses Act 1863 also provided model clauses. However, unlike the model clauses provided by the 1845 Acts, the model clauses provided by the 1863 Act only applied where they were specifically incorporated into a special Act for a particular railway.

[3] Highway (Railway Crossings) Act 1839, s 1; Railways Clauses Consolidation Act 1845, ss 47 and 61; Railways Clauses Consolidation (Scotland) Act 1845, ss 40 and 52;

[4] Railways Clauses Act 1863, s 5.

could only be made by private legislation or in some cases light railway orders, both of which involved "costly and time consuming procedures".[5] The new order-making procedure was seen as a better way of enabling such changes to be made.

5.6 The 1983 Act authorises the Secretary of State to make level crossing orders for the protection of those using a level crossing. In practice, the power to make level crossing orders is now frequently exercised by the Office of Rail Regulation under an Agency Agreement between the Secretary of State and ORR.[6]

5.7 An order can make such provision as the Secretary of State considers "necessary or expedient for the safety or convenience of those using the crossing". As we mentioned in Part 1, this power reflects the need to strike a balance between safety considerations and matters of convenience.

The definition of "level crossing" in the 1983 Act

5.8 The 1983 Act defines a "level crossing" as any place where a railway crosses a "road" on the level.[7] This definition is, of course, much narrower than the definition we have adopted for this project, as it is intended to operate only for the purposes of the 1983 Act order-making power. As we mentioned briefly in Part 1, there are, however, important differences in the definition of "road" in relation to England and Wales, on the one hand, and in relation to Scotland, on the other.

5.9 In relation to England and Wales, a "road" is "any highway or other road to which the public has access".[8] This definition covers all highways, including non-vehicular ones. The term "road to which the public has access" extends the definition to cover ways that can properly be described as "roads" (a matter of fact) where the public has lawful access by permission or tolerance.[9] Therefore, in relation to England and Wales, the 1983 Act applies to all public level crossings (where the railway crosses a highway) *and* some private level crossings where the public has been granted access (or takes access not unlawfully) to the level crossing, even though there is no public right of way over the level crossing.

5.10 The question is – in how many cases does the public have lawful access to private level crossings in England and Wales? We think it unlikely that there will be many cases. It is not enough that the public has access to a private level crossing as a matter of fact. The owner must permit the public to use the right of way. It is not sufficient for permission to extend to the landowner's employees or other specific licensees. Alternatively, the public use, while not permitted, must not be unlawful in the sense that it would negative the acquisition of a right of way

---

[5] *Hansard* (HL) 30 March 1983, vol 440, col 1660-1661.

[6] Agency Agreement dated October 2008.

[7] Level Crossings Act 1983, s 1(1).

[8] Level Crossings Act 1983, s 1(11). The definition of "road" is the same definition as is used in road traffic legislation: see for instance Road Traffic Act 1988, s 192(1) and Road Traffic Offenders Act 1988, s 98.

[9] *Clark (A P) and Others v Kato, Smith, and General Accident, Fire and Life Assurance Corporation plc and Cutter v Eagle Star Insurance Co Ltd* [1998] UKHL 36, [1998] 4 All ER 417.

by prescription.[10] We think it is unlikely that many purely private crossings (where there is no highway or road) fall into either of these categories. On the other hand, one situation where a level crossing might fall within these categories is where a single crossing accommodates both a private road and a highway in the form of a footpath or bridleway. Although it would be a matter of fact, in the vast majority of such cases we would expect the footpath or bridleway to cross the railway on the same line as the private road. At that point (even if not elsewhere), the private road would be a "road to which the public has access".

5.11 In relation to Scotland, "road" is defined in section 1(11) of the 1983 Act as having the same meaning as in section 151(1) of the Roads (Scotland) Act 1984. Accordingly, it is defined as "any way...over which there is a public right of passage...by whatever means". This definition would include footpaths and bridleways. Recent guidance on the meaning of the term "public right of passage" was provided by the decision of the Inner House, of the Court of Session in the case of *Hamilton v Dumfries and Galloway Council*.[11] The Court took the view that before a right can be said to be a "right of passage", it must be "no less extensive, and no less enforceable, than a right of way".[12] In other words, a public right of passage does not automatically exist over a way to which the public has access by permission; in order for there to be a public right of passage, a right of way must be capable of being established over the way in question. The effect of this decision is that, in relation to Scotland, and unlike the position in England and Wales, where the railway crosses a way over which the public has lawful access, but no enforceable right of way, the level crossing concerned is *not* covered by the Level Crossings Act 1983.

5.12 The consequence of the definitions of "road" is that in England and Wales the 1983 Act does not, we think, apply to the majority of private level crossings, as they involve neither a highway nor a road to which the public has lawful access. In Scotland, in view of the recent case law on the meaning of "public right of passage", the 1983 Act does not apply to any private level crossings.

Level crossing orders

5.13 Level crossing orders apply to *individual* level crossings. The Secretary of State can specify such protective equipment as considered necessary for the "safety or convenience of those using the crossing".[13]

5.14 The main steps in the order-making procedure are contained in section 1 of the 1983 Act. However, these are supplemented by guidance issued by ORR.[14]

5.15 The Secretary of State may make an order either following a request by the railway operator (currently Network Rail for the mainline network) or without such

---

[10]   This is discussed further in Part 12.

[11]   2009 SC 277.

[12]   See paragraph 61 of Lord Reed's judgment.

[13]   Level Crossings Act 1983, s 1(2).

[14]   ORR, *Guide to Level Crossing Order Submissions* (Issue 2 January 2008), http://www.rail-reg.gov.uk/upload/pdf/lx-submiss_guide2.pdf (last visited 27 June 2010). A note at the beginning of the guidance states that it is "issued as informal guidance and does not have legal authority".

a request.[15] In most cases the order is made following a request from the operator.[16] However, in some cases this may obscure what is actually happening – the operator may have been placed under a duty to make a request, ORR having given written notice to the operator to do so.[17]

5.16 It should be noted that if ORR issues a notice requiring the railway operator to request an order and the operator fails to do so, ORR has two options: it may issue an improvement or prohibition notice under HSWA 1974 to require compliance with the notice,[18] or it may advise the Secretary of State to make an order without a request.[19]

5.17 Under section 1 of the 1983 Act, before making an application for an order, the railway operator is required to give notice to the local traffic authority in whose area the level crossing is situated and to ORR of its intention to apply for an order. The notice of intention should be accompanied by a draft of the order sought specifying the period (not less than two months) within which the local traffic authority and ORR may make representations to the Secretary of State. If the Secretary of State makes the order without a request from the operator then the same consultation requirements apply. Before making the order, the Secretary of State must consider any representations made, provided that they are made within the specified time period.

5.18 A level crossing order may require the crossing operator or (following amendments to the 1983 Act by the Road Safety Act 2006) the local traffic authority, or both, to provide, maintain and operate specified protective equipment at or near the crossing.[20]

5.19 An order may include provisions relating to protective equipment that is already in place. Under section 1(2)(b) of the 1983 Act, requirements as to the operation of the railway at or near the crossing may be imposed on the operator.

5.20 Regulation 3 of the Level Crossings Regulations 1997,[21] made under section 15

---

[15] Level Crossings Act 1983, s 1(6).

[16] "Operator" is defined in s 1(11) of the Level Crossings Act 1983 in effect to mean the operator of the railway network, that is, Network Rail, heritage and private operators.

[17] Level Crossings Act 1983, s 1(6A). This appears to be a somewhat cumbersome procedure.

[18] Health and Safety at Work etc Act 1974, ss 21 and 22. ORR is made responsible for issuing improvement and prohibition notices under the Health and Safety (Enforcing Authority for Railways and Other Guided Transport Systems) Regulations 2006, SI 2006 No 557, reg 4(4).

[19] ORR, *Guide to Level Crossing Order Submissions* (January 2008) p 17, para 5.

[20] Section 1(11) of the 1983 Act adopts the definition of "local traffic authority" in the Road Traffic Regulation Act 1984. According to s 121A(5) of the 1984 Act, the term means in England and Wales a traffic authority other than the Secretary of State, who in turn is the traffic authority for every highway for which he or she is the highway authority under the Highways Act 1980. In other words, "local traffic authority" is usually the relevant county council or metropolitan district council. In relation to Scotland the local traffic authority is a traffic authority other than the Secretary of State or the Scottish Ministers. In other words, it is the council as constituted under section 2 of the Local Government etc Scotland Act 1994 within whose area the road is located.

[21] SI 1997 No 487.

of HSWA 1974, imposes a duty on the railway operator to ensure that the requirements of a level crossing order under the 1983 Act are complied with.[22] If an order is not complied with, ORR may issue the railway operator with an improvement notice under section 21 of HSWA 1974 or a prohibition notice under section 22 of the Act, or prosecute the railway operator.[23] Improvement and prohibition notices may be used to enforce level crossing orders because the 1997 Regulations create a duty on the operator of a railway to comply with a level crossing order. Section 15 of HSWA 1974, as read with section 53 of the Act, provides that regulations made under section 15 of the Act are "health and safety regulations". In terms of section 53, health and safety regulations are "relevant statutory provisions" for the purposes of the Act. Accordingly, the 1997 Regulations are health and safety regulations and hence "relevant statutory provisions". Sections 21 and 22 of HSWA 1974 allow the use of improvement or prohibition notices as part of the enforcement powers under the Act where "relevant statutory provisions" are contravened.

5.21 An improvement notice requires the operator to remedy the situation within a specified time. Prohibition notices are issued where ORR considers that there is a risk of injury to a person as a result of an activity. The notice directs the operator to stop activities until matters specified in the notice have been remedied. The legislative route to the use of improvement and prohibition notices under HSWA 1974 in connection with enforcement of a level crossing order is extremely complicated. We discuss this further below.

The relationship between special Acts and level crossing orders

5.22 The relationship between special Acts and level crossing orders is governed by section 1(3)(b) of the 1983 Act, as read with section 1(4A). Section 1(3)(b) provides that while an order is in force in relation to a level crossing:

> subject to any exceptions specified in the order, any provision made by or under any enactment as to the crossing … and imposing requirements as to … protective equipment at or near the crossing, the supervision of the crossing … or the operation of the railway at or near the crossing shall not apply in relation to the crossing.

5.23 Where a level crossing order is in force, (and subject to any provision in the order to the contrary) section 1(3)(b) *disapplies* any requirements in special Acts (or, subject to section 1(4) and (4A), in other legislation). What it does not do is *repeal* existing enactments. Consequently, in the event of a level crossing order ceasing to be in force, any provision in an enactment which makes provision in relation to the crossing will once again apply to that crossing.

---

[22] It should be noted that a breach of a level crossing order is an offence under regulation 3 of the Level Crossings Regulations 1997, SI 1997 No 487 and so can be prosecuted as an alternative to issuing an improvement or prohibition notice under HSWA 1974.

[23] In Scotland, prosecution is a matter for the Procurator Fiscal. It is worth noting that the Inner House of the Court of Session in *Clegg v Rogerson* 2008 SLT 345, held that a railway operator may be liable in the law of negligence, despite having fulfilled specific requirements, for example as laid down in a level crossing order.

Orders under the British Transport Commission Act 1957 and the Transport Act 1968

5.24 Orders made under section 66 of the British Transport Commission Act 1957 or section 124 of the Transport Act 1968 and in force immediately before 1 April 1997 are saved by section 1(10A) of the Level Crossings Act 1983.[24] Such orders have effect as if they had been made under the 1983 Act. Henceforth, we do not generally refer to orders under the 1957 and 1968 Acts, but they should be understood as being included when we refer to orders under the 1983 Act.

GENERAL SAFETY REGIME

5.25 In this section we consider the general legislation which regulates health and safety in the UK and how this interacts with the railway-specific safety provisions referred to in the preceding section. While railway safety is governed by the general scheme under HSWA 1974, special Acts and level crossing orders continue to play a role in regulating safety at level crossings.

5.26 Part 1 of HSWA 1974 introduced a general statutory framework regulating health and safety in the UK and established the Health and Safety Commission (HSC) and Executive (HSE).[25] Part 1 of HSWA 1974 does four things of particular relevance to the regulation of level crossings:

(1) it sets out general duties in relation to health and safety;[26]

(2) it provides powers to make health and safety regulations, which allow for tailored provision to be made in respect of particular industries or settings;[27]

(3) it contains a power to issue guidance in the form of approved codes of practice;[28] and

(4) it creates an enforcement regime for the general duties and regulations made under Part 1 of the Act.[29]

5.27 The general purposes of Part 1 of HSWA 1974 are set out in section 1(1). These include:

(a) securing the health, safety and welfare of persons at work;

(b) protecting persons other than persons at work against risks to health or safety arising out of or in connection with the activities of persons at work ... .

---

[24] Although section 66 of the 1957 Act and section 124 of the 1968 Act have been repealed, orders made under those provisions may still be in existence.

[25] Health and Safety at Work etc Act 1974, s 10(1). The HSC/HSE were subsequently abolished, and a new Health and Safety Executive was created: Legislative Reform (Health and Safety Executive) Order 2008 (SI 2008 No 960).

[26] Health and Safety at Work etc Act 1974, ss 2-4

[27] Health and Safety at Work etc Act 1974, s 15.

[28] Health and Safety at Work etc Act 1974, s 16.

[29] Health and Safety at Work etc Act 1974, ss 18-26.

5.28   Section 1(2) of HSWA 1974 envisaged that regulations and codes of practice made under the Act would "progressively replace" existing legislative provisions relating to health and safety. Schedule 1 to HSWA 1974 lists a number of "existing statutory provisions", such as the Offices, Shops and Railway Premises Act 1963 that are to continue in force until they are progressively replaced under Part 1 of HSWA 1974.

Part 1 of HSWA 1974 and the general health and safety duties

5.29   The general health and safety duties set out in sections 2-4 of HSWA 1974 are relevant to level crossings. These provide for:

(1)   general duties on employers to do all that is reasonably practicable to protect the "health, safety and welfare at work of all of [their] employees" (section 2);

(2)   general duties to ensure that, in conducting their business, employers or self-employed persons do not endanger the health and safety of those not in their employment (section 3); and

(3)   general duties relating to those who have control of non-domestic premises, in relation to those who use such premises who are not their employees (section 4).

5.30   For the purposes of this project, sections 3 and 4 are particularly relevant. Neither is limited to the protection of employees. Section 3 in particular is aimed at protecting the general public against risks to health and safety caused by undertakings.

5.31   We now consider the application of HSWA 1974 to each of the following:

(1)   railways;

(2)   highways/roads; and

(3)   other duty-holders in relation to level crossings.

Application of HSWA 1974 to railways

5.32   It was not until the Railways Act 1993 that the system for securing safety on the railways generally was fully assimilated with the HSWA 1974 system. Up until that time, British Rail and other rail operators, as employers, were covered by the general duties in Part 1 of HSWA 1974 and regulations made or enforced under the Act.[30] However, the specific legislation governing railway safety had not been brought into the HSWA 1974 system until the enactment of section 117 of the Railways Act 1993. That section deemed a list of provisions relating to railway safety to be "existing statutory provisions" within the meaning of Part 1 of HSWA 1974, thus bringing them into the general scheme of the Act and applying its enforcement provisions to them. The Level Crossings Act 1983 is one of the listed provisions.

---

[30]   Health and Safety Commission, *Ensuring Safety on Britain's Railways* (1993).

5.33 It appears that initially there was also some doubt as to whether the "general purposes" set out in HSWA 1974 applied to certain safety matters relating to the railways. However, HSE considered themselves to be responsible for enforcing the the general duties under HSWA 1974 in relation to the railways, since the coming into force of HSWA 1974.[31] But to resolve the possible doubt section 117(2) of the 1993 Act specified that, "[i]f to any extent they would not do so apart from this subsection", the general purposes of HSWA 1974 would include a widely-stated set of railway safety purposes.

5.34 As noted above, section 117 of the Railways Act 1993 deems the Level Crossings Act 1983 in its entirety to be an "existing statutory provision". Section 53 of HSWA 1974 defines an "existing statutory provision" as:

> [T]he provisions of the Acts mentioned in Schedule 1 which are specified in the third column of that Schedule and of the regulations, orders or other instruments of a legislative character made or having effect under any provision so specified.

5.35 In law, therefore, all orders made under the Level Crossings Act 1983 are caught by the definition in HSWA 1974 of "existing statutory provisions" and so are subject to the enforcement provisions of HSWA 1974. Under HSWA 1974, HSE is in most cases the enforcement authority as regards compliance with the Act. However, in relation to certain aspects of railway regulation, ORR is the enforcement authority. Regulations make ORR the "enforcing authority" and set out ORR's enforcement responsibilities in relation to safety on the railways, including level crossings.[32]

5.36 The Level Crossings Act 1983 gives the Secretary of State power to make provision in a level crossing order "for the safety *or convenience* of those using the crossing".[33] This opens up the possibility that there are two sorts of orders, or parts of orders, under the Level Crossings Act – "safety" orders and "convenience" orders. On the face of it, the notion of an order making provision for "convenience" would seem to go beyond the concerns of HSWA 1974, which is only concerned with health and safety. But in practice, the line between "safety" and "convenience" will frequently be blurred or non-existent. The overall objective of the Level Crossings Act 1983 is to enable the Secretary of State to make orders to "provide for the protection of those using the level crossing". Even an adjustment made to protective equipment to make it more "convenient" is still *about* ensuring safety, which is the overall function of the protective equipment. Orders making provision as regards the "convenience" may be necessary to prevent ill-disciplined use of a crossing. But the reason for this is a safety one – ill-disciplined use is a threat to the safety of crossing users. It is therefore understandable that the law does not make separate provision for the enforcement of "safety orders" and "convenience orders"; and the assimilation of both to the safety regime under the 1993 Act is rational and appropriate.

---

[31] See Health and Safety Commission, *Ensuring Safety on Britain's Railways* (1993).

[32] Railways Act 2005, sch 3, paras 2 to 4; The Health and Safety (Enforcing Authority for Railways and Other Guided Transport Systems) Regulations 2006, SI 2006 No 557, reg 3.

[33] Level Crossings Act 1983, s 1(2).

Application of HSWA 1974 to highways/roads authorities

5.37 The large majority of public level crossings involve highways/roads which are the responsibility of local authorities, acting as highway or roads authorities. In a small number of cases, the highway authority will be the Secretary of State (who exercises these functions in England through the Highways Agency), or Welsh Ministers. In Scotland, local councils are roads authorities in respect of most roads in their area, although in the case of trunk roads in Scotland, the Scottish Ministers are the roads authority.[34] Where the highway or roads authority is the relevant local authority this is normally referred to as the local highway/roads authority. The legal consequences will be the same where the highway or roads authority is not a local authority.

5.38 The relevant general duty in Part 1 of HSWA 1974 is found in section 3, which provides:

> It shall be the duty of every employer to conduct his undertaking in such a way as to ensure, so far as is reasonably practicable, that persons not in his employment who may be affected thereby are not thereby exposed to risks to their health or safety.

5.39 The key phrase is "conduct his undertaking". The expression is not defined in the Act. It is a matter of fact, about which there are no "rigid rules".[35]

5.40 The performance of statutory functions by local authorities counts as "conduct" of its "undertaking" for the purposes of section 3 of HSWA 1974 in England and Wales.[36] We believe the same approach would be taken by the Scottish courts if the matter were to come before them. However, the nature of the "undertaking" of a statutory authority is not necessarily the same as that of a private individual. We are not aware of any authority directly on the point. However, we consider that what does and does not count as the "undertaking" of a local highway/roads authority will depend not only on the objective facts of the case, but also on the form and limits to the functions of the local highway/roads authority which are engaged by the case. Section 3 operates by instructing local authorities how to "conduct" their "undertaking" (that is, that they should do so in such a way as to ensure they minimise risks to health and safety). But to determine what a local highway/roads authority's "undertaking" is, one must look to its statutory functions. The application of section 3 will be determined by the way in which the "undertaking" of a local highway/roads authority is defined.

5.41 The "functions" of local highway/roads authorities include both powers and duties. The distinction may be important in determining whether an act or an omission is included within the notion of "conduct" in section 3.

---

[34] In relation to the vast majority of public roads in Scotland, the roads authority is the local council constituted in terms of section 2 of the Local Government etc (Scotland) Act 1994 within whose area the road is located. The only exceptions to this apply in relation to special roads, trunk roads and roads created by the Scottish Ministers in terms of section 19 of the Roads (Scotland) Act 1984.

[35] *R v Associated Octel Co Ltd* [1996] 4 All ER 846 at 852.

[36] *R (Hampstead Heath Winter Swimming Club and Another) v Corporation of London and another* [2005] 1 WLR 2930.

5.42   The key *duty* of local highway authorities (and where appropriate the Secretary of State as highway authority) in England and Wales is that contained in section 41 of the Highways Act 1980; that is, the duty to maintain the highway. Maintain includes repair. In Scotland a similar duty is placed on local roads authorities (and where appropriate the Scottish Ministers as roads authority) under sections 1 and 2 of the Roads (Scotland) Act 1984. In discharging its duty to maintain, a local highway/roads authority must be conducting its undertaking under section 3 of HSWA 1974. But if that is so, then the ambit of section 3 will be coterminous with that of section 41 of the 1980 Act and sections 1 and 2 of the 1984 Act. That means that if an act or omission is not covered by section 41 or sections 1 and 2, because of some qualification or exception to the duty, then neither would it be part of the conduct of the authority's undertaking. This is important, because the duty to maintain does not include a duty to erect road signs, nor to paint warnings on the surface of the road.[37] Under section 65 of the Road Traffic Regulation Act 1984, traffic authorities have a power, but not a duty, to erect traffic signs.[38]

5.43   The extent to which a public authority can be judicially reviewed in relation to its use of a power is limited. The Administrative Court will intervene, on an application for judicial review if, for example, the authority contravenes or exceeds the terms of a power, uses a power for an objective other than that for which it was conferred, or does something that is not authorised by the power.[39] The law in Scotland is similar. If a decision-making process is procedurally flawed then its decision will also be reviewable. But, if the section 3 duty only comes into play when public authorities are exercising public law powers or duties, section 3 cannot be used to require more than public law would. If a decision not to exercise a power to erect a sign at a level crossing was flawed in a public law sense, then the section 3 duty would bite, and the authority may be liable under health and safety law as well as public law. But health and safety law cannot expand on the underlying public law position. Section 3 cannot be used to transform the power to erect signs into a duty to erect signs.

5.44   Local highway/roads authorities *are* under a relevant duty (for the purposes of section 3 of HSWA 1974) set out in section 39 of the Road Traffic Act 1988.[40] This requires a relevant local authority to prepare and carry out a programme of measures to promote road safety, to undertake studies of accidents and, in light of them, take appropriate action to prevent accidents. Such action would include the exercise of the authority's powers to erect signs or paint warnings on roads. Section 39 has been described as the statutory recognition of professional risk assessment processes.[41] However, individuals cannot sue highway authorities for breach of this duty (nor is there a parallel common law duty of care in negligence), unlike the duty to maintain the highway discussed above. Rather,

[37]   *Lavis v Kent County Council* (1992) 90 LGR 416 (CA); *Gorringe v Calderdale Metropolitan District Council* [2004] UKHL 15, [2004] 1 WLR 1057.

[38]   The power under section 65 is placed on traffic authorities. Traffic authorities in England and Wales are broadly equivalent to highway authorities. In Scotland traffic authorities are broadly equivalent to roads authorities.

[39]   See generally H Woolf, J Jowell, A le Sueur, *De Smith's Judicial Review* (6th ed 2007) para 5-002.

[40]   Section 39 of the 1988 Act confers duties on "relevant local authorities" but in practice such authorities are the same as local highway/roads authorities.

[41]   *Great North Eastern Railway Limited v Hart* [2003] EWHC 2450 (QB) at [54].

section 39 is a "target duty" giving the authority a wide discretion.[42]

5.45 Carrying out the kind of risk assessments envisaged by section 39 is a purely public law duty. If a local authority failed to discharge the duty, it could be judicially reviewed. Discharging the duty (and the failure to do so) would also, therefore, be within the "conduct" of the authority's "undertaking", and so the duty in section 3 of HSWA 1974 would be engaged. However, the section 3 duty cannot go beyond the underlying statutory duty. In our view, the duty would be discharged by the proper undertaking by the authority of the kind of risk assessments contemplated by section 39. It would be a very rare case in which a specific failure to provide a sign at a level crossing would be judicially reviewable on the basis that it was a breach of the duty under section 39.

5.46 We consider that the consequences of this are as follows. First, where a highway authority is bound by the duty to maintain, it would be in breach of its responsibilities under section 3 of HSWA 1974 if in doing so it endangered the health and safety of non-employees.[43] Just as a failure to act can be a breach of the duty to maintain, so a failure to act could open a highway authority to liability under section 3 if the failure endangered health and safety in the same way. The result of this is that the enforcement procedures under HSWA 1974, including prosecution for criminal offences, could be used to prevent highway authorities failing to protect safety by adequately maintaining the highway (as required by section 41 of the Highways Act 1980) at a level crossing.

5.47 Second, the extent to which section 3 can be used in relation to the erection of signs and painting of warnings on the road is significantly more limited. Neither the power to erect signs under section 65 of the Road Traffic Act 1988, nor the duty to undertake risk management under section 39 of the 1988 Act, are likely in most cases to *require* a traffic authority to erect a specific sign at a particular level crossing (provided the decision-making process concerned was not flawed).

Application of HSWA 1974 to other duty-holders in relation to level crossings

5.48 A wide variety of people hold rights of way over the railway. Many of these rights are exercised for work-related purposes. Commonly, a private level crossing will have been created to accommodate a landowner in using the land on each side of the railway, for example, for agricultural purposes. Where the rights of way are exercised for employment or self employment purposes, section 3 of HSWA 1974 will apply. That section applies to both employers and the self-employed in the "conduct" of their "undertaking" and therefore they would be under a duty to do all that is reasonably practicable to ensure that, in their use of the level crossing, they do not expose others to safety risks.

5.49 However, where the use of a private crossing is not related to a business or other undertaking, clearly there will be no duty imposed on a user by HSWA 1974. This will occur, for example, where a person has a right over the railway at the level crossing to allow ordinary social access to his or her property.

---

[42] *Gorringe v Calderdale Metropolitan District Council* [2004] UKHL 15, [2004] 1 WLR 1057.

[43] Subject to the test under the Health and Safety at Work etc Act 1974 which requires duty-holders to minimise risk so far as is reasonably practicable.

Regulations under HSWA 1974

5.50 Section 15 of HSWA 1974 gives the Secretary of State a wide power to make regulations regarding health and safety matters for any of the general purposes in Part 1. ORR, as the safety regulator for the railways, has a duty to submit to the Secretary of State "such proposals as it considers appropriate for the making of regulations for [the] railway safety purposes".[44] It seems to us that the power in section 15 of HSWA 1974 is sufficiently broad to allow regulations to be made imposing obligations on highway/roads authorities in connection with the placing of signs and other warnings at level crossings, where to do so would further the safety purposes of HSWA 1974.

5.51 The Railways and Other Guided Transport Systems (Safety) Regulations 2006[45] were made under section 15 of HSWA 1974. Those Regulations require railway operators to maintain a safety management system.[46] The duty to maintain the safe operation of level crossings would fall within the safety management system. The Railway Safety (Miscellaneous Provisions) Regulations 1997,[47] which make provision for the safe operation of railways and other guided transport systems, were also made under section 15 of HSWA 1974. Taken together these Regulations and the safety management system provide a basic safety framework for railway operators.

Codes of practice under HSWA 1974

5.52 Section 16 of HSWA 1974 gives HSE the power to approve and issue codes of practice providing practical guidance with regard to compliance with the requirements of the Act.

5.53 Although breach of a code of practice issued under section 16 of HSWA 1974 is not itself a criminal offence, the codes can play an important role and may be admissible as evidence in criminal proceedings relating to a breach of health and safety duties. Thus a breach of a code can, in effect, provide *evidence* of a breach of a duty under the Act, which itself amounts to a criminal offence. Further, the burden of proof is reversed so that a breach of a code will be taken as sufficient evidence of a breach of the provision as charged, unless the employer can prove it was complied with in another way. In other words it is for the employer to prove the matter.

5.54 When ORR became the safety regulator for the railways, the Railways Act 2005 specifically excluded HSE from issuing approved codes of practice under section

---

[44] Railways Act 2005, sch 3, para 2(5).

[45] The Railways and Other Guided Transport Systems (Safety) Regulations 2006 (SI 2006 No 599) implemented the European Railway Safety Directive (2004/49/EC). The aim of the Directive was to provide a common framework for railway safety across Europe. Under the Regulations, railway operators and infrastructure managers must maintain safety management systems and hold a safety certificate/authorisation issued by ORR before they are allowed to operate on the railways.

[46] The Railways and Other Guided Transport Systems (Safety) Regulations 2006, SI 2006 No 599, reg 3.

[47] The Railway Safety (Miscellaneous Provisions) Regulations 1997, SI 1997 No 553.

16 of HSWA 1974 in relation to "railway safety purposes".[48] However, the equivalent power was not given to ORR. This means that at present approved codes of practice under HSWA 1974 cannot be issued in respect of railway safety matters. We are not aware of the reasons why the power was not transferred to ORR at the time of the Railways Act 2005.

THE RELATIONSHIP BETWEEN LEVEL CROSSING-SPECIFIC RULES AND HSWA 1974

Relationship between level crossing orders and HSWA 1974

5.55 Public level crossings are subject to three main sources of regulatory control:

(1) the original special Act, typically from the nineteenth century, which often lays down very specific rules about gates, gatekeepers and so on;

(2) orders made under the Level Crossings Act 1983. Not all public crossings have orders, so for those crossings the 1983 Act has only potential rather than actual relevance; and

(3) HSWA 1974 and regulations made thereunder.

There may be no conflict between these three. But if there is a conflict, which prevails?

Relationship between level crossing orders and special Acts

5.56 Section 1(3) of the 1983 Act provides:

> While an order is in force under this section in relation to a level crossing ... (b) any provision made by or under any enactment as to the crossing ... shall not apply in relation to the crossing.

That means that a level crossing order trumps the provisions of the special Act. The relationship between level crossing orders and earlier special Acts is therefore clear. What is less clear is the relationship between special Acts and level crossing orders on the one hand and HSWA 1974 on the other.

Relationship between level crossing orders and HSWA 1974

5.57 As enacted, the 1983 Act did not mention HSWA 1974. But in 1997 the 1983 Act was amended[49] by the addition of section 1(4A) which provided that: "Nothing in subsection (3)(b) above affects any provision made by or under Part I of the Health and Safety at Work etc Act 1974." That means that a level crossing order (at least such an order made after 1997) does not trump HSWA 1974. But subsection (4A) does not go so far as to say that HSWA 1974 trumps a level crossing order. Perhaps that is implied. Alternatively, it might be possible to argue that as the general duties under HSWA 1974 contain a "so far as reasonably practicable" for the purposes of those provisions qualification, the terms of any level crossing order must be taken into account in determining what is

---

[48] Health and Safety at Work etc Act 1974, s 16(1A), inserted by Railways Act 2005, sch 3, para 9.

[49] By the Level Crossings Regulations 1997, SI 1997 No 487.

"reasonably practicable". Such an argument, if successful, would lead to the conclusion that there could be no conflict and therefore the order would remain effective.

Relationship between special Acts and HSWA 1974

5.58 There is nothing in HSWA 1974 that specifically deals with the relationship between special Acts and HSWA 1974. The general rule of statutory interpretation is that later legislation prevails over earlier legislation.

5.59 But there is an opposing principle, that the general does not derogate from the specific:

> Where the literal meaning of a general enactment covers a situation for which specific provision is made by another enactment contained in an earlier Act, it is presumed that the situation was intended to continue to be dealt with by the specific provision rather than the later general one. Accordingly the earlier specific provision is not treated as impliedly repealed.[50]

5.60 On the basis of that principle it might be argued that the general provisions of HSWA 1974 do not prevail over the specific provisions of the special Acts.

5.61 Our impression is that in the railway industry the assumption is that the provisions of a level crossing order take precedence over special Act provisions, failing which HSWA 1974 applies. We mention this as background information not because it is in itself a legal argument.

5.62 Our conclusion is that the current position is far from clear. In Part 8 we invite comments on whether safety should be regulated by HSWA 1974 alone or whether the current system of regulation should be retained, subject to improvements being made to that system. **Depending on the outcome of consultation, we suggest that if the current system of regulation is to be retained, the relationships between special Acts, level crossing orders and HSWA 1974 duties should be clarified for the future.**

---

[50] F A R Bennion, *Bennion on Statutory Interpretation* (5th ed 2008) p 306.

PART 6
CLOSURE OF LEVEL CROSSINGS

INTRODUCTION

6.1 We now turn to consider the legal framework which allows a level crossing to be closed. By closure we mean the extinguishment[1] of the right to use the way which crosses the railway on the level. A level crossing can be closed with or without a replacement crossing. The Transport and Works Act 1992 (in England and Wales) and the Transport and Works (Scotland) Act 2007 contain provisions providing for closure with or without replacement.

6.2 In relation to closure with replacement, railway-specific provisions have frequently combined provision for closure of a level crossing with provision for a replacement bridge or underpass across the railway.[2] However, this still requires the removal of the right to use the way which crosses the railway on the level and the creation of a new right of way across the bridge or underpass.

6.3 Current legislation relating to highways in England and Wales distinguishes between closure, and closure with diversion of the way which crosses the railway.[3] In both cases, the public right of way over the level crossing will be extinguished, but in the second, the way is diverted to another place on the railway line. There are no equivalent statutory provisions applying to Scotland.

6.4 Closure is also necessary when reducing the status of a level crossing from public to private. In such a case the public right of way has to be extinguished.

6.5 A further key distinction in relation to closure of level crossings is that between public and private level crossings. Where a public right of way exists over a crossing a formal legal procedure involving public consultation is usually necessary. There are specific legislative provisions relating to the closure of public level crossings. By contrast, a private right over a way may be extinguished by a simple agreement with the holder(s) of the right. We discuss the closure of private crossings in detail in Parts 11 and 12, in connection with discussion of rights of way.

TRANSPORT AND WORKS ACT 1992 AND THE TRANSPORT AND WORKS (SCOTLAND) ACT 2007

6.6 Transport and works orders[4] may, among other things, provide for the "…extinguishment of rights over land, whether compulsorily or by agreement".[5]

---

[1] The term "extinguishment" is the term used in England and Wales. In Scotland the term "extinction" is used. However, the terms are synonymous. In this consultation paper we refer to "extinguishment".

[2] For example, Railways Clauses Act 1863, s 7.

[3] Highways Act 1980, ss 118A and 119A respectively.

[4] Made under the Transport and Works Act 1992 or the Transport and Works (Scotland) Act 2007.

[5] Transport and Works Act 1992, sch 1, para 4, and Transport and Works (Scotland) Act 2007, sch 1 para 4.

Accordingly, such orders can be used to extinguish a right of way over a crossing, or divert the right, creating a new right along a different route. This power applies both to public rights of way and private rights of way. There is also a power of compulsory acquisition of land, and a power of compulsory imposition of encumbrances on land. The procedure under the Transport and Works Acts can be used in respect of public and private crossings.

6.7 The advantage of a transport and works order is that closure either with or without diversion or replacement can be effected in a variety of situations. There is no restriction on the use of the order-making procedure.[6] However, the making of an order is subject to the requirements in section 5(6) of the 1992 Act (as regards England and Wales) and in similar terms in section 7 of the 2007 Act (as regards Scotland). Section 5(6) provides that:

> An order under section 1 or 3 above shall not extinguish any public right of way over land unless the Secretary of State or Welsh Ministers[7] is/are satisfied –
>
> (a) that an alternative right of way has been or will be provided, or
>
> (b) that the provision of an alternative right of way is not required.

6.8 The closure of a level crossing may be included in a transport and works order as part of a scheme for major works. Transport and works orders can also be used solely for the purpose of closing individual level crossings. However, we are only aware of a TAW/S order having been used to close a *single* level crossing in a small number of cases, in which there was no opposition to the closure.[8]

6.9 Nevertheless, the observations we have made above on the limitations of transport and works orders, to the effect that they are, in practice, too expensive and time-consuming to suit these purposes, are also relevant in this context.[9]

THE HIGHWAYS ACT 1980 (ENGLAND AND WALES)

6.10 Sections 118A and 119A of the Highways Act 1980[10] provide powers for councils to make orders for the stopping up and diversion of footpaths and bridleways which cross a railway.

---

[6] By way of contrast, ss 118A and 119A of the Highways Act 1980 (which apply in relation to England and Wales alone) only allow the way over a crossing to be extinguished or diverted in the interests of safety of members of the public.

[7] As mentioned in Part 2, functions under the Transport and Works Act 1992 in relation to Wales, are devolved to Welsh Ministers. Hereafter in this Part where we refer to the Secretary of State in respect of functions under the 1992 Act, the reference should be read as meaning Welsh Ministers in respect of the exercise of those functions in Wales.

[8] Examples of TAW/S orders which contain provisions relating to closure (and replacement) are: the Network Rail (West Coast Main Line) Order 2003, SI 2003 No 1075, arts 7-9 and the Felixstowe Branch Line and Ipswich Yard Improvement Order 2008, SI 2008 No 2512, arts 16-18. We are aware that transport and works orders have also been used in individual cases to provide for the reduction in status of public level crossings to private level crossings.

[9] See Part 4.

[10] Sections 118A and 119A were inserted by section 47 of the Transport and Works Act 1992.

Section 118A of the Highways Act 1980 (rail crossing extinguishment orders)

6.11 Section 118A of the 1980 Act provides for the stopping up of footpaths and bridleways crossing railways. As mentioned above, it gives councils the power to stop up a footpath or bridleway in the interests of safety of the public using or likely to use the level crossing. Section 118A allows for the extinguishment of the right of way across the railway at the level crossing, and as much more of it as is expedient, until it intersects with a similar right of way.[11]

6.12 The order is made by the council and confirmed by the Secretary of State or in relation to Wales, the Welsh Ministers,[12] unless unopposed, in which case there is no need for the Secretary of State to confirm it.

6.13 Under section 118A(4), the council should not make an order (nor the Secretary of State confirm one) unless they are satisfied that it is "expedient to do so having regard to all the circumstances". In particular they should have regard to:

(1) whether it is reasonably practicable to make the crossing safe for use by the public, and

(2) what arrangements have been made for ensuring that, if the order is confirmed, any appropriate barriers and signs are erected and maintained.[13]

6.14 The process for making an order can be initiated by a council or may be the result of a request from a member of the public or the railway operator. There is a procedure allowing the Secretary of State to make an order where the council does not initiate one. Where the railway operator makes a request for an order under section 118A, if the council have neither submitted it to the Secretary of State nor taken a decision themselves within six months of the request, then the Secretary of State can take the decision without consulting the council.[14]

6.15 Under section 118A(5), when making an order at the request of the operator of the railway, the council may require the operator to enter into an agreement to defray or apportion the costs of additional barriers or signs.

Section 119A of the Highways Act 1980 (rail crossing diversion orders)

6.16 Section 119A of the 1980 Act is similar to section 118A, except that it also makes provision for the diversion of the footpath or bridleway. It allows the council to make an order (subject to confirmation by the Secretary of State when it is opposed) to extinguish the right of way and create a new path for the right of way

---

[11] Under section 116 of the Highways Act 1980 the magistrates' court has power to order the stopping up of a vehicular highway as well as a footpath and bridleway and this may be requested by a developer or other person.

[12] As mentioned in Part 2, in relation to Wales, functions under sections 118A and 119A of the Highways Act 1980 are devolved to Welsh Ministers. Hereafter in this Part where we refer to the Secretary of State in respect of functions under those provisions, the reference should be read as meaning Welsh Ministers in respect of the exercise of those functions in Wales.

[13] Highways Act 1980, s 118A(4)(a).

[14] Highways Act 1980, s 120.

to effect its diversion.[15]

6.17   So far as the right of way across the level crossing itself is concerned, the procedure and grounds for closure are the same for sections 118A and 119A of the 1980 Act. However, there are slight differences where an order is made on the Secretary of State's own initiative without having received an order for confirmation from a council. In such cases, the Secretary of State has power to order that the railway operator defray or contribute to the costs consequent on the order.[16]

Provisions relating to the stopping up of highways under general highways legislation

6.18   Sections 118 and 119 of the Highways Act 1980 give a general power to councils to order the stopping up, or stopping up with diversion, of a footpath or bridleway on the ground that it is not needed for public use. These powers apply to any highway, footpath or bridleway, not just those over a railway. In addition, under section 116 of the 1980 Act a highway authority can apply to a magistrates' court to have a highway stopped up or diverted if it is unnecessary or can be diverted so as to make it nearer or more convenient for the public. Under section 117, another person, such as a developer, may request that the highway authority makes such an application.

Section 48 of the Transport and Works Act 1992

6.19   In relation to England and Wales only, section 48 of the Transport and Works Act 1992 applies where a closure or diversion application under section 6 of the 1992 Act or a request under section 120(3A)(b) of the Highways Act 1980 has been made.[17] Section 48 enables the Secretary of State to require the operator to provide a new tunnel or bridge (or improve an existing one) at or near the level crossing. However, section 48 is limited by the following factors:[18]

    (1)   It only applies to footpath and bridleway crossings;

    (2)   The railway operator has to have made an application for closure or diversion of the right of way over the crossing; and

    (3)   The Secretary of State is of the opinion that the crossing constitutes a danger to members of the public using it or likely to use it.

6.20   Section 48 is not, however, designed to be a general power for dealing with closure of level crossings.

---

[15]   Highways Act 1980, s 119A(2)(b).

[16]   Highways Act 1980, s 120.

[17]   An application under section 6 of the 1992 Act is for a transport and works order to be made under section 1 of the 1992 Act. A request under section 120(3A)(b) of the 1980 Act is a request for a rail crossing extinguishment order under section 118A of the 1992 Act or a rail crossing diversion order under section 119A of the 1992 Act. As none of these provisions apply to Scotland, section 48 of the 1992 Act does not apply in practice in relation to Scotland.

[18]   Transport and Works Act 1992, s 48(1).

6.21 Under section 48(6) of the 1992 Act, the railway operator is not in breach of an order if it fails to meet its requirements but has used its "best endeavours" (including seeking a transport and works order under section 1).[19]

Closure and diversion of public crossings in Scotland: The Roads (Scotland) Act 1984

6.22 By contrast with England and Wales, there is no specific provision in Scotland for the stopping up or diversion of ways, whether vehicular or non-vehicular, which cross a railway on the level. Section 68 of the Roads (Scotland) Act 1984 confers a *general* power on roads authorities to stop up a "road" as defined in the Act.[20] The definition covers both vehicular and non-vehicular ways over which a public right of passage exists.

6.23 It seems that the power in section 68 of the 1984 Act could be used to close any public level crossing to which it applies. The power is exercisable by a roads authority either on its own initiative or at the request of any person. An order may be made where the relevant roads authority is of the opinion that the road has either become dangerous to the public or that it has or will become unnecessary. Before making an order the roads authority must satisfy itself that a suitable alternative road exists or that no alternative road is needed.

6.24 An order under section 68 of the 1984 Act may provide for the stopping up of a road, subject to the reservation of a means of passage along the road for pedestrians, cyclists or both. If the road is to be stopped up because it has become dangerous to the public, it may not be safe to reserve a means of passage for pedestrians and cyclists. It will be for the roads authority to decide whether or not any such reservation is appropriate in the circumstances of the case, taking account of its implied duty to promote road safety.[21]

6.25 There is no general provision in the Roads (Scotland) Act 1984 for diversion of a "road" within the meaning of the Act. The default position appears to be that where a new road provides an alternative route to an existing road, section 68 of the 1984 Act could be used to stop up the, now unnecessary, existing road. Certain specific provisions for diversion do exist under the 1984 Act, but apply only in a very narrow range of circumstances not relevant to level crossings.[22]

6.26 Section 152(2) of the 1984 Act empowers a roads authority to order the redetermination of the means of exercise of a public right of passage. In effect, it extends the power conferred on roads authorities by section 1 of the 1984 Act; section 1(1)(a) allows roads authorities to determine the means of exercise of a

---

[19] Transport and Works Act 1992, s 48(7). We are not aware of an instance where section 48 has been used.

[20] This is qualified to the extent that the Roads (Scotland) Act 1984 does not confer any power or duty in respect of a public path created by agreement in terms of section 30 of the Countryside (Scotland) Act 1967 (section 151(3) of the 1984 Act). As discussed further below, separate provision exists for both the stopping up and diversion of such paths, in so far as they remain in existence.

[21] A Faulds, T Craggs and J Saunders, *Scottish Roads Law* (2nd ed 2008) p 131, para 9.3.3.

[22] Roads (Scotland) Act 1984, section 69. See also section 12 allowing stopping up, diversion or improvement of a "side road" which crosses or enters the route of a main road or is affected by the construction or improvement of a main road.

public right of passage over a "public road". The power under section 1, and therefore the power under section 152(2), applies only in relation to "public" roads. Under the 1984 Act, a "public road" means a road which the roads authority has a duty to maintain.[23]

6.27 Section 152(2) of the 1984 Act seems to cater for the situation in which, although section 68 does not apply (for example, the road in question has not become dangerous to the public), a roads authority nevertheless wishes to re-determine the means of exercise of the public right of passage over the road. For example, this section could be used if a roads authority wished to prohibit vehicular passage over a level crossing which was not particularly unsafe or unnecessary, while retaining pedestrian use.

Closure and diversion of public crossings: The Roads (Scotland) Act 1984, Countryside (Scotland) Act 1967 and the Land Reform (Scotland) Act 2003

6.28 In relation to ways in Scotland over which the public right of passage is by foot only, or by foot and on horseback, in general the Roads (Scotland) Act 1984 will apply as described above.

6.29 However, the 1984 Act does not apply in relation to public paths created by agreement under section 30 of the Countryside (Scotland) Act 1967. Section 30(3) of the 1967 Act defines a public path as "a way which is a footpath or bridleway or a combination of those". A public path may be created by agreement, in general between the local planning authority and the owner of the land crossed by the path. Alternatively, a public path may be created by order, where the relevant planning authority is satisfied that it is expedient to create a new public path but considers that it is not practicable for an agreement under section 30 to be reached.

6.30 Sections 34 and 35 of the 1967 Act make provision respectively for the stopping up and diversion of such paths by planning authorities. The stopping up power under section 34 is exercisable where it appears to the planning authority that the public path should be stopped up on grounds that it is no longer needed for public use. The power to divert a public path under section 35 may be invoked where the relevant planning authority is satisfied by the owner, tenant or occupier of land crossed by a public path that it is expedient that the line of the path, or part of it, should be diverted to secure the efficient use of the land crossed by the path, or other land held in addition to it, or in order to provide a shorter or more convenient path across the land.

6.31 The system of public paths has been replaced, for the most part, by the system of "core paths" provided for in the Land Reform (Scotland) Act 2003.[24] A core path is "a path, waterway or any other means of crossing land … which is set out in a [core path] plan adopted under section 18 [of the 2003 Act]".[25] Section 17(1) of

---

[23] Roads (Scotland) Act 1984, s 151(1).

[24] Provision for public paths is made by sections 30 to 38 of the Countryside (Scotland) Act 1967. Whilst these provisions have now been repealed for most purposes, they remain subject to a savings provision provided for in paragraph 7 of Schedule 2 to the Land Reform (Scotland) Act 2003. As a result of the savings provision certain paths continue to be governed by the 1967 Act and are still known as "public paths".

[25] Land Reform (Scotland) Act 2003, s 32.

the 2003 Act requires each local authority to maintain a plan showing all of the routes in its area which have been designated as core paths. In terms of section 17(2) these may include rights of way by foot, horseback or pedal cycle.

6.32 Section 5(6) of the 2003 Act expressly provides that access rights do not constitute a public right of passage for the purposes of the definition of "road" in section 151(3) of the Roads (Scotland) Act 1984.

6.33 Prior to their designation as core paths, certain routes may have been covered by pre-existing public rights of way. On that basis, it appears that a public right of passage for the purposes of the Roads (Scotland) Act 1984 exists over such routes.[26] Section 5(3) of the Land Reform (Scotland) Act 2003 makes it clear that such pre-existing rights are not diminished or displaced by the presence of access rights under section 1 of the 1984 Act. As a result, access rights and public rights of passage for the purposes of the Roads (Scotland) Act 1984 may co-exist over certain core paths.

6.34 It seems reasonably clear that access rights under the Land Reform (Scotland) Act 2003 exist automatically over any route that is designated as a core path. It also seems clear that access rights do not ordinarily exist over railways and private level crossings.[27] However, in terms of section 7(1) of the 2003 Act, where land has been designated as a core path the section 6 exclusions do not apply. As a result, although access rights would not *ordinarily* exist over a private level crossing, such rights *will* exist where a way over a private level crossing has been designated as a core path. The Land Reform (Scotland) Act 2003 is discussed further in Part 12.

Town and Country Planning

Town and Country Planning Act 1990 (England and Wales)

6.35 As we note in Part 9, on planning, there are also circumstances in England and Wales where a level crossing could potentially be closed through the operation of section 247 of the Town and Country Planning Act 1990, as the consequence of a planning decision. However, we have no evidence of this having been done. In addition, local planning authorities have power under section 257 of the 1990 Act to stop up or divert footpaths and bridleways where it is necessary in order to carry out works authorised under planning permission.

Town and Country Planning (Scotland) Act 1997

6.36 In relation to Scotland, section 207 of the Town and Country Planning (Scotland) Act 1997 provides an equivalent power for a planning authority to stop up or divert "roads", as defined in the Roads (Scotland) Act 1984,[28] (other than trunk roads and special roads included in a scheme drawn up by the Scottish Ministers) where this is thought necessary for the carrying out of a development.

---

[26] Applying the approach of *Hamilton v Dumfries and Galloway Council* 2009 SC 277, it would seem that in so far as a public right of way exists over any given route, a public right of passage for the purposes of the Roads (Scotland) Act 1984 will be deemed to exist.

[27] This is as a result of the operation of section 6(1)(d) of the Land Reform (Scotland) Act 2003.

[28] Roads (Scotland) Act 1984, s 151.

Section 208 of the 1997 Act makes identical provision for the stopping up and diversion of footpaths and bridleways.

Specific provision incorporated into special Acts

6.37 Section 7 of the Railways Clauses Act 1863, which applies equally to England, Wales and Scotland, may have been specifically incorporated into a special Act. This gives the Secretary of State the power to require a railway company to carry a "turnpike or public carriage road" (now, essentially a public vehicular right of way) over or under the railway by means of a bridge or underpass, instead of on the level. The power could be exercised at any time after the passing of the special Act where it appears to the Secretary of State necessary in the interests of public safety.

6.38 The power in section 7 of the 1863 Act is narrow, in a number of respects. It is only exercisable where certain types of public vehicular way cross a railway on the level; it does not provide for the replacement of footpath or bridleway crossings with bridges, nor does it cover private level crossings. The only ground on which replacement may be required is where it is necessary in the interests of public safety. Furthermore, the power is only exercisable where the existing level crossing is to be replaced. Issues relating to the stopping up or diversion of the right of way over the crossing are not covered.

6.39 We are not aware of any modern use of section 7 of the 1863 Act. We think it unlikely that there are any public vehicular crossings so unsafe that a requirement to close them under section 7 would be imposed on the railway operator nowadays. The primary argument for replacement of a public vehicular level crossing nowadays is that it would be more efficient to do so.

6.40 In terms of funding such a bridge or underpass, section 16(1) of the Railway and Canal Traffic Act 1888 contains a provision which allows for funding agreements where either the Secretary of State or Scottish Ministers has exercised a power in any public general Act or a power in a special Act to require a railway undertaker to build a bridge. However, we are not aware of any modern use of section 16 in connection with level crossings.

Road-rail partnership groups

6.41 It is relevant to discussion about closure of level crossings to mention recent initiatives in fostering co-operation among the interested parties, through the establishment of road-rail partnerships.

6.42 Road-rail partnership groups are formed voluntarily by agreement, usually among Network Rail, a local authority (in its capacity as a highway or roads authority) and other bodies. There is also a road-rail partnership between Network Rail and the Highways Agency for England and Wales. Representatives of local highway/roads authorities involved in road-rail partnership groups are likely to include road safety managers, planners, rights of way officers and strategy/policy managers. Network Rail representatives will typically include those with expertise in such areas as operational risk management, asset maintenance and route enhancement. The aim of road-rail partnership groups is to promote collaborative working in connection with matters relating to level crossings, including closure. Indeed, joint identification of opportunities for the closure of crossings has been one of the key achievements of road-rail partnership groups to date. We discuss these groups further in Part 8.

Provisional conclusions on the current legislation relating to closure of public level crossings

6.43 In relation to England and Wales, the provisions of the Highways Act 1980 relating to stopping up only apply to public footpaths and bridleways, rather than public vehicular ways, and are limited to safety reasons. However, as discussed above, the Highways Act 1980 does provide for a magistrates' court to order the stopping up or diversion of a highway in certain circumstances. Nevertheless, the 1980 Act does not adequately address all the situations where a public right of way over a level crossing may need to be extinguished or diverted.

6.44 Similarly, in Scotland, the general stopping up provisions of the Roads (Scotland) Act 1984 are restricted to grounds of safety and necessity. There is no provision which relates specifically to level crossings. It also seems that there is a gap in provision for the diversion of ways (over which there is a public right of passage) which are neither "core paths" under the Land Reform (Scotland) Act 2003 nor "public paths" under the Countryside (Scotland) Act 1967. It should also be noted that the powers of stopping up and diversion in relation to both "public paths" and "core paths" are not exercisable on safety grounds. Rather they are exercisable only on the basis of consideration of convenience of the public and the effect of stopping up or diversion upon the land over which the path runs.

CLOSURE OF PRIVATE LEVEL CROSSINGS

6.45 A private level crossing can be closed by agreement between the railway operator and the owner of the right of way over the railway. There are no means by which a private level crossing can be compulsorily closed against the wishes of the owner of the right of way, apart from the order-making powers under the Transport and Works Act 1992 and the Transport and Works (Scotland) Act 2007 or by compulsory purchase.[29] It is unlikely that a system designed for much larger scale works, would be used solely for the closure of a single *private* level crossing. We are not aware of any such use.

6.46 We deal in detail with the nature of these rights of way, and the means by which they may be extinguished, in Parts 11 and 12, where we also discuss the power of the Lands Tribunal for Scotland to discharge servitudes. We merely note here that there are substantive differences in the law between England and Wales, and Scotland.

---

[29] This is discussed in more detail in Part 8.

PART 7
THE CASE FOR REFORM

INTRODUCTION

7.1 In this Part we move from an account of the current law to consider the case for reform. We start by setting out what we consider the key aims of the regulatory regime for level crossings should be, and then consider regulatory approaches generally and whether the current regime satisfies the basic requirements. Finally, we outline briefly recent work on cost-benefit analysis of retaining level crossings as against closing them.

AIMS OF LEVEL CROSSING REGULATION

7.2 There are some requirements that are common to all regulatory regimes. They should be clear, consistent and transparent. However, there are also requirements specific to level crossings which are determined by the physical engineering involved and the responsibilities and aims of both regulators and regulated.

7.3 **We provisionally propose that the regulatory regime for level crossings should aim to:**

    (1)   ensure safety at level crossings;

    (2)   promote the efficient operation of railways and, where present, highways/roads, taking account of the need to strike a balance between the interests of rail, road and other users;

    (3)   allocate duties and responsibilities appropriately amongst the various actors; and

    (4)   provide appropriate means to define rights of way at level crossings in so far as feasible, and to extinguish them where necessary.

7.4 So far as is possible, any changes should fit into and take into account the existing legal structures at a level crossing, for instance the provisions of highways/roads and planning legislation.

7.5 **We welcome views on whether these objectives provide an appropriate guide for reform. Would any other objectives be appropriate?**

7.6 To achieve its primary aims, the regulatory regime should include appropriate and proportionate procedures for the permanent closure of level crossings by the extinguishment of rights of way over crossings with or without diversion or replacement with a bridge or underpass. Such procedures should allow the economics in relation to each level crossing to be taken into account in making decisions about closure and replacement. However, economic arguments should not be the only matter taken into consideration.

7.7 Where regulatory action involves interference with rights or land administered by another public body, for instance a highway/roads authority, there should be a suitable dispute-resolution mechanism.

7.8 The regulatory regime should be capable of apportioning costs where appropriate between the railway, public bodies and, where relevant, private actors such as developers.

7.9 Where settlement under the dispute-resolution mechanism is not possible, there should be some other form of mechanism that encourages settlement. If settlement is not possible and it is still thought necessary to interfere with private rights and interests, there should be a clear mechanism for doing this, including an appeal structure and, where necessary, provision for compensation.

REGULATORY APPROACHES

7.10 In recent years, a considerable literature on regulatory theory has developed. Central government has adopted its own approach to regulatory theory, which has informed developments in administrative practice and legislation. We do not think it appropriate to rehearse at length the different approaches to regulation in this paper. We have, however, prepared a short paper setting them out and considering their application in the context of level crossings.[1] In the rest of this section, we consider some of the broad lessons we have drawn.

Regulatory structure and regulatory content

7.11 We suggest that a helpful way to look at regulation is to break it down into consideration of the interdependent concepts of "structure" and "content". Some approaches focus on the powers of the actors involved and the relationship between them. Other approaches focus on the content of regulation.

General versus specific rules

7.12 Some rules use a broad approach and generally applicable provisions, such as the general principles set out in HSWA 1974. At the other end of the spectrum are very specific rules. For example, level crossing orders made under the Level Crossings Act 1983 contain specific provision about the safety measures to be put in place at individual crossings.

7.13 At present, the general rules under HSWA 1974 do play a role in relation to level crossings. It is, however, probably more accurate to see the practice under the current law relating to the regulation of level crossings as exemplifying the specific approach, with separate provision potentially made for each level crossing.

Regulatory structure

7.14 In relation to level crossings, there is a number of important public sector actors. For current purposes, they include the Secretary of State and Scottish Ministers, the Welsh Assembly Government and local authorities. As mentioned earlier in the consultation paper, the Office of Rail Regulation is the economic and safety regulator for the railways.

---

[1] The paper is available on our websites at www.lawcom.gov.uk and www.scotlawcom.gov.uk.

7.15 It would be fair to say that the course of post-privatisation history has been more difficult for the railways than other privatised industries, and the regulatory structure has undergone significant changes, most recently in the aftermath of the collapse of Railtrack plc. It follows from what we have said above that our provisional view is that there should not be wholesale institutional change to the identities, roles and responsibilities of these key actors. In particular, we would not propose a new "level crossings regulator".

7.16 We do propose changes to the powers and duties of the existing actors and, as a consequence, the relationships between them. We see these changes as building on their existing roles and responsibilities.

7.17 The recent history of rail regulation also suggests that we should not automatically assume regulatory stability. Whilst it seems likely that there will always need to be a safety regulator for the railways, we cannot assume that ORR as presently constituted will always fulfil that function. If legislation results from this project, it is likely therefore to have to be adaptable to different institutional arrangements over time. For this reason, we have sought to ensure that our provisional proposals would work in the context of existing institutions, whilst also being capable of adapting to any new arrangements.

Regulatory content

7.18 Modern approaches to regulation would suggest an alternative to prescriptive legal provision for individual level crossings. The alternative approach would involve greater use of general regulations that can easily be amended. Later in the consultation paper we propose adopting such an approach in relation to level crossings.

7.19 The benefits of such a general approach would accrue to both regulator and regulated, in the form of a simpler, more accessible and more proportionate regulatory regime. Reliance on general regulations, which could be amended from time to time to take account of advancements in technology or safety provision, would remove the need to update individual provision in relation to safety at level crossings.

ANALYSIS: THE CASE FOR REFORM

7.20 As we have seen, the law governing level crossings is far from clear, consistent and accessible. The current provisions governing level crossings are scattered in public general Acts, private Acts, secondary legislation and administrative orders.

7.21 Reliance on individual level crossing orders prescribing specific safety measures, which must be complied with exactly, can potentially limit the timely reaction to developments in safety technology. For example, a report of the Rail Accident Investigation Branch might show that a simple change to the lighting at public level crossings or an alteration to the warning sounds would make level crossings safer. A regulatory regime based on individual orders, as at present, could only react to such a general recommendation by altering each of the existing level crossing orders, and possibly making orders where none previously existed. This seems an unnecessary burden to place on both the regulator and the regulated.

7.22 We suggest that the current regulatory regime should be reformed in order, among other things, to address the problem associated with making generic changes to the safety provision at level crossings.

7.23 At present, the absence of general regulations under HSWA 1974, applying to all or at least most level crossings, means that where there is no level crossing order in respect of a level crossing, only the general duties in Part 1 of HSWA 1974 or the special Act apply to govern safety provision at that crossing.

7.24 It should be remembered that the general duties in HSWA 1974 were intended to be amplified over time by regulations and approved codes of practice that would set out the safety requirements for individual industries. The only regulations made under section 15 of HSWA 1974 specifically in relation to level crossings are the Level Crossings Regulations 1997.[2] However, these regulations were merely a vehicle for amending the Level Crossings Act 1983, not an attempt to use regulations to provide a framework for regulating safety at level crossings.

7.25 Although we suggest that general regulations under HSWA 1974 would be desirable, these would need to be supported by approved codes of practice under the Act. Following the Railways Act 2005, there is no power for any institution to make codes of practice under section 16 of HSWA 1974 for "railway safety purposes". Given the current nature of level crossing regulation, this may not constitute a problem. Individual level crossing orders specify the exact safety measures that should be put in place at a level crossing. Codes of practice are designed to amplify and provide detailed guidance on general regulations. If there were a move to greater reliance on general safety regulations under HSWA 1974, we suggest that it would be important for there to be approved codes of practice alongside the regulations.

7.26 We do not think that the current distinction between public and private level crossings is appropriate for all purposes. The distinction means that, in relation to safety, there are different sets of tools open to the regulator, depending not on the risk factors present at a particular level crossing but on the legal nature of the way that crosses the railway. For safety purposes, it is not helpful to distinguish between public and private level crossings. As mentioned above, orders under the Level Crossings Act 1983 can be made in respect of public level crossings but only those private level crossings in England and Wales to which the public has lawful access and no private level crossings in Scotland. We would seek to ensure that as regards safety, future regulation should be more flexible in its approach.

7.27 As we discussed in Part 5, the current system of regulating safety is complicated by the fact that safety is governed by the general duties in Part 1 of HSWA 1974, in addition to the specific provisions in special Acts or level crossing orders. We suggest that a simpler and clearer approach to safety regulation is required.

7.28 As we explored in Part 6, the current highways legislation in England and Wales only allows for the extinguishment of rights of way across the railway to be ordered in restricted circumstances, mainly for safety reasons. As a result the possibility of a level crossing being closed, with or without replacement, is limited.

---

[2] Level Crossings Regulations 1997, SI 1997 No 487.

7.29 While the order-making process under section 1 of the Transport and Works Act 1992 or section 1 of the Transport and Works (Scotland) Act 2007 can be used, as we also set out in Part 5, the procedure is potentially expensive and time-consuming and not appropriate for the closure of individual level crossings. The procedure appears to be more suitable where closure of level crossings is part of a larger engineering project.

7.30 **We provisionally think that the current regulatory regime should be reformed as it does not sufficiently recognise the potentially competing interests affecting level crossings and does not adequately cater for all level crossings.**

ECONOMIC MODELLING OF LEVEL CROSSINGS

7.31 It is possible to use an economic model to assess the costs and benefits of replacing a level crossing with a bridge or underpass, against alternatives such as doing nothing or upgrading safety provision.

7.32 The costs which must be taken into account include: those associated with maintaining the level crossing, the cost of delay to road and rail users, the cost of accidents at the crossing, and the cost of construction and subsequent maintenance of any alternative.

7.33 The delay caused to drivers at a public vehicular level crossing can be expressed in economic terms relatively easily. The two main approaches are to calculate either the lost productivity of those individuals delayed or the amount that they would be willing to pay not to be delayed. At a theoretical level, these approaches should give identical figures. However, this will not always be the case in practice. The Transport Research Laboratory undertook a major research project in 2008 into the impact of traffic delays at level crossings with a view to finding ways to reduce the delays.[3]

7.34 While it is vital that level crossings be closed to road traffic in order to allow trains to pass, this has to be balanced against the need to avoid undue delay to traffic on the road network and the possible dangers associated with tailbacks at level crossings. Some public level crossings are closed for up to 45 minutes in the hour and this can cause tailbacks on the roads approaching the crossings, with resultant traffic delays. This raises the question as to whether the balance between use of the railway and use of the roads crossing railways is fair and appropriate.

7.35 Delay to trains is difficult to attribute to a single level crossing. Generally speaking, trains will only be delayed If there is a sufficient number of level crossings on a particular stretch of track to justify a reduction in the line speed. Removing a single crossing will in most cases not affect the line speed decision. On the other hand, delay consequent on accidents at or damage to a level crossing is more readily quantifiable, although this would have to be balanced against any delay occasioned by damage to bridges.

7.36 Moreover, it is possible to express the potential cost of accidents at level

---

[3] E Delmonte and S Tong, Traffic Research Laboratory Report No PPR377, *Investigation into traffic delays at level crossings* (December 2008).

crossings in economic terms. This would entail combining the risk of an injury occurring with the economic loss that such an injury would occasion to the injured person and the consequent loss to the wider economy. On this basis, the economic impact of an accident would vary from person to person. In order to extrapolate a wider picture, a standardised cost must be assumed that applies to every death or other injury at a level crossing.

7.37 Finally, there is the risk of catastrophic loss. This is something that both injures a large number of people and results in a significant change in the way in which railways operate. It may have major economic implications. An example is the Hatfield rail accident of 17 October 2000.[4]

The AXIAT model

7.38 The Rail Safety and Standards Board has developed such a model: the *Alternatives to Level Crossings Assessment Tool* or "AXIAT".[5] The model only applies to public vehicular level crossings.[6] It considers the costs of maintaining an existing level crossing against the most favoured alternative and includes quantification of safety and delay costs.[7] The model is in the process of being rolled out across the country. An initial study of the level crossings in four counties in England indicated that there was an initial economic case for replacing 49 out of a total of 288 level crossings (or 17% of the total). Given the low number of public crossings which are currently replaced,[8] such modelling may indicate that replacement should be more fully considered in relation to a greater number of level crossings.

7.39 AXIAT is only one way of modelling the costs and benefits of level crossings. It is designed essentially as a screening tool to identify those level crossings where there is most likely to be a case for replacement. Once a candidate level crossing has been identified, a more detailed site-specific cost/benefit analysis would have to be prepared as a basis for a case for allocation of the necessary funds.

Conclusions on economic modelling

7.40 Any model will necessarily be limited by the inputs chosen and the weight given to each input, and it does not provide an answer as to whether the change suggested is desirable, once all factors are taken into account. Even where there are good *economic* arguments that a particular level crossing should be replaced, other compelling public policy considerations (such as protection of rights of way,

---

[4] Significantly, level crossings carry some 42% of the total risk of such an event happening on the railways: Rail Safety and Standards Board, *Road Rail Interface Special Topic Report 2010* (April 2010) p 5.

[5] See www.rssb.co.uk/SiteCollectionDocuments/pdf/reports/Research/T336_rb_final.pdf (last visited 27 June 2010).

[6] It is not designed to consider public level crossings with bridleways or footpaths, or private level crossings.

[7] We provide further detail in the impact assessment to this consultation paper which is available to download from our websites: www.lawcom.gov.uk and www.scotlawcom.gov.uk

[8] A significant number of level crossings *are* closed each year, but we understand that the large majority are private vehicular crossings which have been bought out by Network Rail and the remainder are all or nearly all footpath and bridleway crossings.

local amenity, and local and national transport policy) may outweigh these arguments.

7.41 Models which, like AXIAT, focus on the costs and benefits to society as a whole risk obscuring the fact that decisions about level crossings are taken by individual actors such as railway operators or highway/roads authorities. Not all of the costs included in the AXIAT model will be borne by every actor. Indeed, some actors currently bear none of the costs associated with maintaining a level crossing, but might have to bear the costs of maintaining a bridge. For such actors, even where level crossing replacement provides general economic benefits, their own cost/benefit analyses may act as a disincentive to agreeing to such a scheme.

7.42 Further, economic models such as AXIAT are designed to show the potential wider benefits of change at a level crossing. AXIAT cannot show that this is an appropriate allocation of public resources, particularly when compared to other options available to highway and roads authorities. Good highways schemes, designed to improve safety and reduce delays, frequently exhibit much higher positive cost/benefit ratios than those typical of even a good case for the replacement of a level crossing using the AXIAT model.

7.43 Nevertheless, the disparity between the (initial) findings of the AXIAT model, and the number of public vehicular level crossings actually closed, suggests that there are features of the legal regime which prevent the economically beneficial closure and replacement of level crossings. As we explored in Part 6, this is likely to be, in part, a result of the limited range of situations where the closure of a level crossing (that is, the extinguishment of the right of way over the crossing) can be ordered.

7.44 Another factor militating against the closure and replacement of level crossings is the lack of time-limits within the decision-making process, which can make funding problematic. Following the White Paper *The Future of Rail*[9] and the Railways Act 2005, the Secretary of State and Scottish Ministers are responsible, in consultation with ORR, for the strategic development and funding of railways. This is done on the basis of five-year "control periods".[10] In determining the objectives for a future control period, specific bids can be made for funds to close level crossings. A problem arises in that the timing in relation to the setting of objectives to be included in the High Level Output Specification (HLOS)[11] does not sit well with the inability of the law to provide reasonable certainty and timetables for decision-making about closure. Therefore, a particular bid might not be accepted as it might be impossible to guarantee that the funds will be spent and the aims achieved by the end of a particular control period.

7.45 Arguably, therefore, a reformed regime should allow the true costs and benefits of closure and replacement to be taken into account within the decision-making process. It is not an appropriate task for a law reform project to secure the

[9] Department for Transport, The Future of Rail (2004) Cm 6233.

[10] The current control period is Control Period 4 (CP4) which runs from 2009-2014.

[11] Schedule 4A to the Railways Act 1993 requires the Secretary of State in relation to England and Wales, and the Scottish Ministers in relation to Scotland, to produce an HLOS (and also a Statement of Funds Available (SoFA)) in order to determine the objectives for the railways and the funding required to meet those objectives.

closure (and replacement) of level crossings. Nor should law reform seek to change the current systems used for the allocation of capital resources to Network Rail or highway or roads authorities. But reform should result in legal provision which facilitates rational decisions on the basis of cost/benefit analysis.

PART 8
SAFETY REGULATION, CLOSURE & OTHER REFORM PROPOSALS

INTRODUCTION

8.1   In this Part we provisionally propose the reform of four aspects of level crossing regulation. First, we propose a fundamental change to the system of safety regulation at level crossings. Second, we suggest a new mechanism allowing for the closure of level crossings, with or without replacement. Third, we consider whether there is a need for other mechanisms to manage change at level crossings. Fourth, we ask whether there should be a simplified mechanism to allow for new level crossings. Having put forward these substantive proposals, we consider what should become of existing special Acts and level crossing orders. Finally, we consider the position of heritage and private railways.

8.2   The proposals aim to address the criticism that the law relating to level crossings is over-complicated and outdated and that there are insufficient or overly burdensome processes for either allowing or requiring change, which includes closure.

SAFETY REGULATION

Safety regulation: general provisions of HSWA 1974, regulations and codes of practice

8.3   As discussed in Part 5, the current safety regime at level crossings is based on individual provisions in special Acts authorising the railway, or on level crossing orders. However, in most cases the general duties under HSWA 1974 apply alongside special Acts and level crossing orders.

8.4   The current system which relies in the main on specific provisions in special Acts and level crossing orders is the sort of regime that it was envisaged would be replaced by the general scheme contained in Part 1 of HSWA 1974. We think that for the future it would be preferable for safety at level crossings to be governed entirely by HSWA 1974 together with regulations and codes of practice made under the Act. We think this approach would afford greater flexibility and allow for generic changes to be made to the protective arrangements at level crossings, thus removing the need to amend or make new level crossing orders. A move to reliance on HSWA 1974 and regulations would represent a significant change from the current more individualistic approach to safety regulation.

8.5   An alternative approach would be to retain the current system subject to making improvements to make the system more flexible. It can be argued that the reason for the relatively good safety record of level crossings in Great Britain is that the current system of regulating safety by means of special Acts and level crossing orders generally works well, and that therefore there is no need for fundamental change to the way in which safety is regulated.

8.6   In our view the relatively good safety record is likely to be the product of the effective implementation of safety standards, particularly by HM Railway Inspectors (now part of the Office of Rail Regulation's Railway Safety

Directorate). The issue is not about the need to enforce standards on a crossing-by-crossing basis (if necessary). Rather, the issue is about what is the best way legally to generate those standards. The inspectors will generally have a clear view about the engineering solution necessary at any given level crossing. Our provisional view is that it is likely to be better that that standard should become the legal standard by the application of the flexible apparatus of HSWA 1974, rather than through the inflexible means of making level crossing orders (where that is possible). In relation to those private level crossings for which a level crossing order cannot be made the point is even clearer. If the optimal engineering arrangements do not accord with the requirements of a special Act, there is currently no practical way (HSWA 1974 general duties aside) to require the railway operator or the highway/roads/traffic authority to put those arrangements in place.

8.7 One of the advantages of the current system of safety regulation is that in general there is a document in the form of either a special Act or level crossing order which sets out the safety requirements tailored to individual level crossings. This enables the railway operator and the highway/roads/traffic authorities to know exactly what is required in terms of safety provision. Certainty about the individual requirements for level crossings may have advantages, particularly in relation to enforcement. A possible problem with level crossing orders and special Acts is that they are not readily available to the public or to others who might be interested to know what safety provision is required at a particular level crossing. However, that problem could be overcome, for example, by providing that level crossing orders should be statutory instruments. We discuss this matter later in this Part.

8.8 As we have seen, at present level crossing orders cannot be made for all level crossings. In particular they cannot be made in respect of private level crossings in Scotland and can only be made in respect of private level crossings in England and Wales to which the public has lawful access. However, as mentioned earlier, in most cases safety at such crossings is governed by the general duties under HSWA 1974. But there is currently a gap in the safety regulation of private level crossings where the adjoining landowner is not employed or self-employed in respect of the land. In that case the provisions of HSWA 1974 do not apply, because HSWA 1974 only imposes duties on employers or self-employed persons in relation to their undertaking.

8.9 We accept that there is some force in the arguments for retaining the current system of safety regulation, but provisionally do not see them as compelling. The vast majority of sites creating risks to health and safety manage without a document having the force of law. A HSWA 1974-based system may well allow for the generation of documents specific to particular sites or processes. Under the proposed HSWA 1974-based system, if it were felt appropriate to allow for formal documents to make specific provision about safety matters, the regulations could enable such documents to be made where it was considered necessary for particular level crossings. Another form of specific document would be an enforcement notice under HSWA 1974, should a dispute arise as to what the appropriate safety measures were, or as to their implementation.

8.10 We accept that it may be that changing to a HSWA 1974-based system would leave gaps that the current system of safety regulation does not (we consider this further below). But if that were the case, then the solution might be to adapt the HSWA 1974 system in so far as it would apply to level crossings, rather than retain the current approach to regulating safety at crossings. We make the following provisional proposals regarding the regulation of safety at level crossings:

8.11 **We provisionally propose that the regulation of safety at level crossings should be governed entirely by the general scheme of HSWA 1974.**

8.12 **However, if consultees consider that it would be preferable to retain the current system of regulating safety at level crossings, what changes should be made to improve the system?**

8.13 If consultees agree with our provisional proposal above, it would involve the following matters, discussed later in this Part:

(1) statutory provision to revoke level crossing orders and to disapply the provisions in special Acts in so far as they deal with safety at level crossings;

(2) statutory provision to give the Secretary of State power, where appropriate to repeal or amend provisions of individual special Acts in so far as they deal with safety at level crossings;

(3) the making of regulations under section 15 in relation to safety at level crossings;[1]

(4) statutory provision to give the Office of Rail Regulation (ORR) the power to make approved codes of practice under HSWA 1974; and

(5) the making of codes of practice under the new section 16 power by ORR (we appreciate that in practice it would be a matter for ORR as to whether or not to exercise the power to make codes of practice).

Safety regulator

8.14 As mentioned earlier, ORR is the safety (and economic) regulator for the railways. It would clearly be counter-productive and impractical to separate railway safety generally from safety at level crossings. However, there may be an argument for separating safety at level crossings from other aspects of highway/road safety. Unlike the railways, there is no single regulator for road safety. As we have seen, level crossing orders may impose requirements not only on the railway operator, but also on the appropriate traffic authority.[2] As ORR makes and enforces level crossing orders it is already responsible not only for regulating the railway aspects of level crossings, but also the highway/road aspects of level crossings. For these reasons we think it appropriate that under a HSWA 1974-based system ORR should continue to be the safety (and economic)

---

[1] As mentioned in Part 7, regulations have been made under s 15 of HSWA 1974 in relation to level crossings, namely the Level Crossings Regulations 1997, SI 1997 No 487. However, these regulations amended the Level Crossings Act 1983, rather than making free-standing provision for safety at level crossings.

[2] Following the amendments to the Level Crossings Act 1983 by the Road Safety Act 2006.

regulator for railways including level crossings.

8.15 **We therefore invite consultees to comment on our provisional proposal that ORR, as the safety regulator for the railways, should remain as the body with overall responsibility for safety regulation at level crossings.**

Regulations under HSWA 1974

8.16 As a result of the Railways Act 2005, ORR already has the power to propose that regulations should be made under section 15 of HSWA 1974. We propose that new regulations should be made under this power and that they should be used in place of individual obligations in level crossing orders and special Acts. Under the new regulations the safety obligations should be placed on the railway operator.

8.17 **If our preferred option of moving to a HSWA 1974-based system of regulating safety is accepted, we propose that regulations should be made by the Secretary of State under section 15 of HSWA 1974 in relation to level crossings.**

Approved codes of practice under HSWA 1974

8.18 As we have previously observed, the power to make approved codes of practice under section 16 of HSWA 1974 was removed from HSE by the Railways Act 2005 but not conferred on ORR. As we stated in Parts 5 and 7, we think that codes of practice would be useful in a HSWA 1974-based system, in order to provide practical guidance to support the regulations mentioned above.

8.19 **If our preferred option of moving to a HSWA 1974-based system of regulating safety is accepted, we propose that ORR should be given the power to issue approved codes of practice under HSWA 1974 in relation to level crossings.**

8.20 Clearly it would be inappropriate for us to specify the technical content of any regulations and codes of practice. The regulations and codes of practice would work together. The regulations would make substantive provision to secure the safety of people at level crossings, while the codes of practice would contain practical guidance with respect to the requirements in the regulations. Codes of practice could not make substantive provision. The use of regulations and codes of practice in this way would provide flexibility to take account of the differing circumstances and safety risks at individual crossings. The proper balance between them would be a matter for ORR and the Department for Transport. However, we suggest that together, regulations and codes of practice should be able to make sufficient provision to ensure safety at different types of level crossing.

The position of highway/roads and traffic authorities under a HSWA 1974-based system of safety regulation

8.21 The Level Crossings Act 1983 was amended by the Road Safety Act 2006 to allow level crossing orders to impose obligations on local traffic authorities.[3] As

---

[3]   Road Safety Act 2006, s 50(2).

mentioned earlier, ORR is responsible for enforcing duties under level crossing orders, including those imposed on local traffic authorities.

8.22 If we move to a system based on HSWA 1974, we must therefore consider the extent to which local traffic authorities[4] can be bound by that system, as operated by ORR.

8.23 We discussed in Part 5 the extent to which the general duties in HSWA 1974 currently apply to highway and roads authorities. We also said there that we thought that the regulation-making power in section 15 of HSWA 1974 was broad enough to include regulations imposing specific duties on these authorities.

8.24 The remit of ORR in relation to safety is set out in the Railways Act 2005.[5] The Act describes the role of ORR in terms almost identical to those used of HSE in HSWA 1974, but confines it to "railway safety purposes". Those purposes include "securing the proper construction and safe operation" of [the railway] and "protecting the public (whether or not they are passengers) from personal injury and other risks arising from the construction and operation of [a railway]".[6] It will be recalled that HSE is responsible for enforcement of the "general purposes" in section 1 of HSWA 1974, which include "protecting persons other than persons at work against risks to health or safety arising out of or in connection with the activities of persons at work".

8.25 ORR's duties are very broadly defined. The general duty is defined as "to do such things and make such arrangements as it considers appropriate for the railway safety purposes" and "to assist and encourage persons concerned with matters relevant to any of those purposes to further those purposes". A specific duty is to submit from time to time "such proposals as it considers appropriate for the making of regulations for railway safety purposes" under, among other powers, section 15 of the 1974 Act.[7]

8.26 ORR therefore has the power to submit proposals to the Secretary of State for regulations to be made under section 15 of HSWA 1974 which would be binding on highway/roads or traffic authorities, where the purpose of the regulations is to ensure the safety of the public at level crossings.

8.27 Similarly, if ORR were given powers to issue approved codes of practice under section 16 of HSWA 1974 by reference to the same definition of "railway safety purposes", those codes of practice could provide guidance to highway/roads or traffic authorities; and failure to follow the guidance would have the consequences in any criminal proceedings set out in section 17 of HSWA 1974.

Enforcement and highway/road and traffic authorities

8.28 As mentioned in Part 5, the Health and Safety (Enforcing Authority for Railways and Other Guided Transport Systems) Regulations 2006 make ORR responsible

---

[4] The traffic authority will in most cases be the local authority/council, which in turn will be the highway authority (in England and Wales) or the roads authority (in Scotland).

[5] Railways Act 2005, sch 3, para 2.

[6] Railways Act 2005, sch 3, para 1(2).

[7] Railways Act 2005, sch 3, para 2.

for the enforcement of the "relevant statutory provisions" namely, Part 1 of HSWA 1974, regulations made under section 15 of HSWA 1974 or any of the "existing statutory provisions", to the extent that they relate to the operation of a railway.[8]

8.29 Under the proposed HSWA 1974-based system, if the Secretary of State were to make new regulations under section 15 of HSWA 1974 for the "railway safety purpose" of protecting the safety of the public at level crossings, enforcement of those regulations would "relate to" the operation of the railway. Therefore, by virtue of the 2006 Regulations mentioned above, ORR would be responsible for enforcement of the new regulations including against the highway/road or traffic authority.

8.30 It is not so clear, however, whether ORR would be responsible for enforcement of a breach by a highway/roads or traffic authority of its duties under section 3 of HSWA 1974 at a level crossing. First, as we showed in Part 5, the extent to which such an authority would be under a section 3 duty at all depends on the extent of its public law duties. But second, even if there were a breach of section 3 by virtue of, for instance, a failure to maintain the highway/road adequately at a level crossing, could it be said that it was a breach relating to the operation of the railway?

8.31 On balance, we think it could. First, this is what a natural reading of "relating to the operation of the railway" would suggest, without further analysis. Such a breach would "relate", in the sense of "have to do with" or "be connected with" the operation of the railway at the level crossing. Second, even if one analyses the legal position, it may indeed be true that the underlying statutory duty is fundamentally about the highways or roads duties of the authority and not a *function* relating to the operation of the railway. However, while that duty establishes what the content of the authority's "undertaking" is, section 3 itself is an instruction as to how the authority is to conduct itself in its undertaking. The failure to conduct its undertaking at a level crossing with due regard to the safety of the public "relates" to the operation of the railway (in so far as the risks concerned arise because of the operation of the railway).

8.32 However, we consider that the alternative is also arguable. If a breach of section 3 of HSWA 1974 at a level crossing were *not* enforceable by ORR because it did not relate to the operation of the railway, then HSE would remain the enforcing authority. Safety on the rail and road networks at level crossings is inextricably linked, and in our view is best regulated by a single authority. It would be unsatisfactory if ORR were responsible for enforcing against railway operators, while responsibility for enforcing against highway/roads or traffic authorities rested exclusively with HSE.

8.33 **We therefore ask consultees whether it would be desirable expressly to provide that a breach of section 3 of HSWA 1974 at a level crossing should be subject to enforcement by ORR, not HSE.**

Private level crossings: other business use and enforcement

8.34 Where a private level crossing is used by a business user (whether as an

---

[8] Health and Safety (Enforcing Authority for Railways and Other Guided Transport Systems) Regulations 2006, SI 2006 No 557, reg 3.

employer or self employed person) in connection with the land, for example to get to a field on the other side of the railway line, section 3 of HSWA 1974 will apply. Any unsafe use of the level crossing by such a user would breach section 3 of HSWA 1974 if it compromised the safety of people not in the user's employment. Such a breach would relate to the operation of a railway and thus be enforceable by ORR. If our proposed HSWA-based system were to be introduced, and if the Secretary of State were to make regulations under HSWA 1974, a breach of those regulations by such a business user would also be subject to enforcement by ORR.

8.35 Activities undertaken by a business otherwise than at a level crossing, (for example, where a farmer uses machinery in fields to harvest grain) would be regulated by the Health and Safety Executive (HSE). If an accident occurs whilst a farmer is harvesting grain in a field bisected by the level crossing, the HSE will investigate the accident. In most cases, the activity concerned would be covered by either "existing statutory provisions" or regulations under section 15, as well as the general duties.

8.36 Where a breach takes place on a level crossing, for example where a farmer takes a tractor over the level crossing to get to adjoining fields, ORR would be responsible for enforcement. Where a breach takes place on adjoining land as outlined in the previous paragraph, HSE would be responsible for enforcement. There may be circumstances where a breach of HSWA 1974 takes place partly on a level crossing and partly on adjoining land. In such a situation does ORR or HSE currently have jurisdiction to enforce HSWA 1974?

8.37 Although the question is a difficult one we take the view that, as the current law stands, in relation to a breach at a level crossing (or anywhere else on the railway) ORR's enforcement jurisdiction would take precedence over that of HSE.

8.38 Under the proposed HSWA 1974-based system of safety regulation, concurrent jurisdiction of HSE and ORR might appear to be more attractive than ORR having exclusive jurisdiction. It may be, for instance, that a business user is alleged to have breached one of the relevant provisions while on a level crossing as well as on the land on either side of the crossing. It would seem to be preferable if one prosecution could deal with the whole course of conduct, rather than HSE having jurisdiction in relation to either side of the level crossing and ORR having jurisdiction in relation to the crossing itself. It would be much easier to have a single prosecution if HSE had concurrent jurisdiction with ORR in relation to the crossing. While of course concurrent jurisdiction would require some understanding between ORR and HSE about which of them would enforce in particular cases, to avoid both declining to do so, that seems the sort of issue that can adequately be dealt with by sensible working arrangements, for example they may wish to agree a memorandum of understanding or protocol regarding their respective functions.[9] **We ask consultees the following question:**

8.39 **Would it be desirable for ORR and HSE to have concurrent jurisdiction for**

---

[9] A Memorandum of Understanding was agreed between HSE and ORR in April 2006 to "ensure effective co-ordination and co-operation between these organisations in relation to the regulation of health and safety, including policy matters and the enforcement of health and safety law, on railways, tramways and other guided transport systems in Great Britain".

enforcement of breaches of the general duties under HSWA 1974 or "relevant statutory provisions" where the breach occurs partly at a level crossing; or should ORR's railway-specific jurisdiction oust that of HSE?

Private level crossings: non-business users

8.40 Some private level crossings are not used by the owner of the right of way for any business use, but are used for ordinary day-to-day and social access to their property. In this situation, under our proposed HSWA 1974-based system of regulation, the railway operator would be subject to the duties under HSWA 1974 including any regulations and approved codes of practice, but the owner of the right of way would not be.

8.41 We would expect that most private level crossings would be governed by a special Act and some might be governed by a level crossing order, where in England and Wales the public has lawful access over the right of way. As we have mentioned, level crossing orders cannot be made in relation to private level crossings in Scotland.

8.42 However, there is one situation where it would be necessary to retain the safety provisions in special Acts. At present in England and Wales, a level crossing order may be in force in relation to a level crossing dividing land owned or tenanted by a person who is not employed or self-employed in connection with the land. We propose that if the HSWA 1974-based system of regulation were to be adopted, level crossing orders should be revoked and special Acts should be disapplied in so far as they make provision for safety at level crossings. In relation to the case outlined above, HSWA 1974 would not apply to the landowner (because the landowner would not be undertaking any business in connection with the land). Thus there would be a gap in the regulation of safety at such a level crossing. In order to avoid this gap, it would be necessary to continue to apply the provisions of the special Act dealing with safety rather than disapply them. Another option would be for primary legislation to provide that HSWA 1974 would apply in such a situation. But we do not think that this option is attractive as it would be contrary to the general approach of HSWA 1974 which is to impose duties as regards safety matters on employers and self-employed persons. Alternatively, the existence of appropriate criminal penalties for misusing such a private level crossing might be sufficient.

8.43 **We invite consultees to comment on the problem that HSWA 1974 cannot apply to owners of rights of way over private level crossings who are not business users.**

8.44 **Do consultees think that a move to a HSWA 1974-based system would create problems in practice?**

Safety and convenience

8.45 As we observed in Part 5, the overriding purpose of a level crossing order is to provide for the protection of those using the crossing.[10] However, an order may make provision for the convenience of those using the crossing as well as for their safety.

---

[10] Level Crossings Act 1983, s 1(1).

8.46 We suggested in Part 5 that in practice there is unlikely to be a very sharp distinction between safety and convenience. At present, convenience is a matter which is taken into account in level crossing orders in setting out the protective arrangements that are to be put in place at individual level crossings. The question as to how convenience could continue to be taken into account would arise if there were a move to reliance on HSWA 1974 for the regulation of safety in relation to level crossings. This would arise because at least on one view, HSWA 1974 is concerned with safety matters only. In this section, therefore, we consider those situations in which it is *possible* that the loss of the "convenience" limb in the Level Crossings Act 1983 would be a significant matter and ask whether in practice it is.

8.47 There would only be a gap if some legal provision is required to induce one of the two parties at the level crossing – the railway operator and the highway/roads or traffic authority – to do something it would not otherwise do. One would not expect to have to compel the railway operator to make provision to enhance efficiency (with due regard to safety) on the railway, because the railway operator has an interest in doing so. Similarly, the highways/roads or traffic authority should not have to be required to act in the interests of those using the highway or road (again, the balance between efficiency and safety being properly a matter for that authority). There are however, two possible situations in which there might be a "convenience gap".

Situation 1: action by the railway operator for the convenience of highway/road users

8.48 The first situation is where it might be necessary to bind the railway operator to do something purely for the convenience of highway/road users at a level crossing. This might include requiring the railway operator to make provision to enhance the usability of the crossing for those with particular mobility needs. While currently the Disability Discrimination Act 1995 would oblige the railway operator to make appropriate provision for people with disabilities, there is no requirement to make adjustments to accommodate other users who may have particular mobility needs, such as people with push-chairs, cyclists or horse riders.

Situation 2: action by the highways/roads/traffic authority for the convenience of rail users

8.49 Conversely, there might be circumstances in which it is necessary to bind the highway/roads or traffic authority to do something, unconnected with safety, to enhance the efficiency of the railway (assuming that a more efficient railway would be more "convenient" to rail users of the crossing). While a logical possibility, it is not easy to envisage an example of such a situation.

8.50 If a certain engineering enhancement were conducive to efficiency on the railway, but was neutral as to both safety and the convenience of highway/road users, then it would be reasonable to expect the railway operator to pay for it. If, therefore there were no resource disincentive to making the enhancement, it seems unlikely that it would be necessary for there to be provision to compel the highway/roads authority to make the enhancement. There is only one situation that we can see where it might be necessary to compel the highway/roads authority to undertake the enhancement and where therefore there might be a gap. That is where the highway/roads authority was considering undertaking work which required a balancing exercise to be carried out between the convenience or efficiency of rail users and that of highway/road users. In that situation it would be the highway/roads authority that would make the decision to undertake the work but in reaching that decision the highway/roads authority would not be required to take the interests of the railway into account.

8.51 **We ask consultees to consider whether there is a "convenience gap" in our proposal to replace reliance on special Acts and level crossing orders with a HSWA 1974-based system. If so, how should the gap be closed?**

8.52 **We ask consultees whether in practice it would be necessary to have a legal instrument that would:**

(1) **require rail operators to take safety-neutral steps to enhance the convenience of the users of the highway/road at a level crossing; and/or**

(2) **require highway/roads or traffic authorities to take safety-neutral steps to enhance the convenience of rail users, by enhancing the efficiency of the level crossing for rail use.**

8.53 We suggest there are broadly two options. Either the level crossing-specific HSWA 1974 regulations we have provisionally proposed should be capable of extension to cover such gaps as are identified; or a specific order-making power on the model of level crossing orders should be retained.

8.54 Regulations under section 15 of HSWA 1974 could only cover convenience matters if the statutory power under which the regulations are made enables such provision to be included. The current power in section 15 includes a power to make "incidental" and "supplemental" provisions.[11] This may be sufficient to allow incidental or supplemental provision to be made about convenience matters, provided such matters fell within the general purposes of Part 1 of HSWA 1974. Whether the existing power in section 15 would be wide enough to fill any convenience "gap" is difficult to assess until consultees give us a clearer idea of what, in practice, such a gap might consist of. We suggest that completely free-standing convenience works might not be covered by the power in section 15, but where the convenience works are inextricably linked to safety measures, they probably would be.

8.55 If the "incidental" and "supplemental" provision in section 15 of HSWA 1974 were not wide enough, it would be necessary to extend the power for the purposes of level crossings. Regulations made under the extended power in section 15 would of course be enforceable under HSWA 1974. However, it is difficult to see how non-safety-related convenience issues could sit happily with the health and safety regime under HSWA 1974. It could be argued that enforcement processes designed and developed to deal with health and safety would not be apt to deal with convenience.

8.56 The alternative – the creation of a new power to make orders specific to particular

---

[11] Health and Safety at Work etc Act 1974, s 82(3)(a).

level crossings on the basis of convenience – is also unattractive. It would replicate, albeit in a smaller compass, the crossing-specific regime from which we are provisionally proposing to move away, and would increase rather than decrease the complexity of the law. There would also have to be specific provision to the effect that such a new order would give way to safety concerns, if the two came into conflict over time.

8.57 **Is there a need for provision to enable convenience-related measures to be put in place at level crossings? If so, would it be preferable to:**

(1) **extend the power under section 15 of HSWA 1974 to make regulations, to include considerations of convenience; or**

(2) **create a new power to make separate convenience-related orders for particular level crossings?**

CLOSURE

8.58 We discussed the current provisions relating to closure of level crossings in Part 6. Our approach to closure is based on the view that there is a gap in statutory powers as regards closure of level crossings. It is possible to close level crossings as part of a transport and works (TAW/S) order.[12] But while TAW/S orders can be used to close an individual crossing, they were principally designed for major transport projects including those of national or regional significance. Flexible though they may be, we still consider TAW/S orders too cumbersome, expensive and time-consuming to be used for the closure of a single level crossing for local efficiency or safety reasons.

8.59 At the other end of the scale is the existing power under section 118A of the Highways Act 1980 to stop up footpaths and bridleways over level crossings. Section 118A only applies in England and Wales. There is no equivalent provision in Scotland. The Roads (Scotland) Act 1984 does not contain specific level crossing provisions, but rather general powers to stop up roads. The power in section 118A of the 1980 Act, while designed to be used in relation to individual level crossings, is very limited. It does not apply to vehicular highways or private level crossings. This power relies on the highway authority to make the decision subject to confirmation by the Secretary of State.

8.60 In Part 7 we mentioned that the AXIAT model demonstrates that there is an economic case for closure with replacement of a small but significant minority of public vehicular level crossings. We suggested that there were features of the legal regime that prevented the closure and replacement of public vehicular level crossings and that reform was necessary.

8.61 As regards private level crossings it is not generally considered practical to use a TAW/S order to close such crossings. However, Network Rail has been successful in buying out reasonably large numbers of individual private level crossings on a voluntary basis using a discharge agreement or a deed of release

---

[12] An order under the Transport and Works Act 1992 or the Transport and Works Act (Scotland) Act 2007.

to extinguish the right of way.[13] But it seems likely that in some cases, there will be a good case for the compulsory acquisition of private rights of way over level crossings in order to close them. This may arise where agreement cannot be reached between Network Rail and the owner of the private right of way. There are currently no powers for the compulsory purchase of land in such circumstances. We therefore think that reforms are necessary to enable closure of private level crossings in cases where agreement cannot be reached between the railway operator and the adjoining landowner.

8.62 It has been suggested to us that if a practical and reasonably predictable procedure for level crossing closure was in place, it could potentially lead to very significant savings in the engineering cost of a replacement bridge or underpass. The reason for this is that if the replacement of a level crossing could be planned to take place at the same time as some other engineering work taking place on the railway (or even on the highway/road), then the marginal cost of including the level crossing replacement could be much less than the cost of doing it as a stand-alone project.

8.63 **We provisionally propose a new procedure for level crossing closure orders to allow for closure of both private and public level crossings.** The powers available would include compulsory purchase, and stopping up and diversion in relation to highways/roads. A wide group of actors, including the railway operator, highway/roads authority, and planning authority, in addition to ORR, would be able to apply for an order, which would be made by the Secretary of State or the Scottish Ministers as appropriate. The procedure should include strict time-limits to enhance predictability.

8.64 Proposals for closure of a level crossing may be for closure with or without replacement. Provisionally, we take the view that it is not necessary to have different legal procedures for closure with or closure without replacement. This is because the question as to whether there is to be an alternative will be fundamental to the decision-making about whether or not the order to close should be made. For example, we consider it unlikely that an order for closure of a vehicular highway/road which crosses a railway would often be made without there being provision for a replacement crossing. We note that the AXIAT model, for instance, is unlikely to find an economic case for closure without replacement. So a proposal to close such a level crossing without replacement is unlikely to be acceptable on its merits. However, it may frequently be the case that a private level crossing could be compulsorily closed without replacement where the right of way owner has adequate access to each side of the railway by other means.

Criteria for closure

8.65 As we explored in Part 6, the current criteria for replacing a level crossing under section 7 of the Railways Clauses Act 1863 (safety only), or for the stopping up of a highway under the Highways Act 1980 (England and Wales), or a road under the Roads (Scotland) Act 1984 are very restrictive. Under our new system for closure of level crossings, we think there should be a list of criteria to be taken into account by the decision-maker in deciding whether or not to grant an application for a level crossing closure order. The list would not be a hierarchy, in

---

[13] Extinguishment of rights of way is considered in more detail in Parts 11 and 12.

that no one factor would automatically be more important than another. **We therefore invite views of consultees on the following provisional proposals:**

8.66 **Should there be a list of factors to be taken into account in considering an application for a level crossing closure order?**

8.67 **If so, we would welcome the views of consultees on the following list of factors:**

(1) **safety of users of the crossing (including information as to the incidence of accidents at the level crossing);**

(2) **costs involved in maintenance of the crossing compared with costs involved in closing or closing and replacing the crossing;**

(3) **the effect of closure as opposed to retention (in the case of public level crossings) on the efficiency of the rail and road networks;**

(4) **the effect (in the case of public level crossings) on the integrity of the network of non-vehicular public rights of way;**

(5) **the effect of closure compared to retention of the crossing on the local community;**

(6) **the effect on those holding private rights over the crossing;**

(7) **the usability of the level crossing or its potential alternatives for all level crossing users;**

(8) **the convenience of level crossing users; and**

(9) **the effect on the environment and local amenity.**

8.68 **Should the factors be set out in order of importance? If so, how should they be ordered?**

Decision-making

8.69 The question of who should be the decision-making authority is important because of the need to balance local and national interests with the interests of the railway. This question is the consequence of railways having been seen, at least in modern times, as primarily a national network whilst land, communities and many highways/roads have traditionally been seen as local issues. Level crossings are a visible example of the interface between these potentially conflicting perspectives.

Private level crossings

8.70 The closure of a private level crossing involves the extinguishment of the right of way over the crossing. As we outline in Parts 11 and 12, at present the way over a private level crossing can be extinguished and therefore the level crossing can be closed by agreement (in the form of a deed of release or discharge agreement) between the railway operator and the adjoining landowner. However, agreement between the parties may not always be possible. As we mentioned in

Part 6, apart from the order-making powers under the Transport and Works Acts, there are no means by which a private crossing can be compulsorily closed if the owner of the right of way objects. In that event, our proposed closure procedure would become relevant.

8.71 Given the importance of the issue, we suggest that under the new procedure, an application for a level crossing closure order in respect of a private level crossing should be made to the Secretary of State in relation to crossings in England and Wales and to Scottish Ministers in relation to level crossings in Scotland.

8.72 Under the new procedure, the application for a level crossing closure order would seek compulsory purchase powers (with provision for appropriate compensation) in relation to the landowner's right of way over the crossing. Compulsory purchase of the right of way following a successful application would have the effect of extinguishing the right of way. The body which was to be given the compulsory purchase powers would be specified in the closure order. In the case of a private level crossing, it would almost always be the railway operator.

8.73 Where compulsory purchase powers are applicable, they may be used to purchase land, but they can also be used to purchase an "interest in land", which would include the right of way over the railway. The law of compulsory purchase is not satisfactory.[14] However, we do not consider that it would be practical to suggest an alternative system for level crossings alone.

8.74 In Part 12 we note that the Lands Tribunal for Scotland already has a power to discharge title conditions, including servitudes, without the consent of the dominant owner.[15] This power could be used to close servitude crossings. As we note in Part 12, the power does not extend to crossings that are purely statutory crossings, but it could be so extended by ministerial order. Presumably if a new system is introduced for the *compulsory* closure of private crossings, no such extension would be called for. An extension would in theory be possible, although it might not be desirable to have two possible mechanisms in parallel.

Public level crossings

8.75 In relation to public crossings, an application for a closure order could, where necessary, seek compulsory purchase of land[16] required to build a replacement bridge or underpass. The application could also deal with the apportionment between the parties concerned of the costs of replacement. But an essential

---

[14] The Law Commission has recommended law reform in relation to compulsory purchase: Towards a compulsory purchase code: (1) compensation (2003) Law Com No 286; Towards a compulsory purchase code: (2) procedure (2004) Law Com No 291. An overview of the current law is included in Appendix C of Law Com No 286. In 2005, the Government rejected our proposals on the basis that it was not practicable to find Parliamentary time: ODPM, *Government Response to Law Commission report: Towards a compulsory purchase code* (December 2005).

[15] The Law Commission has suggested the possibility that as regards easements the law in England and Wales should follow the Scottish example: Consultation Paper on Easements, Covenants and Profits à Prendre (2008) Law Com No 186, Part 14. It should be noted that any legislation would apply to easements created in the future only and not to existing easements.

[16] As with a level crossing closure order to close a private crossing, the order would specify the body which was to have the compulsory purchase powers.

element of an application would be a request to stop up or divert the highway or road currently running over the level crossing. In other words, closure would necessitate the stopping up or diversion of the existing highway/road over the crossing.

8.76 An application for a closure order in respect of a public level crossing might seek an order to divert the highway/road on each side of the railway. This could be a small diversion to bring the highway/road into alignment with a replacement bridge or underpass. Or it could be a substantial change to a footpath at some distance from the level crossing designed to ensure the continued integrity of the footpath network once the level crossing that formerly carried the footpath over the railway is closed.[17]

8.77 A decision about closure of a crossing would rest with the Secretary of State or in Scotland, Scottish Ministers. Later in this Part we discuss the implications of this as regards devolution.

8.78 The question arises as to who would decide on the stopping up or diversion. This focuses the issue on a conflict between matters traditionally regulated locally (that is, the vast majority of highways), and those regulated nationally (railways). We suggest that there are three options:

OPTION 1: A FINAL DECISION ON STOPPING UP/DIVERSION BY THE LOCAL HIGHWAY/ROADS AUTHORITY

8.79 Under this option the application for a closure order in respect of a public level crossing would be made to the Secretary of State/Scottish Ministers/Welsh Ministers, (which we will refer to as the "national authority") as appropriate, covering all the proposed elements of the order. The question of stopping up would be referred by the national authority to the local highway/roads authority for decision. The other elements of the order, for example compulsory purchase or apportionment of costs, would be decided by the national authority, but of course would not go ahead if the stopping up was refused.

OPTION 2: A FINAL DECISION ON STOPPING UP/DIVERSION BY THE NATIONAL AUTHORITY

8.80 Again under this option the application for a closure order would be made to the national authority. In relation to the question of stopping up, there would be a requirement for the national authority to *consult* with the local highway/roads/planning authorities and other interested parties, including members of the public who may be affected. But the final decision would rest with the national authority.

OPTION 3: INITIAL DETERMINATION ON STOPPING UP/DIVERSION BY THE LOCAL HIGHWAY/ROADS AUTHORITY, SUBJECT TO AN APPEAL TO THE NATIONAL AUTHORITY

8.81 Once again the application for a closure order would be made to the national authority, but the question of stopping up would be referred for initial decision by

---

[17] In the latter case, the diversion of the footpath might be dealt with under the provisions of the Highways Act 1980 or the Wildlife and Countryside Act 1981 in England and Wales, unless the diversion of the path had a sufficient causal link with the level crossing closure.

the local highway/roads authority. If the local highway/roads authority decided against stopping up, the applicant could ask the national authority to review that decision. The appeal would be on the merits of the application, rather than on grounds that would form the basis of an application for judicial review. The appeal would effectively be a re-determination of the question of stopping up.

8.82 The aim of this would be to retain the initial local focus in connection with decisions about stopping up, whilst also providing for such decisions to be overridden on appeal to the national authority who would seek to balance national and local interests.

DISCUSSION

8.83 It is evident that the local highway/roads authority would be better placed than the national authority to be aware of, and sensitive to, local and community concerns. There is a general legislative preference for decisions about stopping up or diverting highways/roads to be local functions. On the other hand, a local authority could not be expected to take the national perspective of the railway into account. We provisionally consider that option 3 presents the best balance.

8.84 **We provisionally propose that the application for a closure order should be determined in England by the Secretary of State, in Wales by Welsh Ministers and in Scotland by the Scottish Ministers.**

8.85 **In relation to the question as to whether to stop up a highway or road, and whether to divert a highway or road either side of the railway, we suggest three options:**

    (1)   decision by the local highway/roads authority;

    (2)   decision by the Secretary of State/Scottish Ministers/Welsh Ministers but subject to consultation with interested parties and local bodies; or

    (3)   initial decision by the local highway/roads authority, subject to an appeal on the merits to the Secretary of State/Scottish Ministers/Welsh Ministers.

We provisionally favour the third option, but would invite comments from consultees.

Compulsory purchase and deemed planning permission

8.86 The grant of compulsory purchase powers must be limited in time, to minimise the blight on affected land values. We understand that, currently, powers granted under transport and works orders are typically limited to between three and five years. These time limits could well be longer than would be needed in the context of our simpler process. **We therefore invite views from consultees on what time limit for the use of compulsory purchase orders would be appropriate.**

8.87 We have also considered whether a closure order should incorporate deemed planning consent (for example for replacement of a level crossing with a bridge or underpass) as happens in the case of orders under the Transport and Works Acts, which allow for deemed planning consent in some circumstances. We have not reached any provisional view on this matter; rather **we invite views of consultees on whether planning consent should be deemed to be included in a level crossing closure order.**

Apportionment of costs

8.88 The detailed arrangements for funding of level crossing closure is not an issue for us to consider.[18] **However, we make the following provisional proposal:**

8.89 **We provisionally propose that level crossing closure orders should be capable of including provision for the apportionment of the costs of closure and replacement between the statutory authorities concerned.[19]**

8.90 We have considered, but provisionally rejected, a default rule that the promoter should pay unless contrary provision is made in the closure order.

8.91 The proper allocation of costs should be an integral part of the decision-making-process in relation to the level crossing order. Promoters are unlikely to come forward with an application for a closure order without a realistic proposal in relation to funding it; but if an application were made without proposals on funding, it would no doubt be rejected on that basis alone.

8.92 We suggest that section 255 of the Highways Act 1980 may be a suitable model for such a statutory provision. Section 255 provides, in certain circumstances, for the apportionment between the highway authority in England and Wales and the railway owner, of the costs of building a bridge over a railway.

8.93 **We invite consultees to comment on the apportionment of costs of closure and replacement of level crossings.**

Time-limits

8.94 If the maximum benefit is to be gained from a new procedure for the closure of level crossings, then timely consideration of applications would be highly desirable. Cost savings can be achieved if work on closing a level crossing is scheduled to coincide with other work on the track, or indeed on the highway in the vicinity of the track. But such scheduling can only take place if the decision-making on level crossing closure orders can be kept within reasonably short and predictable time-limits.

8.95 **We provisionally propose that the procedure for level crossing closure orders should be subject to short time-limits at each stage, including consideration by the Secretary of State/Scottish Ministers/Welsh Ministers.**

8.96 **We ask consultees for their views on what time-limits there should be for the application process.**

8.97 We offer the following for consideration, without claiming any special merit for them, as appropriately short time-limits for a simple closure order not involving the stopping up or diversion of a highway or road:

---

[18] We discuss the community infrastructure levy in England and Wales in Part 9.

[19] This would include Network Rail as a "statutory undertaker".

(1) serving of application to commencement of consultation: 1 month;

(2) consultation: 12 weeks; and

(3) determination by the national authority (following any further proceedings necessary): 2 months.

8.98 Different time-limits would be necessary in cases where applications for closure involved highways or roads, so as to take account of the time needed in connection with the decision-making process for stopping up including any appeal.

8.99 **We invite views on what the time-limits should be for closure orders including the stopping up or diversion of a highway or road.**

8.100 Where the time-limits are directed at the Secretary of State/Scottish Ministers/Welsh Ministers, we propose that they should be enforced only by public law remedies. If they are directed at the promoter, then failure to adhere to a time-limit should result in the rejection of the application, subject only to a power for the Secretary of State/Scottish Ministers/Welsh Ministers to extend the time-limit in exceptional circumstances.

8.101 Under the TAW/S procedures, "statutory objectors" (those whose private rights are affected and local authorities) have a right to a hearing before a person appointed by the national authority. Where there are other objectors, the national authority must decide whether to hold a public inquiry, a hearing, or to deal with the competing arguments by the exchange of written representations.

8.102 The new procedure we propose is intended to be quicker, cheaper and less onerous on all parties than the TAW/S procedure. Our provisional view is that, in particular circumstances, a hearing might be necessary, but generally the scale of the process would be better suited to proceeding by way of written representations.

8.103 **We provisionally propose that, after the expiry of the consultation period, the Secretary of State/Scottish Ministers/Welsh Ministers should decide whether, exceptionally, to hold a hearing before a person appointed by them. Otherwise, further consideration of competing views should be dealt with by the exchange of written representations.**

8.104 Under the proposed procedure, if it appeared to the national authority that the scale or significance of the proposal was such that a public local inquiry was needed, or that the proposal could be dealt with by a hearing, but that the hearing would be an extended and expensive exercise, then it would be justifiable to refuse the application on the basis that the promoter should use the TAW/S procedures instead.

The relationship between the proposed new procedure and the procedures for transport and works orders

8.105 We do not propose any change to the current system whereby applications for a TAW/S order can include provision for the closure of level crossings, particularly as part of a larger scheme. We think it would be undesirable to have a system which required promoters of such a scheme to obtain a level crossing closure order (to close any level crossings) in addition to a TAW/S order for the other elements of the scheme.

8.106 **Provisionally we do not consider that it is necessary to exclude the possibility of obtaining a TAW/S order where a level crossing closure order may be obtained, or the other way round, but we invite consultees' views.**

8.107 The two systems would operate in tandem. The proposed level crossing closure orders should be easier and cheaper to obtain than TAW/S orders and so would be likely to be the first choice when it was sought to close a single crossing. TAW/S orders would continue to be appropriate where crossings were to be closed as part of a larger scheme. However, if for some reason it were considered easier or more effective to seek a TAW/S order to close a single crossing, there would be nothing to prevent that.

The status of level crossing closure orders

8.108 We have considered whether or not level crossing closure orders should be statutory instruments.[20] We note that currently under the Level Crossings Act 1983, level crossing orders are not statutory instruments. We are not aware of the reason why the 1983 Act did not provide for such orders to be statutory instruments.

8.109 The new level crossing closure orders may well need to contain specific amendments, modifications or disapplications of primary or secondary legislation. One advantage of statutory instruments is that, provided the enabling power is clear, they can make provision of this kind.[21] Another advantage of statutory instruments is that the power to make them includes a power to amend, revoke or re-enact the statutory instrument itself.

8.110 Statutory instruments are classified and numbered in the statutory instrument series. It seems likely that if a level crossing closure order were to be a statutory instrument it would be classified as local rather than as general. The usual practice is that local instruments are not printed and put on sale, nor are they included in the annual printed volumes of statutory instruments. However, one way of ensuring that level crossing closure orders are readily accessible would be to provide that such orders are statutory instruments and that they are to be treated as general instruments for the purposes of printing and publication.[22]

8.111 **We therefore provisionally propose that level crossing closure orders should be statutory instruments and that they should be treated as general instruments.**

Closure of level crossings and devolution: Scotland

8.112 As mentioned in Part 2, the proposed new system of orders dealing with closure

---

[20] Or in Scotland, Scottish Statutory Instruments.

[21] We note that it is possible to amend primary legislation in TAW/S orders, which are statutory instruments.

[22] As a result, such instruments would be available on the website of the Office of Public Sector Information.

of level crossings raises a potential constitutional difficulty as regards the respective powers of the Secretary of State and Scottish Ministers.

8.113 Under the proposed policy options outlined above, the policy intention is that the Scottish Ministers should have the power to make the final decision on closure of level crossings in Scotland. However, as we have seen, in the case of public crossings, closure requires the stopping up of the highway/road which crosses the railway.[23] In Scotland where the roads authority refuses to stop up a road, we propose an appeal to the Scottish Ministers. Under the current devolution arrangements a difficulty would arise in relation to Scotland if, on appeal, the Scottish Ministers refused to order the stopping up of a road. In that situation there would in effect be a conflict between the Scottish Ministers, as final decision-makers on stopping up, and the Secretary of State (who under the current devolution arrangements would have to be the final decision-maker on closure of level crossings[24]). We suggest that this problem might be avoided by means of "executive devolution", as discussed in the following paragraphs in order to enable the Scottish Ministers to make the final decision on closure of crossings in Scotland.

8.114 In some situations it may be desired to give Scottish Ministers the power to carry out certain functions as regards Scotland without changing the reservations in Schedule 5 to the Scotland Act 1998 and therefore without altering the legislative competence of the Scottish Parliament. In these situations the transfer of functions to Scottish Ministers can be effected by means of primary legislation enacted by the UK Parliament. Alternatively, an Order in Council (called a "transfer of functions order") may be made under section 63 of the 1998 Act. Such an order transfers certain reserved functions so that in so far as those functions are to be carried out in or as regards Scotland, they come within the devolved competence of the Scottish Ministers. This process is often called "executive devolution".

8.115 We therefore propose that under the new system for level crossing closure orders, the power for the Secretary of State to make orders as regards level crossings in Scotland should be transferred to the Scottish Ministers by means of executive devolution. In addition to resolving the constitutional difficulty, such a transfer of functions would have the benefit of achieving the more general policy objective that Scottish Ministers should have the power to make level crossing closure orders in respect of both public and private crossings in Scotland.

8.116 **We provisionally propose that under the new system for closure of level crossings, the function of making level crossing closure orders in relation to both public and private level crossings in Scotland should be transferred to the Scottish Ministers.**

---

[23] Stopping up is required in order to extinguish the right of way.

[24] In terms of the health and safety reservation in Schedule 5 to the Scotland Act 1998 (discussed in Part 2 above), the function of making level crossing closure orders on grounds of safety, would rest with the Secretary of State. In cases where a closure order is on grounds other than safety, it would seem that the reservation of railways under the 1998 Act would apply. It is for that reason that executive devolution is required so as to enable the Scottish Ministers to deal with closure orders in Scotland.

Closure of level crossings and devolution: Wales

8.117 A similar constitutional difficulty arises in relation to Wales. The functions previously performed by the Secretary of State in relation to highways in Wales have generally been transferred to the Welsh Ministers. This includes confirmation of stopping up and diversion order under sections 118A and 119A of the Highways Act 1980.

8.118 As explained in Part 2, Welsh devolution has developed in a different way to devolution in Scotland. In particular, while executive devolution is the exception in Scotland, in Wales it is the norm. When considering the introduction of a new power to make level crossing closure orders, it is therefore necessary to consider whether the Secretary of State or Welsh Ministers should exercise the power. In the light of our conclusions in relation to Scotland, it seems clear to us that the same power should be exercised in Wales by Welsh Ministers. In both cases, the devolved administration has both highways/roads and TAWS powers, and therefore we consider that both should be treated in the same way.

8.119 **We therefore provisionally propose that under the new system for closure of level crossings, the function of making level crossing closure orders in relation to both public and private level crossings in Wales should be transferred to the Welsh Ministers.**

OTHER MECHANISMS FOR MANAGING CHANGE

8.120 As we have sought to show in this consultation paper, many different interests come into play in relation to level crossings. We therefore need to consider how to manage the relationship between these interests as they relate to level crossings.

8.121 The management of level crossings does not only involve issues of safety. Other issues arise. In this section, we consider whether there would be advantages in introducing new ways of fostering co-operation and co-ordination as regards matters relating to the ongoing management of level crossings.

Infrastructure agreements

8.122 There may be scope for improving the relationship and in particular consultation and co-operation between the various parties concerned with level crossings. Safety and regulation of level crossings should be seen as more than purely a "railway problem". Rather, it is an issue of joint concern of rail, highway/road and planning interests and other interested parties such as developers, where appropriate dialogue between them would allow the most beneficial solution to emerge.

8.123 Recently, innovative use has been made of "safety interface agreements" in the Australian states. Under the Australian system, it is compulsory for highway and rail authorities to enter into such agreements in relation to all level crossings. These then operate as the principal risk regulators of level crossings.[25]

8.124 We consider that there might be scope to adapt elements of this idea for use in

---

[25] An example of an Australian interface agreement is available to download from our websites: www.lawcom.gov.uk and www.scotlawcom.gov.uk.

Great Britain with the introduction of infrastructure agreements. We suggest that it would probably not be necessary for such agreements to be made compulsory in all situations, unlike in Australia. However, we think that such agreements might be useful where some *major* change is planned at a level crossing, for example where the closure and replacement of a public vehicular level crossing is being proposed. In such a situation there could be a requirement for the interested parties to enter into an infrastructure agreement before an application for closure of a level crossing is made.

8.125 Infrastructure agreements might also be useful where some other major change is contemplated, for example where it is planned to change the protective measures at a level crossing such as from a half-barrier to a full-barrier or vice versa.

8.126 **We invite views of consultees on whether it would be useful to introduce a system of infrastructure agreements for level crossings.**

Road-rail partnership groups

8.127 In recent years, Network Rail has encouraged the creation and development of road-rail partnership groups to consider a wide range of mutual areas of concern, including level crossings. These partnerships often cover fairly large geographical areas involving a large number of level crossings, although that is not necessarily the case. The primary participants are Network Rail and local authorities, but other stakeholders and interested parties may also be involved. Our understanding is that such partnerships have been considered very useful for discussing issues of mutual concern in relation to level crossings. Road-rail partnerships have also been used to some advantage to consider the closure of level crossings.

8.128 The main focus of these partnerships has been on public vehicular level crossings. Clearly there may be more competing interests at play in the case of a public level crossing when compared to a private crossing. However, collaborative arrangements may well have something to contribute to the issues surrounding private crossings.

8.129 We have considered whether it would be helpful for there to be a more formalised mechanism to bring together the key interests at level crossings. The railway operator and the highway/roads authorities will *always* be key interests at public crossings. There will usually be others with an interest, such as the planning authority, other representatives of the local community, developers and voluntary organisations representing interests of those such as walkers and horse riders.

8.130 In this connection we have considered whether there would be benefit in providing for the setting up of new "level crossing panels" which would afford an opportunity for interested parties to come together to discuss relevant matters concerning level crossings. However, a possible disadvantage of this might be that creating new panels would impose undue administrative and financial burdens on those with an interest in level crossings, particularly on voluntary organisations such as those representing ramblers and horse riders. We think that it would be better not to create any new panels but rather to expand on the existing road-rail partnerships. A recent report indicated that the establishment of more road-rail partnership groups in appropriate areas would be beneficial.[26]

8.131   **We provisionally propose the expansion of the role of road-rail partnership groups, as they have proven to be successful in bringing together the various and often competing interests dealing with matters relating to level crossings.**

CREATION OF NEW LEVEL CROSSINGS

8.132   We note the current guidance in relation to TAW/S orders indicates that new level crossings should only be proposed in exceptional circumstances. We are also aware of the policies of both Network Rail[27] and ORR against the creation of new crossings. We provisionally suggest that it would be appropriate to retain the current system for authorising new level crossings under a TAW/S order, or, in England, under the Planning Act 2008, as part of a proposal for a major new railway or some other scheme where, as an exception, a new level crossing is both necessary and safe.

8.133   However, we consider that there may be circumstances where it is desirable to create a single new level crossing over an existing line. For example, there are particular issues about access across the railway in the Highlands of Scotland, both in respect of leisure use of the countryside and access by local communities. In such circumstances, there may need to be a system for the creation of such crossings. For the reasons we explain in Part 12, statutory access rights give rise to significant differences, both practical and legal, between the situation in England and Wales and that in Scotland (although we would add that there may be similar practical issues in parts of Wales and England). In this context, it is possible that in some circumstances it would be safer, more convenient, or both, to create a new level crossing with a non-vehicular public right of way. It might also be necessary or desirable to create a "new" level crossing to replace an existing level crossing nearby where a replacement was justified, but the case for a bridge or underpass could not be made out.

8.134   We provisionally consider that creating a new level crossing in such circumstances is unlikely to require special powers where the railway operator and ORR agree that a crossing should be provided. For instance, it seems that where it is thought necessary to create a footpath crossing to enable walkers to cross the railway line more safely than crossing the track by trespassing at any convenient point, the compulsory acquisition of adjoining land would be unnecessary to accommodate the construction of such a crossing. In such cases the railway operator would simply construct the new crossing.

8.135   The question is therefore whether there should be a more general provision, parallel to our proposed new level crossing closure orders, providing a procedure

---

[26]   E Delmonte and S Tong, Traffic Research Laboratory Report No PPR377, *Investigation into Traffic Delays at Level Crossings* (December 2008).

[27]   It is the policy of Network Rail and the Office of Rail Regulation to avoid the construction of new level crossings where at all possible in the interests of safety. Generally a bridge or underpass will be preferred. See Network Rail's policy: http://www.networkrail.co.uk/documents/4424_level%20crossing%20policy.pdf (last visited 14 June 2010). See also ORR's policy: http://www.rail-reg.gov.uk/server/show/nav.1564 (last visited 14 June 2010).

for the creation, in a legal sense,[28] of new level crossings. For example, in some cases the construction of a new level crossing may entail the acquisition of adjoining land, so there may be a need for compulsory purchase powers. In other situations there may be local pressure for a new crossing but the railway operator (and possibly ORR) are opposed to it. Where such opposition exists, there may be a need for a statutory provision *requiring* the construction of a level crossing. There is also the possibility of an existing private level crossing being made available for public use. These issues arise especially in Scotland, if (as is typically the position) the land on each side of the railway is subject to public access rights under the Land Reform (Scotland) Act 2003, so that a local absence of suitable public crossings may impair the exercise of public access rights. Accordingly, this issue is discussed further in Part 12. Nevertheless the question of new level crossings can arise without reference to the Scottish legislation about public access rights. Hence these issues are general issues and thus relevant to England and Wales as well as to Scotland.

8.136 **Should there be statutory provision requiring the construction of new level crossings on existing railway lines in certain specified circumstances?**

8.137 **If so, should the decision-maker be able to override opposition to the construction of a new level crossing?**

REQUIREMENTS IN SPECIAL ACTS AND LEVEL CROSSING ORDERS

8.138 We need to consider what should be done, if a safety regulation system based on HSWA 1974 were in place, about the requirements in existing special Acts and level crossing orders dealing with safety matters. In particular, the question arises as to whether such requirements in special Acts and level crossing orders can be repealed or revoked or whether they should be disapplied.

8.139 As regards special Acts, so far as we can determine, there are several thousand still in force. In practical terms it would be difficult and time-consuming to repeal them on an individual basis. In any event, special Acts contain non-level crossing-related provisions which are likely to be still effective and necessary, for example those establishing the line of a railway. We have considered whether we should propose the repeal the specific provisions in special Acts dealing with *safety* matters at level crossings in so far as HSWA 1974 would apply in place of those provisions. We have concluded that this would not be advisable. Such a general repeal might have unexpected consequences in relation to provisions of the special Acts and lead to arguments as to which provisions had been repealed and which were still in force. In particular, such a general repeal of this nature would be likely to give rise in Parliament to questions of competency.

8.140 The alternative to *repeal* of the individual safety provisions in special Acts would be a general provision *disapplying* any such provisions. We recognise that one possible disadvantage of this approach would be that the safety provisions in special Acts would continue to have a shadow existence. They would not be repealed but rather would only be deprived of legal effect so long as the disapplication provisions remained in force. However, on balance we are inclined

---

[28] Here we are talking about the need for a procedure to deal with the legal aspects of creating a new level crossing rather than the engineering and physical aspects involved such as barriers, warning lights, and so on.

to think that disapplication of the special Act provisions relating to safety matters would be the safer approach to adopt in the event of a move to reliance on HSWA 1974 as regards safety regulation at level crossings.

8.141 In addition, we think provision should be made to enable the repeal (and consequential amendment) of individual provisions in special Acts in so far as they relate to safety. This would involve conferring on the Secretary of State a power to make orders repealing railway special Acts, or parts of them (and, where necessary, amending them). This power could be used when, for example, consideration had to be given to the terms of a special Act by the Department for Transport, ORR or a railway operator, for some other reason. Repeal could then be considered and effected through a fairly straightforward procedure. Such a power might also make it easier to embark on a more general programme of repeal, if the resources were to become available.

8.142 **We therefore would welcome the views of consultees on our proposal that the provisions in special Acts should be disapplied in so far as they deal with safety at level crossings to the extent that HSWA 1974 applies.**

8.143 **We would also welcome the views of consultees as to whether there should be a power for the Secretary of State to make orders to enable the repeal of provisions in special Acts in so far as the provisions relate to safety matters.**

8.144 As regards level crossing orders, if the HSWA 1974 system were to be adopted such orders would become redundant. **We provisionally propose that all existing level crossings orders should be revoked if the HSWA 1974-based system is adopted.**

HERITAGE AND PRIVATE RAILWAYS

8.145 Our provisional proposals have been largely developed to address the issues we see arising on the mainline railway, where the large majority of level crossings are located. However, we are also aware of the size and significance of the heritage railway sector. Heritage railways are part of the railway industry. But they are also significant players in the leisure and tourism industries. And nearly all are run by voluntary organisations, of which many are charities. Although employing a sizeable workforce, they also rely significantly on volunteer labour. Level crossing safety is a live concern amongst heritage railways. We have not been able to find a definitive figure for the number of level crossings on heritage railways, but understand that there may be as many as 1,000 or 1,500. Many issues are the same as on the mainline, but there are also differences. Heritage trains are typically slower than those on the mainline, and so may pose less of a risk at level crossings. But they are also lighter and may have been built to less exacting safety standards so the danger to the train and its passengers as opposed to, say, a motorist may be greater on a heritage railway.

8.146 There are also a significant number of private railways, mainly in use in docks, factories or other private industrial settings. Again, we have no definitive figure for level crossings on private railways, but we think there are far fewer than on heritage railways. It may be that there are different, perhaps fewer, safety and regulatory issues for private railways. But at the same time, these railways are governed by the broad regulatory structure dealing with mainline railways, and come under the oversight of ORR generally.

8.147   **We provisionally consider that our proposals should apply to all level crossings on all types of railway.**[29]

8.148   **However, we would welcome the views of consultees as to whether our provisional proposals should be adapted for heritage railways and private railways and if so, how.**

---

[29]   Readers will recall that the definition of "railway" for the purposes of this project is limited to those where the gauge meets the statutory minimum of 350mm or about 13 ¾".

PART 9
PLANNING: ENGLAND AND WALES

INTRODUCTION

9.1 A development can have an effect on a level crossing, even if the development is not adjacent to it, where it results in an increase in use of the highway network. Any increase in use of the highway can increase the risk associated with the level crossing.

OVERVIEW OF THE SPATIAL PLANNING SYSTEM IN ENGLAND AND WALES

Regional level strategies

9.2 The planning system in England and Wales is "plan-led". Development plans are created at both the regional and local level, taking into account the Secretary of State's policy guidance as set out in planning policy statements.[1] Currently, regional plans, called regional spatial strategies, are prepared by the eight regional assemblies in England and Greater London[2] and seek to integrate planning policy with other policy areas. The Regional Spatial Strategy (RSS) contains a regional transport strategy and should include a consideration of the inter-relationship between transport and infrastructure. Regional planning boards, appointed by the Secretary of State, review and revise the regional spatial strategies.[3] Consultation with planning and transport stakeholders from both the public and private sector is emphasised, as part of the RSS process as is the importance of a robust evidence base. Regional planning boards should have regard to national transport policy statements, including Transport White Papers and other policy documents, including Network Rail's Strategic Business Plan.[4]

Wales

9.3 As set out in Part 2, planning is devolved in Wales. The powers of the Secretary of State have been transferred to the Welsh Assembly Government.[5] The Wales Spatial Plan does not have quite the same role as the regional spatial strategies, although it should be taken into account when creating local development documents. The Planning Act 2008 transferred further spatial planning powers to the Welsh Assembly Government, giving them powers in relation to plans for development and land use. This encompasses both plans created by the Welsh

---

[1] See Planning for a Sustainable Future (2007) Cm 7120, p 6 for a chart giving an overview of the planning system, available at http://www.communities.gov.uk/publications/planningandbuilding/planningsustainablefuture (last visited 27 June 2010).

[2] In London, spatial development strategy and in Wales, Welsh development plan. The Coalition Government has announced a proposal to abolish Regional Spatial Strategies and return decision-making powers to local authorities: HM Government, *The Coalition: our programme for government* (May 2010) which can be found at: http://www.cabinetoffice.gov.uk/media/409088/pfg_coalition.pdf (last visited 27 June 2010).

[3] Planning and Compulsory Purchase Act 2004, s 3.

[4] http://www.networkrail.co.uk/aspx/4355.aspx (last visited 27 June 2010).

[5] National Assembly for Wales (Transfer of Functions) Order 1999, SI 1999 No 672.

Ministers and local plans, including the relationship between the Wales Spatial Plan and local development documents.

Local level plans

Local development frameworks

9.4 A local development framework translates the regional spatial strategy to a local level. It is underpinned by a core strategy which covers a 15 year period. That provides a guide as to where long term investment in infrastructure should take place within the plan area and where development should be located. Consultation with stakeholders, including key infrastructure providers, such as Network Rail, is essential.

9.5 In addition, the local development framework consists of local development documents. They provide guidance in greater detail taking into account the regional spatial strategy and the core strategy for the local development framework. Together the suite of documents is the development plan. Decisions on planning applications must be taken in accordance with the development plan unless other material considerations indicate otherwise.[6]

Local transport plans

9.6 Under section 108 of the Transport Act 2000, local authorities are to prepare local transport plans:

    (1)   Each local transport authority must—

        (a)   develop policies for the promotion and encouragement of safe, integrated, efficient and economic transport facilities and services to, from and within their area, and

        (b)   carry out their functions so as to implement those policies.

9.7 Local transport plans[7] must take account of the regional spatial strategy and should contain evidence of successful joint working with railways actors.[8] Any rail projects included in a local transport plan should include evidence that they have the support of key rail industry partners.

9.8 Under section 109 of the Transport Act 2000 local authorities in England must consult with the operators of any "network or station, or of any railway services, in their area" in relation to the drawing up of local transport plans. This provision came into effect on 9 February 2009.[9] It does not apply in Wales where transport plans must be approved by the Welsh Assembly Government which may only

---

[6]   Planning and Compulsory Purchase Act 2004, s 38(6).

[7]   London boroughs instead have local implementation strategies to implement the Mayor's transport strategy.

[8]   Department for Transport, *Full Guidance on Local Transport Plans: Second Edition* (2006) para 41.

[9]   The Local Transport Act 2008 (Commencement No. 1 and Transitional Provisions) Order 2009 SI 2009 No 107, Art 2(2), sch 2, Pt 1.

approve those which are "consistent" with the Welsh Transport Strategy[10] and "adequate" for its implementation.[11] Approval of the Secretary of State is not required in England.

9.9 When formulating local development documents and transport plans local authorities should explore and identify possible proposals for improving rail travel in liaison with railways actors. This includes proposals for reopening railway lines and creating new stations.[12]

INDIVIDUAL PLANNING DECISIONS AND LEVEL CROSSINGS

Introduction

9.10 When a planning application of significant size is proposed, pre-application consultation takes place by the developer with the community and stakeholders. If required, an environmental statement is prepared. The application is then submitted. It is publicised and further consultation takes place before the planning authority determines the application on its merits. The Secretary of State retains a call-in power for applications of more than local importance.[13]

9.11 Planning decisions are to be made in accordance with the development plan, unless material considerations indicate otherwise.[14] Material considerations will vary depending on the application and must be genuine considerations related to the development and use of the land in the public interest and relating to the application in question.[15] Whether something is a material consideration is a matter of law and ultimately is a matter to be determined by the courts. The weight to be attached to each material consideration in assessing the application is a matter for the planning authority.[16]

9.12 The impact of a development on a level crossing could be a material consideration which the planning authority should take into account. Means of access to a development, availability of infrastructure, and traffic issues are frequently material considerations[17] and it has been held that the safeguarding of land for a road widening scheme can be a material consideration.[18] We think it likely that a planning authority could refuse planning permission because of the adverse impact upon a level crossing.

Consultation with transport actors

9.13 Where a development is likely to result in a material increase in the volume or a

---

[10] Transport Act 2000, s 109A(4)(a).

[11] Transport Act 2000, s 109A(4)(b).

[12] Department of Communities and Local Government, *Planning Policy Guidance 13: Transport* (2001) para 74.

[13] Town and Country Planning Act 1990, s 77. For policy on when this is done see Written Answer, *Hansard,* (HC), 16 June 1999, vol 333, col 138.

[14] Planning and Compulsory Purchase Act 2004, s 38(6).

[15] *R v Westminster City Council ex parte Monahan* [1990] 1 QB 87.

[16] *Tesco Stores Ltd v Secretary of State for the Environment* [1995] 1 WLR 759.

[17] See V Moore, *A Practical Approach to Planning Law* (10th ed 2007) para 12.46.

[18] *Westminster Bank Ltd v Minister of Housing and Local Government* [1971] AC 508.

material change in the character of traffic using a level crossing over a railway, a Transport Assessment must be prepared and submitted as part of the planning application and the operator of the rail network must be consulted.[19] The detail of the assessment will vary with the size of the project. For some developments a simplified transport statement will be sufficient and there is a possibility that no formal process will be required where the transport impact is limited.[20]

9.14   A material increase has been held to be an increase of 5% or less in a congested area.[21]

9.15   Examples of material changes to the transport network that could affect level crossings include:

(1)   changes to the road layout, for example for new residential estates that may cause traffic increases such as to cause tailbacks onto crossings;

(2)   construction of houses, schools and so on that could increase the number of vehicles or pedestrians; and

(3)   construction of industrial or similar premises near to crossings where turning traffic, particularly large or slow moving vehicles, might cause tailbacks.[22]

9.16   In addition, the local planning authority should consult either the Secretary of State or the highway authority before granting planning permission where material changes will result. Consultation should take place, for example, where there would be a material increase in the volume or a material change in the character of traffic entering or leaving a classified road, proposed highway or trunk road. It should also take place where development is likely to prejudice the improvement or construction of a classified road or proposed highway and also where development would involve the formation, laying out or alteration of any means of access to a highway (other than a trunk road).[23]

9.17   During the passage of the Bill which became the Road Safety Act 2006, certain

[19]   The operator of the rail network is defined as including or consisting of the railway operator in question and the Secretary of State for Transport in England or the Welsh Assembly Government in Wales. Town and Country Planning (General Development Procedure) Order 1995, SI 1995 No 419, art 10(e)(ii). See Department for Transport and Department of Communities and Local Government, *Guidance on Transport Assessment* (March 2007).

[20]   Department for Transport and Department of Communities and Local Government, *Guidance on Transport Assessment* (March 2007) http://www.dft.gov.uk/pgr/regional/transportassessments/guidanceonta (last visited 27 June 2010).

[21]   Department of Communities and Local Government, *Planning Policy Guidance 13: Transport* (April 2001) http://www.communities.gov.uk/publications/planningandbuilding/ppg13 (last visited 27 June 2010).

[22]   Circular 9/95 ODPM, quoted in *Note on Planning and Railway Level Crossings* received from the ODPM on 14 March 2005, Appendix 2 of *First Report of the Working Party to the National Level Crossing Safety Group* (September 2006).

[23]   Town and Country Planning (General Development Procedure) Order 1995, SI 1995 No 419, art 10 (e)-(I).

amendments were tabled which would have required consultation with railway undertakers where development might require changes to protective arrangements at level crossings.[24] Consultation was to have been restricted to cases where a crossing was within 15 miles of the proposed development. These amendments were not included in the Bill as enacted.

Planning decisions in practice

9.18　In general it is the responsibility of the local planning authority to decide who to consult, when to consult and when the impact upon a level crossing will result in a "material increase" in traffic. It may be that local planning authorities have inadequate knowledge of the impact of planning decisions on level crossings and the problems that an increase in traffic can present.

9.19　**We would welcome examples or experiences of how consultation works in practice.**

9.20　In practice, the rail operator may be able to take steps to engage in the planning process, as suggested by the National Level Crossing Safety Group.[25] Network Rail can respond to local planning authority consultations on planning applications and suggest conditions or planning obligations to mitigate the effect of developments. They can also monitor emerging plans for development proposals which might have a significant impact on traffic levels at level crossings and propose improvements to level crossings as part of the development plans where necessary.

Planning decisions and closure of level crossings

9.21　As outlined in Part 6, the local planning authority has powers to stop up or divert footpaths and bridleways where it is necessary in order to carry out works authorised under planning permission.[26] This includes footpaths and bridleways which cross a railway. In considering the use of these powers, a local planning authority could consider the impact of a development upon a level crossing and whether this can be mitigated, for example, by stopping up or diverting a footpath.

9.22　Full engagement of all interested parties in consultation processes is desirable. For example, if the traffic over a level crossing increases to the point that the existing protection is no longer adequate, the railway operator may have to upgrade the crossing at its own expense. The upgrade of an automatic half-barrier crossing to a full-barrier could cause greater traffic delays due to the longer "down time" of full-barrier crossings, requiring the local authority to seek alternative traffic systems. If the impact upon the level crossing had been discussed between the relevant actors prior to the development taking place, a more integrated solution might have been found. If changes have to be made after the development has been completed, the cost is likely to be met by the railway operator (with the possibility of a contribution from the local highway

[24]　*Hansard* (HL), 29 November 2005, vol 676, col 139.

[25]　*Note on Planning and Railway Level Crossings* received from the ODPM on 14 March 2005, Appendix 2 of *First Report of the Working Party to the National Level Crossing Safety Group* (September 2006).

[26]　Town and Country Planning Act 1990, s 257. The Secretary of State and Welsh Ministers have a similar power in relation to highways: Town and Country Planning Act 1990, s 247.

authority) and the opportunity of a developer contribution is lost.

9.23 Planning authorities can impose conditions on the grant of planning permission for a proposed development under section 70 of the Town and Country Planning Act 1990. Conditions must be necessary, and "fair and reasonably relate to the permitted development".[27] For example, a planning authority could place a negative condition upon the developer of a housing or industrial development, preventing the project from going ahead until the level crossing had been upgraded or replaced with a bridge. These "Grampian conditions" are permissible even though the works or action required is outside the control of the developer.[28]

9.24 A planning authority may also require the developer to contribute to the cost of the upgrade or replacement level crossing through a section 106 agreement, which we discuss below.

9.25 There appear to be adequate legal tools available in the planning process to protect level crossings and the road network from any impact arising from developments. But we are aware from anecdotal material from the industry that there is a view amongst interested groups that planning authorities do not adequately take into account the impact of proposed developments on level crossings.[29] But concerns remain as to how often consultation and joined-up working between planning authorities and railways actors takes place in practice. As a result, opportunities for collaboration may be lost, and planning decisions may not take into account the need for review of the protective measures at level crossings and consideration of future convenience of crossing users.

9.26 **Do consultees think that the current practice of consultation relating to level crossings is adequate between local planning authorities, railway interests, developers and the public? If not, we would welcome specific examples.**

9.27 **Do consultees think that the current legal requirements for consultation where development affects a level crossing should be modified? If so, what modifications should be made?**

PLANNING LAW AND FUNDING OF INFRASTRUCTURE IMPROVEMENTS

9.28 Development can have a significant impact on the surrounding infrastructure. The planning system in England and Wales incorporates provision for financial contribution by developers in order to mitigate these effects. What follows is a brief outline of the current system of section 106 obligations (also called "section 106 agreements") and the Community Infrastructure Levy and their potential use in relation to level crossings.

Section 106 obligations

9.29 In England and Wales where a planned development requires infrastructure

---

[27] *Pyx Granite Co. Ltd v Ministry of Housing and Local Government* [1958] 1 QB 554.

[28] *Grampian Regional Council v Secretary of State for Scotland and City of Aberdeen* District Council 1984 SC (HL) 58.

[29] See also Department of Communities and Local Government, *Infrastructure Delivery, Spatial Plans in Practice: Supporting the Reform of Local Planning* (June 2008) para 1.26.

changes, funding is usually obtained from the developer by way of an agreement under section 106 of the Town and Country Planning Act 1990 ("section 106 obligation"). This provision allows local planning authorities to negotiate with developers to come to an agreement or obtain an undertaking which:

(1)   restricts the development or use of land in a specified way;

(2)   requires specified operations or activities to be carried out on, under or over the land;

(3)   requires the land to be used in a specified way; or

(4)   requires a sum or sums to be paid to the local authority, on a specified date or dates or periodically.[30]

9.30   A local planning authority may obtain funding for infrastructure outside the boundary of the development site, but the subject matter of a planning obligation must be fairly and reasonably related in scale and kind to the proposed development.[31] The section 106 obligation may require a developer to contribute to the widening of a public highway.[32]

9.31   Section 106 obligations are used to develop public transport infrastructure and development plans may include a policy on such agreements. Such planning obligations may be used in relation to level crossings, although we are not aware of any instance in which this has happened.

9.32   Planning obligations are linked to the development plans outlined above. The development plan should outline the authority's policies in relation to the funding of development proposals. These policies should provide an explanation and a justification for the circumstances in which a local planning authority may seek a planning obligation.[33]

9.33   The practice relating to section 106 obligations varies across the country. Research commissioned by the Department for Communities and Local Government supported concerns that only a very small proportion of developers contributed to infrastructure under the section 106 scheme.[34]

The Planning Act 2008 and the Community Infrastructure Levy

9.34   In April 2010 the Community Infrastructure Levy was brought into force by the Community Infrastructure Levy Regulations 2010[35] under the Planning Act 2008

---

[30]   Town and Country Planning Act 1990, s 106(1).

[31]   Office of the Deputy Prime Minister Circular 5/2005, *Planning Obligations,* para B9.

[32]   *Bradford City Council v Secretary of State for the Environment* [1986] JPL 598 CA.

[33]   Office of the Deputy Prime Minister Circular 05/2005, *Planning Obligations,* para B8.

[34]   Department of Communities and Local Government, *Community Infrastructure Levy, An Overview* (March 2010) para 5. Available at: http://www.communities.gov.uk/publications/planningandbuilding/communityinfrastructurele vy (last visited 27 June 2010).

[35]   Community Infrastructure Levy Regulations 2010, SI 2010 No 948.

across England and Wales.[36] The aim of the levy is to pass on infrastructure costs required by a development to the developers or owners of the land.[37] It is hoped that it will supplement the existing powers relating to section 106 obligations, under the Town and Country Planning Act 1990.

9.35 Funding obtained by way of the Community Infrastructure Levy may be used by the local authority to fund infrastructure development within the local authority's area,[38] and to do things outside its area. Section 216 (7)(d)-(f) of the Planning Act 2008 provides for regulations to be made, enabling a local planning authority to pass money on to another body for this purpose.

9.36 However, the introduction of the Community Infrastructure Levy is discretionary. Each local planning authority can decide whether it wishes to impose the levy and at what level, taking into account the infrastructure, planning and development plans for the area.[39] The impact of the Community Infrastructure Levy can only be assessed once it becomes clear to what extent local planning authorities decide to use this power.

9.37 The Community Infrastructure Levy, and the assessment of the infrastructure needs of an area which would be necessary to implement it, provide an opportunity for discussion of the future of any level crossing in that area.

9.38 **We provisionally think that the current legal provision is sufficient to allow for developer contributions towards closure, replacement or improvement of level crossings. It may be that what is required is guidance, which would be beyond the scope of this project.**

9.39 **Do consultees think that section 106 obligations are appropriate legal mechanisms for obtaining developer contributions for upgrading or replacing level crossing infrastructure?**

9.40 **Will the situation be improved if the Community Infrastructure Levy is adopted by local planning authorities?**

9.41 **If not, what more is needed?**

---

[36] There is no equivalent Community Infrastructure Levy in Scotland.

[37] Planning Act 2008, s 205(2).

[38] Planning Act 2008, s 216.

[39] Department of Communities and Local Government, *Community Infrastructure Levy, An Overview* (March 2010); Department of Communities and Local Government, *Community Infrastructure Levy Guidance: charge setting and charging schedule procedures* (March 2010). Available at: http://www.communities.gov.uk/publications/planningandbuilding/cilguidance (last visited 27 June 2010).

PART 10
PLANNING: SCOTLAND

INTRODUCTION

10.1 As mentioned in Part 9, developments can have an impact on nearby level crossings as a result of the increased use of the road network. As planning is a devolved matter we discuss the issues relating to Scotland separately.

10.2 The main legislation relating to planning in Scotland is the Town and Country Planning (Scotland) Act 1997.[1] The Planning etc (Scotland) Act 2006 amends certain provisions of the 1997 Act. The main change of relevance to discussion of level crossings is in relation to planning agreements, which we discuss below.

10.3 The Scottish Ministers have policy responsibility for planning matters in Scotland. However, the bulk of everyday planning decisions are made by local authorities (who are "planning authorities" for the purposes of planning legislation[2]), with the Scottish Ministers exercising a supervisory function.[3] There are also planning circulars and planning advice notes issued by the Scottish Ministers, which although not legally binding, are often taken into account in local decision-making.[4]

INDIVIDUAL PLANNING DECISIONS AND LEVEL CROSSINGS

10.4 Subject to certain exceptions, an application to a planning authority for planning permission is required where there is "development" of land.[5] The Planning etc (Scotland) Act 2006 introduced new categories of "national", "major" and "local" developments.[6]

10.5 In relation to local developments, the Town and Country Planning (Development Management Procedure) (Scotland) Regulations 2008[7] provide that planning authorities must consult with Network Rail Infrastructure Limited or any other railway undertakers:

---

[1] A commentary on the 1997 Act can be found in J Rowan-Robinson, *Town and Country Planning (Scotland) Act 1997* (2009).

[2] Town and Country Planning (Scotland) Act 1997, s 1.

[3] For example, under s 46 of the 1997 Act, the Scottish Ministers may "call in" planning applications.

[4] For Scottish planning policy see http://www.scotland.gov.uk/Topics/Built-Environment/planning/National-Planning-Policy/newSPP (last visited 27 June 2010).

[5] Town and Country Planning (Scotland) Act 1997, s 28.

[6] Town and Country Planning (Scotland) Act 1997, s 26A(1).

[7] Town and Country Planning (Development Management Procedure) (Scotland) Regulations 2008, SI 2008 No 432.

...where the development is likely to result in a material increase in the volume or a material change in the character of traffic using a level crossing over a railway.[8]

10.6 As we mentioned in Part 9 in relation to planning in England and Wales, we have heard anecdotally that there is a view amongst interested groups that planning authorities do not always take adequate account of the impact of proposed developments on level crossings.

10.7 **We would welcome examples or experiences of how consultation works in practice.**

10.8 We noted in Part 9 that during the passage of the Bill which became the Road Safety Act 2006, amendments were tabled which would have required consultation with railway undertakers.[9] However, as mentioned, those amendments were not included in the Bill as enacted. The question arises therefore as to whether the current requirement under the 2008 Regulations needs to be strengthened or amended to ensure that proper consideration is given by planning authorities before granting planning permission for developments as to the potential impact on level crossings. We therefore ask consultees the following question:

10.9 **Should amendments be made to the requirements under the 2008 Regulations for consultation with Network Rail Infrastructure Limited and other railway undertakers, where development is likely to affect a level crossing to a material degree?**

10.10 In determining an application, the planning authority must have regard to the provisions of any development plan, so far as material to the application, and any other material considerations.[10] There is some uncertainty over the meaning of "material considerations" in this context, as what may be material in a particular case usually turns on the facts.[11] The *weight* to be given to any particular consideration is a matter for determination by the planning authority/Scottish Ministers,[12] and should only be reviewed by the courts where the decision is so unreasonable that no reasonable authority could have come to it.[13] The planning authority must also take into account any representations relating to the application, for example, following consultation with Network Rail as outlined

---

[8] Town and Country Planning (Development Management Procedure) (Scotland) Regulations 2008, SI 2008 No 432, reg 25, read with sch 5, para 9.

[9] Town and Country Planning (General Development Procedure) (Scotland) Order 1992, SI 1992 No 224, art 15.

[10] Town and Country Planning (Scotland) Act 1997, s 37(2).

[11] See generally Rowan Robinson and others, *Scottish Planning Law and Procedure* (2001) para 8.33ff.

[12] *City of Edinburgh Council v Secretary of State for Scotland and Revival Properties Ltd* 1997 SCLR 1112,1998 SC (HL) 33.

[13] This is referred to as *Wednesbury* unreasonableness after the case of *Associated Provincial Picture Houses Ltd v Wednesbury Corporation* [1948] 1 KB 223, an English case which sets out that administrative decisions may be judicially reviewed where an authority has "come to a conclusion so unreasonable that no reasonable authority could ever have come to it" (per Lord Greene at [234]).

above.[14] If the development is likely to have a material impact on the railway, any representations made by Network Rail would be a material consideration.

10.11 Furthermore, the suitability of existing infrastructure will usually fall to be considered in the course of determination of a planning application. Planning authorities would also be required under HSWA 1974 to ensure that decisions of a planning authority, so far as reasonably practicable, do not adversely impact on the safety of those affected by such decisions.[15] On this basis, level crossing safety should be an important factor when determining a planning application.

10.12 If it is decided to grant an application, the grant of planning permission may be "subject to such conditions as [the planning authority] think fit".[16] Section 41 of the Town and Country Planning (Scotland) Act 1997 gives examples of conditions that may be imposed. Circular 4/1998 sets out Scottish Government policy in respect of planning conditions, stating that they must be:

(1) necessary;

(2) relevant to planning;

(3) relevant to the development to be permitted;

(4) enforceable;

(5) precise; and

(6) reasonable in all other respects.

10.13 In the level crossings context, an important issue is whether a planning condition can be imposed to make planning permission conditional on the closure of a particular crossing. In *Grampian Regional Council v Secretary of State for Scotland and City of Aberdeen District Council*,[17] it was held that a condition requiring closure of a section of road was not unreasonable. The case noted a distinction between (i) a positive condition attached to planning permission that the applicant should bring about some circumstance and (ii) a negative condition that the development should not commence until an event had occurred. Whilst road closure was not a matter within the control of the applicants, if the development was in the public interest, refusal of plannning permission would be wrong. Moreover, the existence of statutory provision allowing the stopping up of roads, so as to enable development to be carried out,[18] was seen as supporting the argument that a negative condition relating to road closure was contemplated by the legislature.

10.14 One of the most serious problems arises where a development takes place in the vicinity of a level crossing. Where a development is likely to have a material effect

---

14 Town and Country Planning (Scotland) Act 1997, s 38(1).

15 Health and Safety at Work etc Act 1974, s 3(1).

16 Town and Country Planning (Scotland) Act 1997, s 37(1)(a).

17 *Grampian Regional Council v Secretary of State for Scotland and City of Aberdeen District Council* 1984 SC (HL) 58.

18 Town and Country Planning (Scotland) Act 1997, s 202.

in traffic terms in relation to level crossings in the vicinity, a transport plan would be required. In these circumstances the developer would be required to prepare a transport assessment as part of the planning application, which would enable subsequent consultation with the railway operator to be more meaningful.

10.15 **Should there be a requirement for a transport plan to be produced in connection with an application for planning permission for a development in the vicinity of a level crossing which is likely to have a material effect on the traffic (in terms of volume and/or composition) that uses the level crossing?**

PLANNING DECISIONS AND CLOSURE OF LEVEL CROSSINGS

10.16 Section 207 of the Town and Country Planning (Scotland) Act 1997 permits planning authorities to stop up or divert any "road" (within the meaning of the Roads (Scotland) Act 1984), unless it is a trunk road within the meaning of the 1984 Act, or it is a special road provided by the Scottish Ministers under that Act. This may only be done if the planning authority is satisfied that it is necessary to do so in order to enable the development to be carried out in accordance with planning permission. Section 208 provides a similar power in respect of footpaths and bridleways. Section 208 is of use principally in relation to public paths under the Countryside (Scotland) Act 1967 (in so far as such paths continue to be classed as public paths under the 1967 Act) and some core paths under the Land Reform (Scotland) Act 2003, which fall outside the scope of the Roads (Scotland) Act 1984.[19]

10.17 Where replacement of a level crossing with a bridge or an underpass is preferable to stopping up or diverting the way, the power contained in section 189 of the 1997 Act allows a planning authority to:

acquire compulsorily any land in their area which:

(a) is suitable for and is required in order to secure the carrying out of development, redevelopment or improvement;

(b) is required for a purpose which it is necessary to achieve in the interests of the proper planning of an area in which the land is situated.

10.18 A common obstacle to replacement of a crossing is the need to acquire land for construction purposes, for example, to allow for approaches to a bridge. Section 189 of the 1997 Act gives planning authorities the power, where necessary, to acquire such land compulsorily.

10.19 There may be a need for more involvement of local planning authorities in the decision as to when closure of a crossing is appropriate, and whether any replacement such as a bridge or underpass is necessary. This is especially true where closure and/or replacement of a crossing are required as a result of development. In such cases, Network Rail has no powers to stop up roads or

---

[19] See Roads (Scotland) Act 1984, s 151(3)(a). As we mention in Part 12, although there may be a public right of passage over a core path, there will be some core paths over which no public right of passage exists. These will also fall outwith the scope of the 1984 Act.

compulsorily purchase land. This means that Network Rail is dependent on the planning authority exercising its powers of compulsory purchase. An authority is required to consider whether there would be a compelling case that compulsory acquisition would be in the public interest before being able to exercise its powers of compulsory acquisition.

10.20   **Our provisional view is that any future procedure governing closure of level crossings should aim to involve planning authorities in the decision to close or replace a crossing (in particular where development is a factor necessitating closure).**

10.21   In Part 8, we have provisionally proposed a closure procedure that would provide compulsory purchase powers, for example when extra land is required to build a replacement bridge or underpass. Also in Part 8 we invite consultees to comment on whether it would be useful to introduce infrastructure agreements for level crossings. Such agreements might facilitate co-operation between all the parties involved in closure, including planning authorities and railway operators.

PLANNING LAW AND FUNDING OF INFRASTRUCTURE IMPROVEMENTS

10.22   As mentioned in Part 9, the Community Infrastructure Levy applies in England and Wales only and there is no equivalent to it in Scotland.

Roads (Scotland) Act 1984

10.23   Section 48 of the Roads (Scotland) Act 1984 allows a roads authority to enter into an agreement with any person willing to contribute to the construction or improvement of a road. The authority may have regard to any such contributions when deciding whether to construct a new road or undertake improvement to an existing road. In practice, it appears that agreements under section 48 are only infrequently used to secure contributions from developers.[20]

Agreements under section 75 of the Town and Country Planning (Scotland) Act 1997

10.24   Section 75 of the Town and Country Planning (Scotland) Act 1997 provides for agreements between a planning authority and a developer, aimed at making a proposed development more acceptable to the planning authority.[21] At present, such agreements represent an important vehicle for funding infrastructure improvements. Planning agreements can be used to fund transport infrastructure. For example, if upgrade or replacement is required to a level crossing as a result of a development, as mentioned above, planning authorities could consider securing a contribution towards the cost of this from the developer.

10.25   It should be noted that sections 23 and 24 of the Planning etc (Scotland) Act 2006 substitute new provisions for section 75 of the 1997 Act regarding planning agreements. The Scottish Government is consulting on proposed Regulations to

---

[20]   McMaster and others, *An Assessment of the Value of Planning Agreements in Scotland*, Scottish Government Social Research (2008) p 2.

[21]   Section 23 of the Planning etc (Scotland) Act 2006 provides for amendments to section 75 of the 1997 Act to introduce planning obligations similar to those in England and Wales. However, section 23 is not yet fully in force.

implement sections 23 of the 2006 Act. In terms of the new section 75, in future planning agreements will be referred to as "planning obligations". However, the new planning obligations will be broadly equivalent to the current planning agreements.[22]

10.26 Despite the limitations placed on planning agreements by the Scottish Government *Circular 12/1996*, in *City of Edinburgh Council v Secretary of State for Scotland and Others*[23] Lord Clyde applied the approach adopted in the English case of *Tesco Stores Ltd v Secretary of State for the Environment,*[24] mentioned in Part 9 above. This case appears to significantly broaden the scope for a planning agreement to influence the outcome of a planning application.

10.27 Where a development might impact upon its infrastructure, Network Rail may request that the planning authority conclude an agreement under section 75 of the 1997 Act regarding, for example, funding a crossing replacement. Where a development causes a material impact on the surrounding infrastructure, particularly on roads in the area of a development, it seems reasonable to expect the developer to contribute to the costs involved in improving or changing the infrastructure provided that is necessary for the development to proceed.

10.28 **Are there any legal obstacles to the use of agreements (in particular, planning agreements under section 75 of the Town and Country Planning (Scotland) Act 1997) to secure contributions from developers towards level crossing infrastructure? Are there any other improvements which could be made in this area?**

---

[22] The consultation period is due to finish at the end of July 2010. The consultation paper is available at: http://www.scotland.gov.uk/Publications/2010/04/26150418/0 (last visited 27 June 2010).

[23] *City of Edinburgh Council v Secretary of State for Scotland and Revival Properties Ltd* 1997 SCLR 1112; 1998 SC (HL) 33.

[24] [1995] 1 WLR 759.

PART 11
RIGHTS OF WAY AND ACCESS ISSUES: ENGLAND AND WALES

INTRODUCTION

11.1 We deal with this topic separately for England and Wales, and for Scotland, mainly because the law relating to public and private rights of way and to "access rights"[1] is different. Moreover, there are certain variations that are not legal differences as such. For example, access is more of a public issue north than south of the border.

11.2 In relation to England and Wales, this Part outlines various issues concerning rights of way over railways and suggests some specific reforms.

PRIVATE RIGHTS OF WAY OVER THE RAILWAY

The nature of private rights of way

11.3 Private rights of way in the law of England and Wales are generally examples of easements;[2] easements give one landowner the right (rather than merely a permission) to do something on another's land.[3] Easements can arise either by grant (by one landowner to another) or through long use, known as prescription.

Level crossings that intersected existing rights of way

11.4 When the railways were constructed, in many cases they cut across existing rights of way. There is no general provision for private rights of way similar to that in section 46 of the Railways Clauses Consolidation Act 1845, which specifies how a public road should be crossed. However, where a private right of way for a horse or a carriage existed prior to the construction of the railway and was to be severed by it there was an obligation under section 53 of the Railways Clauses Consolidation Act 1845 to create and to maintain a substitute way, if the clause was not excluded in the special Act.[4] If substitution was not put in place then damages could be recovered by any person entitled to such a right by virtue of the model clause provided by section 55 of the Railways Clauses Consolidation Act 1845. If a substitute way was put in place by the provision of a level crossing, then the easement remained; the crossing would be an easement crossing. It would continue in its original form unless extinguished.

---

[1] This is the term used by the Land Reform (Scotland) Act 2003.

[2] In Scotland these are referred to as "servitudes".

[3] In the law of England and Wales an easement must be appurtenant to land; it cannot be held "in gross", that is, owned simply by an individual without being attached to that person's land: *Re Ellenborough Park* [1956] Ch 131 at [163], see also C Harpum, S Bridge and M Dixon, *Megarry and Wade: The Law of Real Property* (7th ed 2008) paras 27-004 to 27-019.

[4] Railways Clauses Consolidation Act 1845, s 53 applies to both public and private ways.

The user-worked level crossing (UWC) on a private road at Bratts Blackhouse on the freight only Saxmundham to Sizewell line in Suffolk: note the absence of telephones or other warning devices, so that the user has to judge whether it is safe to cross by looking out for approaching trains.

Credit: Rail Accident Investigation Branch.

Level crossings that gave rise to private rights of way

11.5 As we said in Part 1, the Railways Clauses Consolidation Act 1845 provided for what was to happen when private interests were affected by the building of the railway. A level crossing could arise, as we said above, where the railway cut across a pre-existing private right of way. Alternatively the railway might have bisected land owned by the same landowner. Special Acts establishing the railway line automatically included the 1845 Act model clauses, unless they were specifically excluded.[5]

11.6 Where the railway bisected a piece of land, the special Act would provide for how this interference with land should be dealt with. The combination in a special Act of model clauses and specific provisions gave great flexibility to the railway company and the owners of adjoining lands. In some cases the interference was dealt with by the payment of compensation to the landowner and/or occupier, in which case the need for a level crossing would not arise. If not, then the special Act did not normally define a specific structure, as it would generally do for public rights of way, but instead contained an outline power to do "accommodation" works.

11.7 The majority of special Acts incorporate section 68 of the Railways Clauses Consolidation Act 1845 for this purpose. This, so far as is relevant, states that:

---

[5] Railways Clauses Consolidation Act 1845, s 1.

The company shall make and at all times thereafter maintain the following works for the accommodation of the owners and occupiers of lands adjoining the railway; (that is to say)

> Such and so many convenient gates, bridges, arches, culverts, and passages, over, under, or by the sides of or leading to or from the railway, as shall be necessary for the purpose of making good any interruptions caused by the railway to the use of the lands through which the railway shall be made;
>
> …
>
> Provided always, that the company shall not be required to make such accommodation works in such a manner as would prevent or obstruct the working or using of the railway, nor to make any accommodation works with respect to which the owners and occupiers of the lands shall have agreed to receive and shall have been paid compensation instead of the making them.

11.8   Against that background, we can say generally that two types of private level crossing came into existence.

11.9   In many cases, the conveyance of land to the railway company (often as a result of compulsory purchase) contained an express grant to the landowner of a right of way across a level crossing, the latter of course to be constructed as part of the railway company's obligation to carry out accommodation works.

11.10   In other cases, there was no specific grant in the conveyance. Section 68 of the Railways Clauses Consolidation Act 1845 does not confer any specific right of way; so in these cases a right to use the crossing has to be implied. Such rights are not easements, since they are created neither by grant nor by prescription, but are clearly akin to easements. It is not clear how far they differ from easements nor how much of the law of easements can be applied to them.

11.11   The case law on the issue is also unclear, referring at times to such interests as easements, and at other times as interests akin to easements. In some cases the courts have referred to purely section 68-based rights of way as easements, as in *Taff Vale Railway Company v Gordon Canning*.[6] The use of the word "easement" in a judgment, however, is not necessarily conclusive as to the nature of the right.

11.12   In *South Eastern Railways v Cooper*,[7] the Court of Appeal described the landowner's right as an easement and analysed it as such. In *Cooper* the right of way was provided for in the conveyance and, as well as connecting the two portions of the landowner's severed land, was intended to connect the land to a diverted highway. The court distinguished interests which are not contained in the conveyance and depend on section 68 of the Railways Clauses Consolidation Act 1845 alone, which the court referred to as "mere accommodation works".

---

[6]   [1909] 2 Ch 48.

[7]   [1924] 1 Ch 211.

11.13 Whether the conveyance in fact constitutes the grant of the right of way as an easement or merely records what is to be done pursuant to section 68 of the Railways Clauses Consolidation Act 1845 will depend upon how the court construes the wording of the conveyance. The different approaches which may be taken are seen in the case of *British Railways Board v Glass*,[8] where the majority in the Court of Appeal took the view that the conveyance granted an easement which was a right of way for all purposes. Its wording differed from section 68, requiring the railway company to allow the landowner to pass rather than to actually build and maintain a level crossing. In his dissenting judgment, Lord Denning viewed the conveyance as merely recording the exceptions to the landowner's waiver of his rights under section 68 of the 1845 Act and that therefore this did not constitute a grant but was a "mere accommodation way".[9]

Extent of private interests over a level crossing

Easement crossings

11.14 Where the right of way is provided for in the conveyance, the extent of the interest will be specified in the conveyance itself. In general, where an interest is granted by deed the courts have been generous in construing the extent of the right. For example, in *British Railways Board v Glass*[10] there was a grant in the following terms:

> A right of crossing the said railway to the extent of twelve feet in width on the level thereof with all manner of cattle to and from one part of the said close of land ... to the other part of the same close severed by the said line or railway.

11.15 The reference to cattle was seen as expanding rather than limiting the right, since the right to cross with cattle was regarded as being more extensive than a footpath or bridleway.

11.16 Where a right of way granted by a conveyance is in general terms, this right appears to be good for all purposes, even those which differ widely from that for which the crossing was used when the railway was first constructed. In *British Railways Board v Glass*,[11] the owner could use the crossing, which was originally a purely agricultural crossing, for the purpose of allowing access to a caravan site on the severed piece of land. The only limitation to this was capacity of the railway to grant the right. A railway company cannot grant an interest over the railway which would be incompatible with the statutory purposes for which the land was originally granted to the railway company; that is, "incompatible with the working of the railway".[12]

---

[8]   [1965] Ch 538.

[9]   [1965] Ch 538 per Harman LJ.

[10] [1965] Ch 538.

[11] [1965] Ch 538.

[12] *British Railways Board v Glass* [1965] Ch 538 at 554 (Lord Denning). See also *TRH Sampson Associates Ltd v British Railways Board* [1983] 1 WLR 170; [1983] 1 All ER 257 at 261, this was said to mean that an interest, "could not be construed in such a way as to obstruct the proper working of the railway".

11.17   The issue of incompatibility is also encountered in relation to the granting of public rights of way, which is discussed further below. It would appear that there would have to be substantial interference with the working of the railway for the interest to be considered incompatible. There seems to be no example in the cases where it has been decided that the railway company did not have the capacity to grant the interest claimed over a level crossing. Lord Denning, dissenting in *British Railways Board v Glass,* gave the example of putting a factory on the land with "multitudes of people and convoys of lorries over the crossing" as a use which would be incompatible with the working of the railway, but these were not the facts in that case. Further, in *South Eastern Railway Company v Cooper*[13] it was considered that an increase in burden from agricultural use to access to a sandpit was compatible with the continued working of the railway. However, this case has been distinguished as the interest in question also provided access to a road which had been diverted.

11.18   Therefore the permitted use of a right over a railway granted in a conveyance is determined by the right as granted at the time. First, the wording of the grant must be construed. Second, if the grant is considered to be a general grant of a right of way the court must consider whether such a grant is compatible with the working of the railway and the limitations on the right imposed by the physical characteristics of the way itself.[14] For example, a right of way over a narrow way cannot support the passage for 14 large trucks per day.[15]

11.19   The fact that a right of way crosses a railway line is an important characteristic of the way. Thus it is part of the factual background against which the extent of a general grant of a right of way should be considered.

Statutory rights of way over level crossings

11.20   Where the right to cross is not expressly granted but has to be implied from the statute, it appears that the persons who can use the crossing are the owner and/or the occupier of the adjoining lands together with "those claiming under" the owner or occupier.[16] This would include such people as those delivering to the owner/occupier and visiting friends.[17]

11.21   Further evidence that the use is not limited is given by section 74 of the Railways Clauses Consolidation Act 1845, which provides for the initial right to cross the railway until the accommodation works are completed, unless the owner or occupier of the land has accepted compensation as an alternative to being allowed to cross the railway. Section 74 refers to such a right for:

> the owners and occupiers of such lands, and other persons whose right of way shall be affected by the want of such communication, and their respective servants.

[13]   [1923] 1 Ch 211.

[14]   K Gray and S F Gray, *Elements of Land Law* (5th ed 2008) para 8.92 and J Gaunt QC and The Hon Mr Justice Morgan (eds), *Gale on the Law of Easements* (18th ed 2008) para 9.62.

[15]   *White v Richards* (1994) 68 P & CR 105.

[16]   Railways Clauses Consolidation Act 1845, s 74

[17]   *Greenhalgh v British Railways Board* [1969] 2 QB 286 at [292].

11.22 This clearly envisages persons, other than the owner and occupier, needing to cross the railway.

11.23 The offence under section 75 of the Railways Clauses Consolidation Act 1845 provides that "any person" who fails to fasten the gate at such a crossing commits an offence, thus acknowledging that persons other than the owner or occupier may be passing across the crossing.

11.24 The following people would, therefore, be entitled to use a level crossing constructed in accordance with section 68 of the Railways Clauses Consolidation Act 1845:

(1) the owner and occupier of adjoining land, as it is to them that the duty under section 68 is owed; and

(2) those "claiming under" the owner and occupier of adjoining lands, including those who are there with the permission of the owner, for example, servants, guests or people delivering to the owner;[18] and those who had a pre-existing right of way granted by the owner or occupier.[19]

11.25 As to the way in which the statutory right of way may be used, where there is no evidence of the agreement in the conveyance it is necessary to go back to the provisions of the statute and to look at use at the time of construction of the railway to determine the extent of the interest.

11.26 In *TRH Sampson Associates Ltd v British Railways Board* the court observed that:

Section 68 is in terms designed for the purposes of making good any "interruptions caused by railway to the use of the lands through which the railway shall be made" which suggests, at first glance at least, that one has to start by considering the use to which the land was then being put in order to ascertain the use that was "interrupted".[20]

11.27 In *Great Northern Railway v M'Alister* the court said:

The owner of the adjoining lands was entitled, when the railway was made, to a convenient passage over the railway sufficient to make good, so far as possible, any interruption which the construction of the railway caused by severance in the working of his farm, including, I should say, any alteration or extension of that working which could or ought to have been contemplated by the parties when the accommodation works were made and accepted.[21]

11.28 Because an interest under section 68 of the 1845 Act has its extent determined by the type of use that has occurred, it bears some similarities with a right of way acquired by long use. However, the use made of the crossing merely allows the

---

[18] *Greenhalgh v British Railways Board* [1969] 2 QB 286 at [292].

[19] See C Sara, *Boundaries and Easements* (4th ed 2008) para 14.22.

[20] [1983] 1 WLR 170 at [174] to [175].

[21] [1897] 1 IR 587 at 602.

extent of the rights to be determined; it is not the source of the right itself, which of course is the statute. This point was made in *TRH Sampson Associates Ltd v British Railways Board:*[22]

> The case before me is not concerned with any question of a prescriptive right … It is obvious that a prescriptive right depends upon, and indeed, stems from, user over a period, so that the actual extent of that use governs the nature of the right acquired by prescription: and it may be that some of the judges, particularly in the older cases, have consciously or unconsciously drawn a parallel between a section 68 statutory right and a right acquired by prescription.

Extension or change of use

11.29 Can the permitted use change over time? There are two possible ways in which this could happen. First, the original grant may be deemed to cover wider usage than that which originally took place. Second, a user may have acquired different rights over a way by prescription. It appears that this may be possible where the original right is statutory.[23] It does not seem that an easement granted as a right of way to a limited extent (for example, to pass on foot only) can be extended by prescription to encompass a different use; that would amount to excessive use of the easement, creating a nuisance, which could be prevented by injunction.

> It is critical to determine the extent of the right which the dominant owner is entitled to enjoy. Use which goes beyond the right will amount to a trespass on the servient land … Use which goes beyond the right is generally termed "excessive" … The extent of a right acquired by grant depends upon the terms of the grant properly construed in the light of all relevant factors.[24]

11.30 In either case, there are limits to how extensive an interest over a railway may be. No interest may be acquired which the railway is not capable of granting. It appears that this is a fundamental limit which applies no matter how an interest is acquired, even if the interest when originally granted was framed as a general right of way. If, on the other hand, the interest granted was not a general right of way, change of use now seems only to be permissible if it does not substantially increase the burden on the railway, compared to the burden imposed by the interest as originally granted.

Statutory right of way crossings

PERMISSIBLE EXTENDED USE

11.31 Where a right is based purely on the statute, the extent of the permitted use is defined by the use at the time the crossing was constructed. Any extension of use is also determined by reference to this starting point. Any extended use will only be permissible if it does not substantially increase the burden on the

---

[22] [1983] 1 WLR 170 at 181.

[23] *British Railways Board v Glass* [1956] Ch 538.

[24] J Gaunt QC and The Hon Mr Justice Morgan (eds), *Gale on the Law of Easements* (18th ed 2008) para 9-02.

railway.[25] Accordingly, later cases have allowed changes of use, provided that the use does not substantially increase the burden on the railway.[26] In judging this, it is clear that there is a difference between an accommodation bridge, where the only burden on the railway would be a possible increase in maintenance costs, and a level crossing, where there are serious safety and operational concerns linked to changed or increased use.[27]

11.32 It appears that quite a substantial increase in the burden on the railway will be required before the use is deemed excessive and therefore impermissible. For example, in *Taff Vale Railway Company v Gordon Canning* the use was deemed excessive where a crossing across a busy line was being used as a means of access for a tennis club. However, it was made clear that the interest was not so limited as to allow use of the crossing for agricultural purposes only. Whether the burden is substantially increased is a question of fact to be determined in each case.

11.33 The burden of proof is on the rights-holder to show that the increased use does not constitute a substantial increase in burden on the railway.[28]

WHERE A MORE EXTENSIVE INTEREST IS CLAIMED BY PRESCRIPTION

11.34 Where it is claimed that an easement has been acquired by prescription, in addition to the statutory right of way, the nature of the easement is determined by the use made of the way by the claimant.

11.35 The right claimed to be acquired by prescription cannot be a right which the railway could not have granted due to it being incompatible with the proper working of the railway, as prescription is based on the fiction that there was an express grant which has since been lost. In the case of *British Railways Board v Glass*,[29] the Court of Appeal clearly thought that it was possible to acquire a further right over the railway by prescription. The test of compatibility with the proper working of the railway as described above will apply.

11.36 The acquisition of an easement by prescription can be prevented by the railway operator prohibiting the increased use within the 20 year prescriptive period, or allowing it by express permission.[30]

11.37 Consultees should note that the Law Commission's Consultation Paper on Easements, Covenants and Profits à Prendre[31] proposed the abolition of the fiction of express grant, although this would not have retrospective effect. If that proposal is implemented, it will be necessary to make express provision to the

[25] *Great Western Railway Co (GWR) v Talbot* [1902] 2 Ch 759 and *TRH Sampson Associates Ltd v British Railways Board* [1983] 1 WLR 170.

[26] *Taff Vale Railway Company v Gordon Canning* [1909] 2 Ch 48.

[27] *TRH Sampson Associates Ltd v British Railways Board* [1983] 1 WLR 170 at [266].

[28] *TRH Sampson Associates Ltd v British Railways Board* [1983] 1 WLR 170 at [266].

[29] [1965] Ch 538.

[30] Because the use made of the way, in order to support a claim of prescription, must be made without the owner's permission.

[31] Easements, Covenants and Profits à Prendre (2008) Law Commission Consultation Paper No 186. The Final Report is to be published in 2011.

effect that it is not possible to prescribe for an easement over a level crossing if that is incompatible with the proper working of the railway.

11.38 A further alternative would be to prohibit the acquisition by prescription of further private rights over level crossings.

11.39 **Do consultees think there should be a statutory prohibition on the future acquisition of private rights of way over the railway by prescription?**

Easement crossings

11.40 As we explained above, the only limitation upon the extent of an easement granted by the railway company seems to be its capacity to do so. A right of way may be granted for a limited purpose, but it may be in general terms and for all purposes.

11.41 Can the route of such a right be varied? In England and Wales, the route of an easement can only be varied by agreement between the parties (the owners of the dominant and servient tenements). Even where a proposed deviation is small and the alternative route equally convenient for the dominant owner, an interference with an easement will still be actionable. In *Dudley Heslop v Bishton and Others* it was held that where a right of way had been obstructed, the existence of an equally convenient right of way effectively did not extinguish the underlying right or any part of it. The servient owner could not unilaterally by provision of a new right grant a new interest and compel the dominant owner to use it.[32]

11.42 This is so whether the easement is recorded in a deed or not. There is no option to appeal to a court or tribunal. The alteration of the route of an easement involves both the grant of a right of way over the new route and the extinguishment of the old route; whilst a party may unilaterally grant a private right of way they cannot unilaterally extinguish one.[33] The provision of an alternative right of way may affect the remedy available,[34] but it does not affect the nature of the right or prevent its obstruction being actionable. Agreement is therefore the only way to vary an easement.

11.43 The Law Commission's Consultation Paper on Easements, Covenants and Profits à Prendre included proposals to extend the jurisdiction of the Lands Tribunal so as to enable it to extinguish or modify an easement, including the power to change the route of the easement.[35]

11.44 Reform of the law relating to change of use

---

[32] [2009] EWHC 607.

[33] *Dudley Heslop v Bishton and Others* [2009] EWHC 607 at [22]-[24].

[34] As in *Greenwich Healthcare NHS Trust v London and Quadrant Housing Trust and others* [1998] 1 WLR 1749 and [1998] 3 All ER 437, where the court refused to grant an injunction where an alternative and more convenient route was provided. Allowing the development to go ahead would achieve a public objective and rights holders had not objected to the proposals.

[35] Easements, Covenants and Profits à Prendre (2008) Law Commission Consultation Paper No186. The Final Report is to be published in 2011.

11.45　We think it would be useful to both rights-holders and railway operators to have a clearer understanding of what constitutes excessive - and therefore tortious - use in relation to private level crossings, even though this must remain a question of fact in each case.

11.46　As mentioned above, where a right is provided for in a conveyance and that conveyance is construed to be a separate grant of an easement, the general law of easements will apply. However, that easement bears certain characteristics which are unique to rights over level crossings, due to the existence of the railway.

11.47　We do not think it possible to change the extent of existing rights, nor to abolish them; to do so would be contrary to principle and might also, if accomplished without compensation, amount to a breach of Article 1 of Protocol 1 to the European Convention on Human Rights, which protects the right to peaceful enjoyment of possessions.

11.48　What constitutes excessive use of a private right of way is a matter of fact. However, we do think there may be scope to articulate a non-exhaustive list of factors which should be taken into account by the courts when deciding whether, as a matter of fact, a change or increase in use amounts to a substantial increase in the burden on the railway such as to constitute excessive use.

11.49　**We provisionally propose that there should be a statutory list of factors which should be taken into account by courts when deciding whether changed or increased use of a private level crossing amounts to excessive use.**

11.50　**We provisionally propose the following factors:**

(1)　**impact on safety of the railway and crossing users;**

(2)　**the operational requirements of the railway, including how heavily used the railway line is;**

(3)　**whether the use is of a substantially different character to the original use;**

(4)　**the frequency of use compared to the original frequency of use; and**

(5)　**whether the use will have such an impact upon the railway as to require expenditure on the part of the railway operator.**

11.51　**Do consultees think there should be such a statutory list of factors to be taken into consideration when construing the extent of a general right of way?**

11.52　**If consultees agree that there should be a list of factors, is the list above satisfactory or are there any other key factors which should be taken into account when assessing whether increased use of a private level crossing amounts to excessive use?**

Closure of private level crossings

11.53 As was seen in Part 6, there are no statutory provisions dealing directly with the closure of crossings over which a private right of way exists. The closure of such a level crossing is generally carried out by agreement between the railway operator (usually Network Rail) and the person or persons who hold the interest. There is also the possibility (in England and Wales at least) of implied release by abandonment. In Part 12 we will discuss the concept of negative prescription in Scots law. Such a concept does not exist in the law of England and Wales, where abandonment is the only passive route available for relinquishment of a private right of way.[36]

Express release: agreement

11.54 As outlined above, in principle at least, the railway company and landowner or occupier should be able to vary an agreement on what accommodation works are "necessary". This should be possible for those level crossings where the right of way over the railway is a right akin to an easement, just as it is possible for easements.[37]

11.55 The parties cannot agree that further works should be carried out by the railway company after five years (or the end of the prescribed period if different).[38] However, there appears to be no reason why the parties could not agree that the works are no longer required, that compensation is sufficient to make good the interruption and therefore agree to closure of the level crossing. If the crossing is no longer deemed to be "necessary for the purpose of making good any interruptions caused by the railway" then there will no longer be a duty to maintain placed on the railway company. Therefore, they may close the level crossing. The duty to fence would ensure that the tracks at the former crossing did not go unprotected.

11.56 The Rail Safety and Standards Board's *Guidance on Level Crossings Interface Requirements*[39] gives information about the procedure to be followed with respect to private level crossings. The guidance states that where the land is in single ownership either side of the crossing, there may be a deed which defines a class of authorised users. However, this is generally not the case in practice.[40] If there is such a deed, any beneficiary of a right granted by the deed, landholder and anyone having a legitimate interest in the crossing must agree to the closure (that is, the extinguishment of their rights).[41] The agreement may make provision for alternative access and/or compensation, and should be contained in an executed

---

[36] J Gaunt QC and The Hon Mr Justice Morgan (eds), *Gale on the Law of Easements* (18th ed 2008) para 12.66.

[37] It was considered so in *Midland Railway Company v Gribble* [1895] 2 Ch 827.

[38] Railways Clauses Consolidation Act 1845, s 73.

[39] Rail Safety and Standards Board, *Guidance on Level Crossings Interface Requirements* (GK/GN0692, Issue 1, February 2010). Available at: http://www.rgsonline.co.uk/Railway_Group_Standards/Control_Command_and_Signalling/Guidance_Notes/GKGN0692_Iss_1.pdf (last visited 27 June 2010).

[40] As above, para A.4.5.1.

[41] As above, para A.4.5.2.

deed of release.[42]

11.57 Where there is no deed identifying users, the same procedures should be followed, as a deed is required at law for the release of an easement. However, with no record of who holds interests over the crossing, it can be difficult to identify the relevant people. In addition to difficulties in identifying those who hold an interest, even if identified all may not agree to the release.

11.58 We do not question the validity of release of rights of way over level crossings, and of corresponding maintenance obligations, by agreement. We think this should continue to be a way to close private level crossings and think that it may be helpful to declare that such agreements are valid in case there is any doubt as to their validity where the right is not an easement.

11.59 **Do consultees think that it would be helpful for the law expressly to state that private rights over a level crossing can be extinguished by agreement between the rights holder(s) and the railway operator?**

Implied release: abandonment

11.60 Where the ownership of land on one side of a level crossing is transferred to another person, a deed of release is said not to be required if no rights in relation to the crossing have been transferred to the new owner or third parties.

11.61 In *Midland Railway Company v Gribble,* a crossing had been built where a farm had been severed by the railway. The right had originally been granted to Y. Y later sold the field on one side of the railway to X without reserving to himself that right or granting X that right in the conveyance. The question subsequently arose as to whether the right had been abandoned and therefore extinguished. The court said:

> He severed his land in such a way as to shew conclusively that this occupation way over the railway was no longer of any use to him, and to shew conclusively that he never intended to use it thereafter. This appears to me to be a clear and distinct abandonment of his right over the railway … he abandoned his easement.[43]

11.62 In *Gribble*, the right had been included in the conveyance and the court certainly refers to the right as an easement, although also emphasising that it was constructed in consequence of section 68 of the Railways Clauses Consolidation Act 1845. It appears that the court, while clearly applying the general law relating to abandonment of easements, did not address the question of whether the right was an easement based on a grant in the conveyance or a right akin to an easement based on section 68 of the 1845 Act. It seems that the court's opinion was equally applicable to both types of right.

11.63 The purpose of the right in *Gribble* was to cross from one side of the farm to the other over the railway. When that use became unnecessary as the farmer only

---

[42] As above, para A.4.5.3.

[43] *Midland Railway Company v Gribble* [1895] 2 Ch 827 at [831] (Lindley LJ).

owned land on one side of the railway, the right was impossible to exercise.[44] As the farmer no longer owned the land on the other side of the railway he no longer needed to access it and so his access was not interrupted by the railway. As is the case with express release above, the crossing was no longer "necessary for the purpose of making good the interruptions caused by the railway".[45]

11.64 The argument could also be framed in terms of the *Re Ellenborough Park*[46] requirements for the validity of easements: it no longer accommodates the dominant tenement to have access across a railway to land on the other side which the owner has no interest in or right of way over.

11.65 This approach was criticised and not followed in Scotland.[47]

11.66 The closure of the railway would not necessarily mean that the purpose was extinct as it may still be necessary to cross the piece of land formerly occupied by the railway tracks. In *Walker* the question to be considered was whether the purpose of particular accommodation works was extinct.[48] As Sara puts it:

> The fact that the railway closes down does not render the ways unimportant. It may be possible for a bridge over a railway to be replaced by a road across the path of the old track, but the need for the way still remains.[49]

11.67 We think that the decision of the court in *Midland Railway Company v Gribble* is correct and that where the land on one side of a crossing over which there is a private right of way is sold without reservation of the right, the right ceases to exist, having been abandoned. We think that this applies to both easement crossings and statutory rights of way crossings. It is notable that in *Gribble* there was no reservation of the right when the land on the other side of the railway was sold. It seems that had there been such a reservation, or a grant of the right to the purchaser of the land, then the right would have continued to exist. In this way rights holders could preserve their rights if they wished.

11.68 **Do consultees agree that the law should be as laid down in *Midland Railway Company v Gribble*? If so, should this rule be given statutory effect, or is it sufficient that it remains a matter of case law?**

PUBLIC RIGHTS OF WAY

11.69 In Part 4, we outlined how highways law, namely the law governing public rights of way including roads, footpaths and bridleways, is relevant to level crossings. In this Part we explore some of the issues in more detail.

11.70 In England and Wales each local authority is required to maintain a "definitive

---

[44] *Midland Railway Company v Gribble* 1895] 2 Ch 827 at [834] (Rigby LJ).

[45] Railways Clauses Consolidation Act 1845, s 68.

[46] [1956] Ch 131 at [163].

[47] *Robertson v Network Rail Infrastructure Limited* Inverness Sheriff Court, 28 May 2007 (unreported).

[48] *R Walker and Sons v British Railways Board* [1984] 1 WLR 805.

[49] C Sara, *Boundaries and Easements* (4th ed 2008) para 14.21.

map" of public rights of way in its area.[50]

General Issues

Introduction

11.71 A highway has been described as "essentially a public right to pass over a defined route".[51] "Essentially" because a highway is also a physical feature of the landscape.

Classification of highways

11.72 At common law, a highway is a way over which there exists a public right of passage.[52] Highways are sub-divided according to the scope of the right of passage, with the key ones being:

(1) "full highway/carriageway": the public has a right of way on foot, with vehicles or riding on or accompanied by a beast of burden;

(2) "bridleway": the same as (1), except that vehicles are not permitted; and

(3) "footpath": the public has a right of way only on foot.

Creation of public rights of way

Dedication of a highway

11.73 In England and Wales a highway can be created by:

(1) statute; or

(2) by dedication and acceptance:

(a) at common law, or

(b) by statute.

11.74 A way constructed under the Highways Act 1980 becomes a highway upon completion, by virtue of the statute and without the need for dedication and acceptance. Land that has been designated by a development plan as the site for a proposed road, or required for the widening of a road may be declared to be a highway by the local authority under section 34 of the Highways Act 1980. Highway authorities may also enter into agreement with landowners for the dedication of the landowner's land as a highway, which is then maintainable at the public expense.[53]

11.75 The owner of the land upon which a railway was constructed is the railway operator. The highway authority may not, therefore, dedicate such land as a

---

[50] "Definitive map" is defined in the Wildlife and Countryside Act 1981, s 53, where the requirements are also set out.

[51] S Sauvain, *Highway Law* (4th ed 2009) para 1-01.

[52] *Ex p Lewis* (1888) 21 QBD 191, 197.

[53] See A Sydenham, *Public Rights of Way and Access to Land* (3rd ed 2007) para 3.1.

highway. However, where the railway operator (as owner of the land) agrees to dedicate a highway over the railway line, the process is uncontroversial.

Dedication and acceptance

11.76 Under common law in England and Wales, the following are amongst the conditions required for the dedication of a way:

    (1)   the dedication must be to the public at large and not to a particular class of person, for example those using the road as invitees or licensees, like postmen, meter readers or tradesmen;[54]

    (2)   dedication may be express or may be implied by public user. Mere use is not sufficient, the use must be:

        (a)   as of right;

        (b)   of sufficient length (this will depend on all the circumstances); and

        (c)   not rebutted by conduct on the part of the landowner, for example, by notices or gates.[55]

    (3)   the grantor (including a body corporate or a statutory body) must have the capacity to dedicate. A highway must be dedicated in perpetuity for "once a highway always a highway";[56] and

    (4)   dedication must be proved by the claimant.

11.77 Proving the requirements for dedication and acceptance is now somewhat easier due to section 31 of the Highways Act 1980. That section simplifies the proof of implied dedication by long use. A right of way can be established if there has been 20 years use of the way over land by the public as of right, without interruption, unless the landowner can show that during that period there was no intention to dedicate. Unlike common law dedication, the burden of proof under section 31 of the Highways Act 1980 is on the landowner to rebut the presumption.[57]

---

[54] A Sydenham, *Public Rights of Way and Access to Land* (3rd ed 2007) para 3.5.3.

[55] A Sydenham, *Public Rights of Way and Access to Land* (3rd ed 2007) para 3.5.7(4).

[56] *Suffolk CC v Mason* [1979] AC 705 at [710] per Lord Diplock.

[57] In *Bakewell Management Limited v Brandwood* [2004] UKHL 14 and [2004] 2 AC 519, it was held that the ability to acquire rights by long user in relation to the acquisition of private rights rested on the ability to lawfully grant the right. Lord Scott of Foscote at [40] considered that similar principles applied in respect of dedication as well as to grant.

A public bridleway crossing (left) and a private road crossing (right) at Poplar Farm level crossing near Attleborough on the Ely to Norwich line. The vehicular gates are manually controlled by a crossing keeper.

Credit: Rail Accident Investigation Branch.

Capacity to dedicate

11.78 In order to dedicate a highway, no matter what the method of dedication, the landowner dedicating it must have the capacity to do so. This will depend upon the original grant of land to the person or body in question. Where land is vested in a body for a particular purpose, it may not dedicate a highway if to do so would be incompatible with the statutory purposes for which the land was vested. As Sauvain puts it:

> Generally, however, the power to dedicate will be considered incidental to and ancillary to any powers which the body might have to own and alienate land.[58]

11.79 The requirement of capacity to dedicate a way over land is reflected in section 31(8) of the Highways Act 1980. Section 31(8) provides that section 31 does not remedy any incapacity of any corporation or other body or person in possession of land for public or statutory purposes (for example operating a railway) to dedicate a way over that land as a highway, if the existence of a highway would be incompatible with those purposes.

11.80 Capacity is a key issue in relation to railways and is explored in the next section.

---

[58] S Sauvain, *Highway Law* (4th ed, 2009), para 2-40.

POSSIBILITY OF A PRIVATE RIGHT OF WAY BECOMING A PUBLIC RIGHT OF WAY

Introduction

11.81   A private right of way and a public right of way can undoubtedly exist over the same way, and this includes level crossings. However, can a public right of way come into being across a railway by force of prescriptive use? It arises in practice mainly where there is in physical existence a level crossing which is, or at least was, a private one but where there has been use by the public. Can there be a prescriptive upgrade?

Capacity to dedicate a highway

11.82   A railway company will only have the capacity to dedicate if doing so would not be incompatible with the purposes for which it was granted the land, namely the building and running of the railway.[59]

11.83   The case of *British Transport Commission v Westmorland County Council*[60] fundamentally changed the interpretation of whether a railway company had the capacity to dedicate a public right of way over the railway. As the Court of Appeal stated in *Thomas v British Railways Board*,[61] prior to 1958 and the *Westmorland* case, no court would have said that a railway could dedicate such a way. It would have been considered as outside the capacity of the railway company to do so because such a way would be thought to interfere with the running of the railway.

11.84   It is, however, worth noting that in *Thomas* the existence of the public right of way was admitted. In considering the application of *Westmorland*, the Court of Appeal was merely outlining how a right which did already exist could have come into being. That said, at present it appears that a railway company does have the capacity to dedicate a public right of way over a level crossing, both expressly and impliedly.

Illegality

Introduction

11.85   A core question in relation to this topic is whether it is possible to imply dedication when the activity amounts to criminal trespass on the railway. It is criminal trespass for someone to be on the railway if not an authorised user and notices are displayed at the nearest station.[62] Here, the distinction between civil illegality and criminal illegality is vital.

11.86   All use of a way which could lead to implied dedication as a right of way, or similarly (in the context of private interests) the acquisition of an easement by prescription, is civil trespass. This is how such rights are acquired. Clearly, such *civil* trespass does not preclude presumptive dedication of a right of way, or

---

[59]   *R v Inhabitants of Leake* (1833) 5 B & Ad 469 at [478].

[60]   [1958] AC 126.

[61]   *Thomas v British Railways Board* [1976] QB 912.

[62]   British Transport Commission Act 1949, s 55. Section 55 does not specifically create an offence, but imposes a penalty for trespass on the railway.

prescriptive acquisition of an easement.

11.87 Whether *criminal* trespass precludes dedication of a public right of way is a more difficult question to answer. The first question which arises in the context of level crossings is whether it is criminal trespass for a person to use a private level crossing when that person is not the authorised user and does not have the permission of the railway. If it is criminal trespass, then the second question, of whether this precludes the presumptive dedication of a right, must be answered. If it is not, then the question will be whether, in such circumstances, the remaining requirements for implied dedication are fulfilled.

Does unauthorised use of a private level crossing constitute criminal trespass?

11.88 As discussed in Part 13, section 55 of the British Transport Commission Act 1949 in practice creates a criminal offence of trespass on the railway providing a warning notice against trespassing is displayed at the nearest station. Our understanding is that the notice requirement will always be fulfilled, because it is standard practice to post such notices at all stations (at least, on the mainline railway), although of course the existence of the notice will still need to be proved. Accordingly, a person who is not authorised to use a right of way over the railway line will be committing the offence, providing a notice is displayed at the nearest station.

11.89 It is worth noting that the overall scheme of the British Transport Commission Act 1949 indicates that it should not be possible to acquire a right over a railway by prescription. Section 57 of the 1949 Act addresses the issue of potential acquisition of rights of way over railway land by prescription, or use (dedication). It provides that no right of way by prescription or use is to be acquired over any road, footpath, thoroughfare or place forming an access or approach to any station, goods-yard, wharf, garage, depot, dock or harbour which are premises of the British Transport Commission.[63]

11.90 It is notable that section 57 of the 1949 Act makes no mention of railway lines or level crossings. However, prior to *Westmorland*,[64] it was not considered possible for the railway operator to dedicate and for the public to acquire a right of way over the railway itself, including at what was known as an "accommodation crossing". Therefore, at the time of drafting of section 57 of the 1949 Act, it may not have been thought necessary to include reference to the railway line, so as to prevent the acquisition by dedication of a right of way over railway lines.

Is presumptive dedication of a highway/public right of way precluded by criminal illegality?

11.91 The general rule under the common law is that implied dedication of a highway or prescriptive acquisition of an easement cannot be presumed from conduct which is criminally illegal.[65] However, the case of *Bakewell Management Limited v Brandwood* made an exception for cases where the dominant tenement could, by

---

[63] The predecessor of the British Railways Board.

[64] *British Transport Commission v Westmorland County Council* [1958] AC 126.

[65] *Cargill v Gotts* [1981] 1 WLR 441.

their own actions, make the conduct legal.[66] In relation to level crossings, the railway company could render the trespass lawful by granting permission to cross. Lord Scott of Foscote stated:

> A statutory prohibition forbidding some particular use of land that is expressed in terms that allows the landowner to authorise the prohibited use and exempts from criminality use of the land with that authority is an unusual type of prohibition. It allows a clear distinction to be drawn between cases where a grant by the landowner of the right to use the land in the prohibited way would be a lawful grant that would remove the criminality of the user and cases where a grant would be an unlawful grant and incapable of vesting any right in the grantee. It is easy to see why, in the latter class of case, long and uninterrupted use cannot give rise to the presumed grant of an easement that it would have been unlawful for the landowner to grant. It is difficult to see why, in the former class of case, the long and uninterrupted user should not be capable of supporting the presumed grant by the landowner of an easement that if granted would have been lawful and effective notwithstanding that the user was contrary to a statutory prohibition. I can see no requirement of public policy that would prevent the presumption of a grant that it would have been lawful to grant.[67]

11.92 Whilst the *Brandwood* case relates to easements, the trespass involved in acquisition by long use is the same for presumed dedication of a highway as for prescriptive acquisition of an easement. In the absence of a warning notice railway companies can treat use as not criminal in the same way as the commons owner did in the case of *Brandwood*.

11.93 However, the *Brandwood* case can be distinguished as it turns on particular circumstances in relation to commons, where there are public policy reasons to allow easements to be acquired. We consider it likely that, in relation to level crossings, the court would find that public policy considerations pointed strongly against upsetting the traditional rule (that implied dedication or prescriptive acquisition of an easement cannot be presumed from conduct which is criminally illegal). The matter is, however, clearly debatable.

Has the implication been rebutted by conduct on the part of the landowner?

11.94 Dedication of a highway requires actual or implied intention to dedicate that highway. If such intention is rebutted by conduct on the part of the landowner, for example, the erection of notices or gates, the highway will not be dedicated.[68]

11.95 Notices are, however, only one way of showing that a landowner did not intend to dedicate the way.[69] What constitutes sufficient evidence of lack of intention to dedicate is a question of fact in each case. The test is an objective one. The

---

[66] [2004] UKHL 14, [2004] 2 AC 519.

[67] [2004] UKHL 14 at [39].

[68] Highways Act 1980 s 31(1) and (3). See also A Sydenham, *Public Rights of Way and Access to Land* (3rd ed 2007) para 3.5.7(4).

[69] Highways Act 1980, s 31, provides further examples itself in subsections (5) and (6).

landowner must communicate his lack of intention to dedicate a public right of way to the users of that way:[70]

> I think that upon the true construction of section 31(1) "intention" means what the relevant audience, namely the users of that way, would reasonably have understood the landowner's intention to be. The test is...objective, not what the owner subjectively intended nor what particular users of the way assumed, but whether a reasonable user would have understood that the owner was intending ... to "disabuse [him]" of the notion that the way was a public highway.

11.96 Whether notices placed at stations would be sufficient to rebut the presumption of an intention to dedicate will depend on the facts in each case. The notices at the nearest station that render the trespass criminal would not, normally, do so. But if we are right that *Brandwood* would not apply to level crossings, such rebuttal would in any event be unnecessary.

11.97 It seems that it may be possible for a private right of way to become a public right of way. Railway companies have the capacity to dedicate and therefore implied dedication can occur.

11.98 As we have said, we think there is a considerable doubt as to whether *Brandwood* would be followed in relation to the implied dedication of a highway over the railway. However, the question is not clear. As with prescriptive acquisition (or extension) of a private right of way, we can see a case for saying that it should not be possible for a highway to be impliedly dedicated over the railway.

11.99 **Do consultees think there should there be a statutory prohibition on the future implied dedication of highways over the railway?**

---

[70] *R (Godmanchester Town Council) v Secretary of State for the Environment, Food and Rural Affairs* [2007] UKHL 28 at [32].

PART 12   RIGHTS OF WAY AND ACCESS ISSUES: SCOTLAND

INTRODUCTION

12.1   We now turn to examine the law relating to rights of way (public and private) over level crossings in Scotland.

12.2   This Part is divided into three sections: private rights of way; public rights of way; and access rights under the Land Reform (Scotland) Act 2003.

PRIVATE RIGHTS OF WAY

Classification of private rights in Scotland

12.3   Private rights of way over a railway may arise either under the general law or by virtue of the special Act establishing the railway.

Common law rights: servitudes

Creation of servitudes

12.4   Any private right of way at common law in Scotland will usually be a servitude of way. Servitudes may be constituted by grant or reservation (express or implied from circumstances) and by positive prescription.[1] Whilst there are other means of constitution,[2] it seems that these are most relevant for current purposes.

12.5   The voluntary grant of servitudes of way over the railway has happened in the past, but we suspect is unlikely to happen in future. The question of whether the grant of access rights over the track is *ultra vires* is explored further below, in the context of grants of public rights of way, and the arguments described apply equally to the grant of new servitudes, discussed below. The view that we come to below is that the grant of access rights over the track is not *ultra vires* and that level crossings are not inconsistent with the proper running of a railway network, and in some cases may even be essential to the continued safe operation of the railway.[3] We do not see any value in precluding track/railway owners from granting servitudes over a crossing. We therefore ask consultees:

12.6   **Do consultees agree that it should be competent for the owner of the railway to grant a servitude of way?**

12.7   The question of the prescriptive creation of a servitude across a railway will seldom arise. Thus if there exists a statutory right of way, the use of that, for however long, could not mature into a prescriptive servitude, because the use would be attributable to the statutory right. But in certain cases the question could

---

[1]   "Positive prescription" means the acquisition of a right by possession or use for the relevant period. In the case of a servitude the relevant period is 20 years: Prescription and Limitation (Scotland) Act 1973, s 3.

[2]   For further detail about the constitution of servitudes, see D J Cusine and R R M Paisley, *Servitudes and Rights of Way* (1st ed 1998) p 353.

[3]   For example, it might be necessary to grant a new servitude over the railway at a particular location as a substitute for other (less safe) crossings at a different location.

arise. For example, suppose that an owner of land adjoining the railway ("X") has a statutory right of way crossing. What happens if a neighbour ("Y") uses the crossing over a period of 20 years, to reach a public road on the other side of the railway? Has a servitude of way been created over the statutory right of way crossing in favour of Y?[4] The issues here are almost indistinguishable from the issues about the prescriptive creation of a public right of way, discussed below. It is not wholly certain whether a public right of way across a railway can be established by prescriptive use, and the same is true for servitudes. We therefore ask consultees:

12.8 **Should it be possible for prescriptive use to create a servitude across a railway?**

Extent and exercise of servitudes

12.9 The exercise of servitude rights must be *civiliter,* that is to say, "in the way least burdensome to the servient tenement",[5] and as with all rights must not create a nuisance. Moreover, the burden on the servient tenement must not be unwarrantably increased.[6] In general, these rules mean that although the original extent of the right to use the crossing cannot be restricted (for example, a pedestrian right cannot be substituted for a vehicular one), an increase in the volume or nature of traffic over a crossing may be prohibited.[7] In the event of any dispute arising, it is likely that the court would have regard to the unique position of level crossings, in particular the need to protect the safety of users and ensure the efficient operation of the railway. It may be that reasonable exercise of a servitude over a level crossing will always be restricted to infrequent use, with light vehicles. In exceptional cases, it is even possible that the principle of *civiliter* exercise could justify the restriction of access due to the potential harm caused to the interest of the track owner.[8]

Variation of servitudes

12.10 At common law, the question of whether the route of a servitude may be varied is determined by whether or not the route has been specified in a deed. Dealing first with the situation where the route *has* been so specified, there is a divergence of judicial views. In *Servitudes and Rights of Way,* Cusine and Paisley refer to the "majority view" and the "minority view".[9] The majority view is that so long as the proprietor of the dominant tenement retains an interest in the existing route of the servitude, the proprietor of the servient tenement may not alter the route or width of the servitude without the consent of the dominant proprietor. Moreover, the

---

4   And over part of X's land, because Y will not be able to reach the crossing without passing over X's land.

5   *Moyes v McDiarmid* (1900) 2 F 918.

6   G J Bell and W Guthrie, *Principles of the Law of Scotland* (10th ed 1899) p 988. See also D J Cusine and R R M Paisley, *Servitudes and Rights of Way* (1st ed 1998) para 12.186.

7   D J Cusine and R R M Paisley, *Servitudes and Rights of Way* (1st ed 1998) para 12.191.

8   See, for example, *Cloy v T M Adams & Sons* 2000 SLT (Sh Ct) 39.

9   D J Cusine and R R M Paisley, *Servitudes and Rights of Way* (1st ed 1998). The "majority" view is set out at paras 12.45 ff and the "minority" view at paras 12.55 ff. Both derive from *Hill v McLaren* (1879) 6 R 1363, the former looking to Lord Moncreiff's opinion in that case, the the latter to Lord Gifford's.

court may not exercise a common law power to vary the route. On the other hand, the minority view indicates that the servient proprietor may still apply to the court to have the servitude varied even if the dominant proprietor retains an interest and refuses to consent to the proposed variation. However, it is suggested that the minority view is unlikely to be followed in practice.[10]

12.11   Where the route of a servitude has *not* been specified in a deed, the common law position is that the route may be varied, providing certain conditions are satisfied. The servitude must be indefinite, meaning that the right is not clearly defined, and there must be no implied contractual agreement that those elements of the servitude that require to be established by extrinsic evidence are not to be varied. Moreover, the substitute route must be as convenient to the current proprietor of the dominant tenement as the original route was. In the context of level crossings, it seems that variation of the level of the way (for example, replacement of a level crossing with a bridge) would be treated as equally commodious.[11] In addition to these requirements, a declarator of the court may be required in limited circumstances, where the proposed change in route is material and extensive in nature.[12]

12.12   There are two further situations in which the route of a servitude may be varied, regardless of whether or not it has been specified in a deed. One such situation is where the proprietor of the servient tenement obtains consent to the variation from the proprietor of the dominant tenement. Alternatively, a servitude may be varied upon application to the Lands Tribunal for Scotland in terms of Part 9 of the Title Conditions (Scotland) Act 2003. There do not appear to be any particular problems which affect level crossings in relation to variation of servitudes.

Extinction of servitudes

12.13   Extinction of a servitude over a railway may arise in a variety of ways. These include express or implied discharge, abandonment, negative prescription,[13] extinction by statute or confusion (that is, the two tenements coming into the ownership of the same person, holding them in the same capacity).[14] There does not seem to be any particular problem with the existing law in relation to closure of servitude crossings, as the general law allows for extinction of the right in a wide range of circumstances. There is no general legal provision however, which would allow *compulsory* extinction of a servitude for example, on safety grounds. But the Lands Tribunal for Scotland has a general jurisdiction to discharge servitudes, as discussed below.

---

[10]   D J Cusine and R R M Paisley, *Servitudes and Rights of Way* (1st ed 1998) para 12.43.

[11]   D J Cusine and R R M Paisley, *Servitudes and Rights of Way* (1st ed 1998) para 12.66.

[12]   D J Cusine and R R M Paisley, *Servitudes and Rights of Way* (1st ed 1998) paras 12.58-12.72.

[13]   "Negative prescription" means the loss of a right as a result of non-exercise for a sufficiently long time. For property rights such as servitudes the relevant period is 20 years: Prescription and Limitation (Scotland) Act 1973.

[14]   See generally D J Cusine and R R M Paisley, *Servitudes and Rights of Way* (1st ed 1998) chapter 17.

Statutory rights of way crossings under the Railways Clauses Consolidation (Scotland) Act 1845

Creation

12.14 As mentioned in Part 4, the creation of private statutory rights of way crossings is provided for in section 60 of the Railways Clauses Consolidation (Scotland) Act 1845:

> shall make and at all times thereafter maintain the following works for the accommodation of the owners and occupiers of lands adjoining the railway: ... Such and so many convenient gates, bridges, arches, culverts, and passages, over, under, or by the sides of or leading to or from the railway, as shall be necessary for the purpose of making good any interruptions caused by the railway to the use of the lands through which the railway shall be made....[15]

12.15 As level crossings were less expensive than bridges or underpasses, this provision led to the construction of a large number of private crossings. Although there is reference to "making good any interruptions caused by the railway to the use of the lands through which the railway shall be made", no specific right to use the crossing is conferred by the legislation. A right of use has to be implied. In practice the provisions are taken as conferring a right of use. While on occasions a conveyance might refer to a right of use under the 1845 Act, the Act itself is relied upon as conferring the actual right.[16]

Nature of statutory rights of way over crossings

12.16 Though a right to use such a crossing can be implied without difficulty, the silence of the legislation means that there is little guidance as to the detailed nature of the right. A reasonable inference would be that the right is a servitude of way.[17] The land belonging to the railway would be the servient property, and the land on each side would be the dominant property. If the right which exists over a statutory right of way crossing is a servitude, that would bring with it a complete set of legal rules, namely those applying to servitudes of way. If it is not a servitude, that would have the opposite result: the statutory right of way over the crossing would be a right of some unknown type. The set of standard answers provided by the law of servitudes would not apply, with consequent uncertainty.

12.17 Whether a statutory right of way crossing is a servitude is uncertain, but on balance it seems that it is not. In *Robertson v Network Rail Infrastructure Ltd*[18] it

---

[15] Railways Clauses Consolidation (Scotland) Act 1845, s 60.

[16] This issue applies equally to bridges or underpasses which were constructed to comply with the terms of the Act, and over which a statutory right of way may exist as a result.

[17] The Railways Clauses Consolidation (Scotland) Act 1845, s 60 also requires the construction of culverts. This looks like a servitude for the drainage of water.

[18] Inverness Sheriff Court, 28th May 2007 http://www.scotcourts.gov.uk/opinions/A161_06.html (last visited 27 June 2010) unreported. In *Network Rail Infrastructure Ltd, Petitioner* 2008 SLT 25 the decision of the sheriff was partially reduced by the Court of Session, so as to allow an appeal on the merits (which would otherwise have been prevented by certain provisions in the 1845 Act), but this does not seem to have affected the substance of the decision. As far as we know, no appeal took place.

was stated that an accommodation crossing[19] was not a servitude. Another case pointing to the same conclusion is *William Dixon v Monkland Railway*,[20] though that case was fact-specific. A special statute conferred something akin to an accommodation crossing right on the pursuers, who made use of it to build their own railway, which extended to land beyond the land that they owned. Had this been a servitude, the benefit could not have extended beyond the boundary of the dominant property.[21] It was held that the benefit did extend as claimed by the pursuers. The case was a special one in a number of respects, one of which was that this was not a crossing regulated by section 60 of the Railways Clauses Consolidation (Scotland) Act 1845, and no definite conclusions can be drawn from it, but it at least further supports the suggestion that statutory rights of way may not be servitudes. Of course, if they are not servitudes that does not mean that aspects of the law of servitudes cannot sometimes be applied to them by analogy.

Extent and exercise of statutory rights of way

12.18   Section 60 of the 1845 Act appears to be limited to the "owners and occupiers of lands adjoining the railway".

12.19   Otherwise, however, the Act is silent as to the extent of any right to use the crossing. We note that the law of servitudes would, in principle, provide guidance on construction of the original extent of the right, and its reasonable exercise.

12.20   On the question of change of use, limited authority exists. In Part 11, we note the case of *Taff Vale Railway Company v Gordon Canning*,[22] a case under the law of England and Wales. The court held that the burden on the railway company could not be substantially increased. The only Scottish case we are aware of is *British Railways Board v Macbeath*,[23] where interim interdict was granted against a crofter who had set up a small caravan park, access to which was across an accommodation crossing.[24] According to Sheriff Principal Ronald Ireland "Occupiers cannot, by changing the use of the land, increase the burden on the proprietors of the railway, because that would be inconsistent with the limited purpose of an accommodation crossing" (that is, a statutory right of way crossing), and he cited the *Taff Vale* decision. It seems likely that the law in this area is substantially the same as in England and Wales.

12.21   Parallel issues quite often arise in connection with servitudes, and despite a

---

[19]   Although it was stated in Part 1 that the term "accommodation crossing" would not generally be used in this consultation paper, it is retained here as this was the term used in the case. The usage denotes a right deriving from Railways Clauses Consolidation (Scotland) Act 1845, s 60, which we are classifying in this consultation paper as a statutory right of way.

[20]   *William Dixon v Monkland Railway* (1840) 2 D 1470, (1840) 12 Sc Jur 675.

[21]   *Scott v Bogle*, FC 6th July 1809; *Irvine Knitters Ltd v North Ayrshire Co-operative Society Ltd* 1978 SC 109.

[22]   *Taff Vale Railway Company v Gordon Canning* [1909] 2 Ch 48. See also *British Railways Board v Glass* [1965] Ch 538 where the owner developed a caravan site, though this case was not a pure accommodation case.

[23]   19 March 1990, R R M Paisley and D J Cusine, *Unreported Property Cases* (2000) p 463.

[24]   Again we retain the term "accommodation crossing" for the reasons given above.

number of reported cases the law is not yet wholly clear.[25] Nevertheless, it could well be argued that the law of level crossings would be better if the law of servitudes, for all its imperfections, were applicable to statutory rights of way.

Excessive use of a statutory right of way over a crossing

12.22 In Part 11 in respect of England and Wales we refer to a list of factors which would be taken into account by courts when deciding whether a change or increase in user amounts to a substantial increase in the burden on the railway. This conceptual approach would be less suitable for Scotland, because it is formulated in terms of remedies rather than in terms of rights and obligations, that is, it formulates the rule in terms of what *courts* are to do.

12.23 **For Scotland, a suitable approach might be something on the following lines:**

> **The use made of the statutory right of way over a crossing is not to be such as would:**
>
> **(1) be unreasonably detrimental to the safety of the railway users and crossing users;**
>
> **(2) interfere unreasonably with the operational requirements of the railway;**
>
> **(3) be substantially different in character (including frequency) as compared with the original use; and**
>
> **(4) give rise to unreasonable expenditure on the part of the railway infrastructure manager.**

12.24 **Would it be desirable to clarify the extent of use permitted under the Railways Clauses Consolidation (Scotland) Act 1845?**

12.25 **If this is the case, would such a list of factors be useful?**

12.26 **Alternatively, would alignment with the law of servitudes be helpful in determining the permissible extent of use of a statutory right of way crossing?**

Extinction of statutory rights of way

EXPRESS RELEASE: AGREEMENT

12.27 There exists a body of law about the discharge of servitudes; in particular a servitude can be discharged by the consent of the dominant proprietor. Here again the position about statutory right of way crossings is a blank. In practice what has happened *de facto* is that the law of servitudes has been applied. Thus if there is a crossing over which a statutory right of way exists and the track owner reaches an agreement with the party who has the benefit of a statutory right of way for the closure of that crossing, what happens is that the benefited

---

[25] See D J Cusine and R R M Paisley, *Servitudes and Rights of Way* (1st ed 1998) chapter 14.

party signs a "discharge agreement"[26] which in substance is much the same as a deed of discharge of a servitude. Given that the legislation says that the track owner "shall make and *at all times thereafter* maintain" the crossing,[27] the question arises as to whether such a discharge is effective only as against the granter, or whether it truly extinguishes the right, so as to be effective against the granter's singular successors.[28] The general view is that singular successors are indeed bound. We incline to think that view correct. Whatever the current law, we ask:

12.28 **Should the law expressly state that the authorised user of a statutory right of way crossing can enter into a discharge agreement with the railway operator validly to extinguish the right to use the crossing, as happens in practice at present?**

12.29 **If so, are any qualifications or exceptions necessary?**

12.30 **In consultees' experience, are there any practical difficulties involved in the current process of extinguishing a right of way over a level crossing?**

12.31 We would add, simply to paint a complete picture, that it can happen that more than one right exists at the same physical crossing (as seen in the photograph at page.[29] For example, a farmer might hold a right to cross with vehicles while there is also a public pedestrian right of way. Naturally, a discharge by the farmer would leave the public right of way intact. Again, if there are two separate authorised users for the same private crossing, a discharge by one does not affect the rights of the other.

THE GRIBBLE ISSUE

12.32 As described in Part 11, in *Midland Railway Company v Gribble*[30] a railway bisected certain lands, and a level crossing was provided by the railway company under section 68 of the Railways Clauses Consolidation Act 1845 (as incorporated into the relevant special Act). A right of way over the crossing was reserved to the owner of the lands and his successors in title in the conveyance to the railway company. Afterwards the owner conveyed his land on one side of the railway to a third party, not mentioning the crossing, and failing to give the purchaser any right of way over the land retained, nor reserving any right of way over the land sold. The land retained by the owner was eventually sold to the defendant, who insisted on his right to use the crossing. The Court of Appeal in England and Wales held that after the division of the land, there was no right to use the crossing. There were, however, conflicting opinions about whether this was due to abandonment of an easement over the crossing, or the fact that the

---

[26] These are referred to as "deeds of release" in England and Wales.

[27] The italicised words were a significant element in persuading the court in *Robertson* not to follow *Gribble* in relation to the severance issue.

[28] This is a technical term of civilian property law. Roughly speaking it means a subsequent owner of the property (but, to be precise, it does not include "universal successors", and it can include holders of "subordinate real rights").

[29] See page 138 for a photograph of a level crossing where both a public bridleway and a private road exist at the same crossing.

[30] [1895] 2 Ch 827.

crossing existed to fulfill a statutory purpose, which ended when the land was divided. Following *Gribble*, Part 11 notes that in *R Walker & Sons v British Railways Board*[31] it was held that the duty to provide fencing under section 68 of the Railways Clauses Consolidation Act 1845 only ended when the purpose of the particular fencing became extinct. However, it is interesting that in *Walker* the fact that the railway was no longer in operation did not mean that the purpose of the fencing came to an end.

12.33 When a case with facts apparently identical to *Gribble* came before the courts in Scotland the opposite was held. In *Robertson v Network Rail Infrastructure Ltd*[32] it was accepted that rights under section 60 of the Railways Clauses Consolidation (Scotland) Act 1845 were a statutory creation, and therefore arguments about the transmission of servitudes were not relevant. The court dismissed the argument that the statutory rights came to an end if division of the property meant that they could no longer be exercised. This was in part on the basis that the statute did not provide for the rights to be extinguished. In part it was on the basis that *Gribble* was decided very much in the context of English conveyancing law. And in part it was on the basis that the *Gribble* rule was unfair. The view taken by Sheriff Mackenzie was not that the right revived after the severed parts were reunited, but rather that the right was never extinguished in the first place.[33]

12.34 The idea that the right is not extinguished is a workable one. Suppose that the land straddling the railway is divided. The land on one side can be called X and the land on the other side can be called Y. The right that survives (on the *Robertson* view) would be in fact be a double right: the right of the owner of area X to cross over Network Rail's land to reach the edge of area Y, and, conversely, the right of the owner of area Y to cross over Network Rail's land to reach the edge of area X. It is true that, having reached that edge, it might be impossible to go further. But equally it might be possible. The owner of X might have a servitude over Y, for example. There might be a public right of way at the edge. Or the owner of X might have a lease of Y. And so on. These are issues as between the owners of X and Y, not Network Rail.

12.35 *Robertson* was, however, only a first-instance decision and is thus of limited authority. Although *Gribble* is an English case, as a decision of the Court of Appeal it has considerable persuasive authority. We think, therefore, that the current law cannot be stated with confidence. Which approach is better in terms of policy is arguable. On the one hand it can be argued that the purpose of a statutory right of way crossing was merely to counterbalance the inconvenience

---

[31] *R Walker & Sons v British Railways Board* [1984] 1 WLR 805.

[32] *Robertson v Network Rail Infrastructure Ltd* Inverness Sheriff Court, 28 May 2007 (unreported).

[33] Sheriff Mackenzie held: "As I do not hold that the accommodation crossing right has been lost it is perhaps not strictly speaking necessary for me to go on to consider whether it could be revived upon the title being reunited. However, if I should be in error and it be held by a higher court that in such a case the statutory right is suspended just because the titles have been split, I confess I cannot see the justice in a new owner of both properties who has repaired the split in title not being able to claim the original right - nothing having otherwise changed and there being no intervening contract between the owners of the lands on both sides of the track and the railway company nor any amending legislation disposing of the right".

caused by the bisection of a single unit of land, and if the bisected parts cease to be a unit, the reason for the existence of the crossing vanishes. To suggest that the extinction of statutory rights of way is governed wholly by the terms of section 60 of the Railways Clauses Consolidation (Scotland) Act 1845 is problematic, as the Act is silent on the issue. The arguments in *Robertson* could even suggest that agreements between landowners and railway operators purporting to discharge the statutory right are actually ineffectual. That would be an unsatisfactory result.

12.36   However, in policy terms, the 1845 Act clearly intended to minimise the disruption caused by the construction of the railway. It is difficult to see why a period of non-use of the crossing (for whatever reason) should remove the protection given by the Act to the "owners and occupiers of lands adjoining the railway". The railway line would form a permanent interference with the land, and so it is arguable that the "accommodations" were intended to be permanent too, or at least to last as long as the railway itself.   The 1845 Act does not suggest any temporal limit to the duty to provide accommodation works: indeed, it talks of maintaining the accommodation works "at all times thereafter". It might therefore be thought that a statutory right of way deriving from such accommodation works should similarly exist indefinitely.

12.37   Law reform is generally prospective only. That creates an immediate difficulty. It seems likely that in the future few new statutory right of way crossings will come into existence, and possibly none at all. For most practical purposes, therefore, to reform the law about existing statutory right of way crossings would mean changing vested rights. As an illustration, suppose that the view were to be taken that *Robertson*[34] accurately reflects the law of Scotland. In that case, if the *Gribble*[35] rule were to be extended to Scotland, authorised users of statutory right of way crossings would suffer a downgrade in the nature of their right. It would be likely that the property protection rules of the European Convention on Human Rights (ECHR) would be engaged with the result that such parties would be entitled to compensation. Having said that, in practice the number of claims might be small. Moreover, it might be argued that since, before *Robertson*, it was widely supposed that *Gribble* represented the law in Scotland as well as in England, anyone who bought land before *Robertson* would have bought at a price which presupposed the *Gribble* rule, and that accordingly for such persons compensation would represent a windfall gain. How strong this latter argument is, may be arguable. The fact that someone may not have realised that she or he had a right does not mean that the right is unprotected by the ECHR.

12.38   Much the same would be true the other way round. Thus suppose that the *Robertson* rule were to be regarded as preferable and were to be extended to England and Wales. In that case, if the *Gribble* rule were to be extended to Scotland, there would be a benefit to the track owner at the expense of the relevant landowners, whose rights would have been lost without their consent The existence of vested rights thus makes reform difficult. Nevertheless, there are strong arguments that the position in England and Scotland should be harmonised. Moreover, the law in Scotland is currently open to doubt. Arguably,

---

[34] Inverness Sheriff Court 28 May 2007 (unreported).

[35] *Midland Railway Company v Gribble* [1895] 2 Ch 827.

legislation could (and should) remove some of the uncertainty regarding statutory rights of way over level crossings. This would be to the advantage of both track owners and the authorised users of statutory right of way crossings. **To test the views of consultees, we ask:**

12.39 **Should the *Robertson* rule (assuming that it correctly states the law) be replaced by the *Gribble* rule, for existing crossings as well as for new ones?**

12.40 **If so (and assuming that that would in fact result in a change in the law)[36] would you agree that the owner of the track would in principle be liable to compensate those who suffered loss as a result? If so, do you have views about how such compensation should be calculated?**

12.41 We mentioned above that there is at least one area – future extinction by agreement or by prescription – where reform would be possible without problems about compensation for variation of vested rights. In the first place, it would be possible to provide expressly that the statutory right of way over a crossing can competently be extinguished by a discharge agreement.[37] We think that this would be merely declaratory of the existing law, but even if we were wrong on that there is no reason why such a facility should not be introduced.

NEGATIVE PRESCRIPTION OF STATUTORY RIGHTS OF WAY

12.42 Servitudes may be extinguished by negative prescription.[38] This leads to the question of whether a statutory right of way over a crossing may similarly be extinguished by negative prescription. It seems that this is a matter which has never been judicially considered. The "all times thereafter" argument indicates imprescriptibility, but the legislation on prescription contains nothing to suggest any exception from the operation of negative prescription for statutory right of way crossings.

12.43 Further, there is the situation where a railway line is disused for a long period, and the track is lifted, but the strip of land remains in the ownership of the railway company (such as Network Rail) and eventually the track is re-laid and the railway is used once again. In the interim period, it might well be that the specific site of the statutory level crossing would have ceased to be used to cross the land over which there was formerly a railway line, because the farmer might take access between the two parts of the farm along the whole length of the former line. Yet it would be unsatisfactory if the re-opening of the railway should leave the land on either side of the railway line (for example, a farm) severed because the statutory right of way had negatively prescribed. On the other hand, where a line has remained in use but a statutory right of way crossing has *de facto* ceased to exist for a long period – perhaps many decades – there is clearly an argument that what is dead in reality should also be dead in law.

---

[36] That is to say, assuming that *Robertson* correctly states the law of Scotland. It would always be open to Network Rail (or other track owner) to argue in a later case that Scots law does in fact accept the *Gribble* rule, and in that case the question of compensation would not arise.

[37] In Scotland these are called discharge agreements whereas in England and Wales they are called deeds of release.

[38] Prescription and Limitation (Scotland) Act 1973, s 8.

12.44 **Would it be useful for there to be express legislative provision as to the extinction of statutory crossing rights by negative prescription? If so, what should the law provide?**

DISCHARGE OF PRIVATE RIGHTS BY THE LANDS TRIBUNAL FOR SCOTLAND

12.45 Under the Title Conditions (Scotland) Act 2003, the Lands Tribunal for Scotland has the power to discharge title conditions.[39] Servitudes are title conditions.[40] Hence where a railway is crossed by a servitude of way, the railway operator (typically Network Rail) could apply for a discharge.[41] But statutory rights of way over level crossings created under section 60 of the Railways Clauses Consolidation (Scotland) Act 1845 are not title conditions[42] and so the Tribunal's jurisdiction does not extend to them.[43] However, the Scottish Ministers have the power to make an order to extend the Tribunal's jurisdiction.[44] Since statutory rights of way crossings are functionally similar to servitude rights of way, there would evidently be a stateable case that the Tribunal's jurisdiction should extend to them. That could be done either by an order under the 2003 Act, or by amending the 2003 Act itself.

12.46 In discharging a title condition, the Tribunal has power to award compensation to the dominant owner,[45] and that would also be the case if the jurisdiction were to be extended to statutory rights of way crossings.

12.47 However, if our proposed scheme for closure of level crossings is introduced, it may be that the extension of the jurisdiction of the Tribunal would not be appropriate.

12.48 **Should the jurisdiction of the Lands Tribunal for Scotland be extended to include statutory rights of way over level crossings created under section 60 of the Railways Clauses Consolidation (Scotland) Act 1845?**

PUBLIC RIGHTS OF WAY

Creation of public rights of way

Statutory creation

12.49 As discussed in Part 6, the provisions of the Countryside (Scotland) Act 1967 relating to public paths created by order or agreement remain in force for certain purposes. A "public path" is defined as a footpath or bridleway or a combination

---

[39] Title Conditions (Scotland) Act 2003, s 90(1).

[40] Title Conditions (Scotland) Act 2003, s 122(1).

[41] The Lands Tribunal for England and Wales does not have equivalent jurisdiction for easements.

[42] They are not mentioned in the definition of "title condition" in s 122(1) of the Title Conditions (Scotland) Act 2003.

[43] Nor does it extend to public rights of way.

[44] Title Conditions (Scotland) Act 2003, s 122(1). See sub-paragraph (g) of the definition "title condition".

[45] Title Conditions (Scotland) Act 2003, s 90(6) and (7).

of the two.[46] "Footpaths" and "bridleways" are in turn defined with reference to the nature of the public rights of way exercisable over them.[47] It would seem that the function of the savings provision which applies in relation to public paths is to enable certain public paths to continue to be recognised, rather than to allow new ones to be created. Nevertheless, it seems clear that to the extent that public paths continue to exist, public rights of way are exercisable over them.

12.50   The Town and Country Planning (Scotland) Act 1997 is also of note. Section 208 of the 1997 Act empowers planning authorities to create an alternative footpath or bridleway (within the meaning of section 47 of the Countryside (Scotland) Act 1967) where it is necessary to close off a footpath or bridleway as a result of a development. Section 208(4) of the 1997 Act expressly provides that the section applies to land which is a core path as it applies in relation to footpaths and bridleways. Section 208 is likely to be of greater significance in practice, given that, as noted above, the provisions of the Countryside (Scotland) Act 1967 relating to public paths have now been repealed for most purposes (both footpaths and bridleways are public paths for the purposes of the Act).

12.51   Section 207 of the 1997 Act makes equivalent provision in relation to roads within the meaning of section 151(1) of the Roads (Scotland) Act 1984, other than trunk roads and special roads. Section 202 confers a similar power on the Scottish Ministers in relation to roads within the meaning of the Roads (Scotland) Act 1984.

The voluntary grant of a public right of way

12.52   The question of whether it would be competent for a track/railway owner voluntarily to grant a public right of way over a way which crosses a railway on the level is probably of little more than theoretical significance. However, it is an issue that can occasionally arise. For reasons given in the following section, we incline to think that the grant of a public right of way is within the powers of track owners. And, if that is the law, we incline to regard it as acceptable. **But to test views, we ask:**

12.53   **Is legislation needed to clarify the power of a track/railway owner to make a voluntary grant of public rights of way?**

Creation of public rights of way by prescription

NO DEFINITIVE MAP

12.54   In England and Wales there is a system whereby each local authority maintains a "definitive map" of public rights of way in its area. No such system exists in Scotland,[48] a fact that has misled some into thinking that there are no public rights of way in Scotland. Whether a similar system should be adopted in Scotland is something on which we express no view. We mention the matter merely by way of background, and to illustrate how in practice it can sometimes

---

[46]   Countryside (Scotland) Act 1967, s 30(3).

[47]   Countryside (Scotland) Act 1967, s 47.

[48]   But the Scottish Rights of Way and Access Society (Scotways) maintains a National Catalogue of Rights of Way, which, though not having official status, enjoys a high non-official status.

be more difficult in Scotland than in England and Wales to know whether an alleged public way is indeed such or not. Thus in *Greenhalgh v British Railways Board*[49] the question of whether a bridge over a railway, which had begun life as an accommodation bridge,[50] had by usage become a public right of way, was resolved by reference to the definitive map. Had the facts which led to the dispute happened in Scotland, that reference would not have been possible.

12.55   A further issue relates to the interaction of the law of level crossings with the law of prescription. This issue relates to whether a public right of way can come into being across a railway by force of prescriptive use. It arises in practice mainly where there is in physical existence a level crossing which is, or at least was, a private one but there has been use by the public for more than 20 years. Has the private right of way morphed into a public one? Or, in other words, has there been a prescriptive upgrade? Any claim that a public right of way has been created would need to get over two hurdles. One is the hurdle of the general law of prescription, and the other is the set of specialities relating to railways.

A private footpath crosses the West Highland line at the user-worked level crossing (UWC) at Corrour station on Rannoch Moor.

Credit: Ramblers Scotland.

---

[49]   *Greenhalgh v British Railways Board* [1969] 2 QB 286.

[50]   This is a bridge over which a statutory right of way originally existed. The term "accommodation bridge" is retained here for the reasons given above in relation to "accommodation crossings".

12.56 As to the first, the usage would have to be "open, peaceable and without any judicial interruption".[51] Usage does not count as prescriptive usage if it is clandestine or merely occasional.[52]

12.57 A public right of way has to be from one "public place" to another.[53] That condition would be satisfied in at least some cases (it might possibly be that the result of the Land Reform (Scotland) Act 2003 is that it would be satisfied in most cases, for it might be that a place where the public can exercise access rights is a "public place" for the purposes of the law of public rights of way; but this is to speculate, and in any event 20 years have not elapsed since the 2003 Act). Each case has to be considered on its own facts, but one can say that in at least some cases the conditions necessary for the creation of a prescriptive public right of way will apply.

RAILWAY-SPECIFIC ISSUES

12.58 The second hurdle consists of the speciality that the ground over which the alleged right arises is a railway ground. Might this mean that prescriptive upgrade cannot operate?[54] There are two main lines of argument here, namely the *ultra vires* argument and the criminal trespass argument.

The ultra vires argument

12.59 The first is the *ultra vires* argument. This argument runs like this: it would be *ultra vires* for a track owner to grant a right of way: *Ayr Harbour Trustees v Oswald.*[55] Therefore such a right cannot arise by prescription: *Ellice's Trustees v Caledonian Canal Commissioners;*[56] *The Corporation of Edinburgh v North British Railway Co.*[57]

12.60 This "no power to grant, therefore no possibility of prescription either" argument has two strands. The first is the "could not competently grant" and the second is the "therefore...". The argument would not work if either were incorrect. In fact, both seem doubtful.

12.61 As for the first strand of the argument, it is not, we think, *ultra vires* to grant a right of way over a railway. If level crossings were inconsistent with the running of a railway there would be no level crossings. It may, however, be that if a *particular*

---

[51] Prescription and Limitation (Scotland) Act 1973 Act, s 3.

[52] See *McInroy v Duke of Athole* (1891) 18 R (HL) 46 and the discussion in D J Cusine and R R M Paisley, *Servitudes and Rights of Way* (1st ed 1998) paras 10-16 and 10-19.

[53] For this not unproblematic concept see D J and R R M Paisley, *Servitudes and Rights of Way* (1st ed 1998) para 20.03 ff.

[54] Those so arguing are in a slightly awkward position, for at the same time they are likely also to argue that the law of prescription *does* apply to railway ground, as far as *negative* prescription is concerned. In our view no actual self-contradiction is involved. The reasons for arguing that *positive* prescription does not apply are irrelevant to *negative* prescription. Thus cherry-picking the prescription legislation is logically possible.

[55] *Ayr Harbour Trustees v Oswald* (1883) 10 R 472, (1883) 10 R (HL) 85, LR 8 App Cas 623.

[56] *Ellice's Trustees v Caledonian Canal Commissioners* (1904) 6 F 325.

[57] *The Corporation of Edinburgh v North British Railway Co* (1904) 6 F 620.

crossing were to give rise to exceptional interference with the operation of the railway, it would be *ultra vires* to grant a right of way.[58] It may be added that Network Rail is a company under the Companies Acts and so presumably not subject to the old rules about *ultra vires*. The same was true of Railtrack plc.

12.62 As to the second strand of the argument, the inference from "no power to grant" to "no possibility of prescription", we think that incorrect too. Prescription is not based on implied grant or on acquiescence. As Lord Watson said:[59]

> The constitution of [a right of way] does not depend upon any legal fiction, but upon the fact of user by the public, as matter of right, continuously and without interruption, for the full period of the long prescription. . . . I am aware that there are dicta to be found, in which the prescriptive acquisition of a right of way by the public is attributed to implied grant, acquiescence by the owner of the soil, and so forth; but these appear to me to be mere speculations as to the origin of the rule, and their tendency is to obscure rather than to elucidate its due application to a case like the present.

12.63 Likewise Johnston:[60]

> Questions have arisen about rights of way across land acquired under statutory powers. It is clear that, if the right of way is inconsistent with the exercise of those powers, the acquiring body has no authority to grant a public right of way. That would be *ultra vires*. It has been held that on the same principle the acquiring body is not capable of acquiescing in the prescriptive acquisition by the public of such a right: "A landowner who has no power to grant has no power to acquiesce".[61] But acquiescence is not really the point. A person without legal capacity cannot grant a servitude, yet positive prescription can run against him. The same ought to be true of legal persons. Accordingly it seems that public rights of way can be established in the normal way over lands acquired under statutory powers.

12.64 Professor Gordon's approach is different, but for the reasons already given we are not able to agree with it:

> The question of the capability of the servient owner to grant a servitude arises both in relation to grant and to prescription, because where a servient owner cannot consent to exercise of the servitude right, no right can be prescribed against him.[62]

---

[58] For this approach, see Lord's Keith's speech in *British Transport Commission v Westmorland County Council* [1958] AC 126.

[59] *Mann v Brodie* (1885) 12 R (HL) 52 at p 57.

[60] D Johnston, *Prescription and Limitation* (1st ed 1999) para 17.26.

[61] At this point Johnston footnotes *Corporation of Edinburgh v North British Railway Co* (1904) 6 F 620, *Kinross County Council v Archibald and another* (1899) 7 SLT 305 and *Ellice's Trustees v Caledonian Canal Commissioners* (1904) 6 F 325.

[62] W M Gordon, *Scottish Land Law* (2nd ed 1999) para 24-54.

12.65 *British Transport Commission v Westmorland County Council*,[63] though a case on the law of England and Wales, is of relevance to Scots law, including *dicta* by Lord Keith. He says that the fact that a public body cannot grant a right does not mean that such a right cannot be created prescriptively.[64] And with reference to *Corporation of Edinburgh v North British Railway Co* he says:

> If Lord Kinnear was intending to lay down as a matter of law that in no circumstances could the public acquire a right of way over railway property, I think, with all respect to the great authority of that eminent judge, that such an opinion is not consistent with the train of authority to which your Lordship on the Woolsack has referred.

12.66 Cusine and Paisley interpret such cases as Corporation of Edinburgh v North British Railway Co thus:

> Notwithstanding the provisions of the 1973 Act, a servitude cannot be acquired by prescriptive exercise alone, nor can a grant be fortified by exercise for the prescriptive period, if the grant or exercise contravenes a statutory purpose.[65]

12.67 They reject the *ultra vires* argument as untenable, and this is their substitute interpretation of the authorities. They do not mention this argument in connection with public rights of way. Other writers, such as Johnston,[66] do not mention this argument. It seems to us a rather speculative approach. Even if it is right (and applies to public rights of way) it seems to us doubtful whether it would be relevant to private crossings, where a level crossing *already* exists.

12.68 The law is not wholly clear, but in our view the first strand of the argument[67] is not correct.

The criminal trespass argument[68]

12.69 The second argument concerns criminal trespass. As discussed in Part 11, section 55 of the British Transport Commission Act 1949 in effect criminalises the use of private level crossings by persons other than the authorised user.

12.70 Does this mean that prescription could not operate? That depends on whether the law says "usage that is an offence cannot be the basis for prescribing a public right of way". We have not found any direct authority for such a rule. The closest rule we have found is a rule in the law of salmon fishing which says that fishing in an unlawful manner[69] cannot give rise to a prescriptive fishing title. This is a fairly obscure rule: Johnston does not mention it, though Cusine and Paisley do. They write:

---

[63] *British Transport Commission v Westmorland County Council* [1958] AC 126.

[64] *British Transport Commission v Westmorland County Council* [1958] AC 126, p 166.

[65] D J Cusine and R R M Paisley, *Servitudes and Rights of Way* (1st ed 1998) para 10.22.

[66] D Johnston, *Prescription and Limitation* (1st ed 1999).

[67] The "could not competently grant, therefore no prescription either" argument.

[68] Criminal offences relevant to level crossings are discussed further in Part 13.

[69] The law has always had complex rules about how salmon may be legally caught.

In several cases dealing with the acquisition of ownership by the operation of positive prescription, it has been held that the possession must not be illegal. That principle should be equally applicable to the acquisition of servitude rights.[70]

12.71 They cite *Mackenzie v Renton*,[71] *Duke of Richmond v Earl of Seafield*[72] and *Maxwell v Lamont*.[73] These cases do indeed support the first quoted sentence, though not in relation to ownership in general, but only to salmon fishing rights. We have found no case in which the principle has been extended to other ownership rights, nor to servitude rights. Cusine and Paisley themselves do not suggest that it applies to public rights of way. It remains to add that in practice if public rights of way have come into being by prescriptive usage that will in many or most cases have happened before the 1949 Act, and before 1949 the relevant statutory provisions appear to have been narrower in scope.[74]

12.72 It might be argued that the "openly, peaceably and without any judicial interruption" requirement of the 1973 Act could be invoked here, on the basis that usage by way of criminal trespass would not be "peaceable". On balance we do not think that such an argument would be sound. "Peaceable" means "not by force or threats". The term "peaceable" translates the "*nec vi*" requirement of Roman law and the older Scots law, which has the meaning just mentioned. However, as mentioned above, there are strong public policy arguments for excluding prescription in such cases. It is difficult to say which approach a court would find persuasive.

12.73 Another provision of the British Transport Commission Act 1949 worth noting is section 57, which provides that:

> ...no right of way as against the Commission shall be acquired by prescription or user over any road footpath thoroughfare or place now or hereafter the property of the Commission and forming an access or approach to any station goods-yard wharf garage or depot or any dock or harbour premises of the Commission.

12.74 It is possible that section 57 was impliedly repealed (in relation to Scotland) by the Prescription and Limitation (Scotland) Act 1973. That is something on which we express no view. But in any event a private crossing will not, we think, fall within the terms of section 57 and accordingly it would appear not to be relevant. We mention it only by way of background information, and to show that anti-prescription legislation – whether desirable or undesirable – has a precedent. It may be added that any right of way already constituted before 1949 would have been unaffected by section 57.

12.75 In Part 11 we discuss the English case of *Bakewell Management Limited v*

---

[70] D J Cusine and R R M Paisley, *Servitudes and Rights of Way* (1st ed 1998) para 10.21.

[71] *Mackenzie v Renton* (1840) 2 D 1078.

[72] *Duke of Richmond v Earl of Seafield* (1870) 8 M 530.

[73] *Maxwell v Lamont* (1903) 6 F 245.

[74] Railway Regulation Act 1840, s 16 and the Regulation of Railways Act 1868, s 23.

Brandwood.[75] Legislation made it an offence to drive without lawful authority on a common. It was held that nevertheless such driving could create an easement.[76] But as we point out in Part 11, this decision is not necessarily determinative of the rather different situation for railways.

Provisional conclusion: prescriptive upgrade

12.76 We think that the argument based on the *ultra vires* doctrine is weak and we incline to dismiss it. The argument based on section 55 of the British Transport Commission Act 1949 is stronger.

12.77 To the extent that public rights of way may *already* have come into being by prescriptive use, that fact cannot be undone. If the public is to be excluded, that means that the general rules – present or future – about closure of public rights of way over level crossings must be invoked.

12.78 But for cases of possible *future* prescriptive creation, the law can be changed. There are clearly drawbacks to the prescriptive creation of public rights across level crossings.[77] The authorised user knows the safety rules; the public may not.[78] Public use means increased use, and increased use may have safety implications. As against this it can be argued that if the public has been using a crossing for over 20 years that suggests that there is no major safety problem.

12.79 Our provisional view is that a public right of way over a private crossing can probably be constituted by prescriptive usage, but we accept that the law is not wholly clear. Whatever the *current* law may be, the question arises as to what the law should be in the future. We therefore ask consultees:

12.80 **Should the public use of a private level crossing be capable of giving rise to a public right of way through the operation of prescription?**

Extinction of public rights of way

12.81 In the context of the level crossings project, it would seem that the most relevant means by which a public right of way may be extinguished are prescription and operation of statutory powers.[79] The various statutory powers which allow closure or diversion of a public crossing are discussed in Part 6, above. It seems that negative prescription will operate to extinguish the right of way where it is unexercised or unenforced for 20 years.[80] The general law in this respect seems broadly satisfactory for the purposes of level crossings, but it might be argued that a level crossing-specific stopping up procedure would be helpful. For this

---

[75] *Bakewell Management Limited v Brandwood* [2004] 2 AC 519.

[76] An easement corresponds to a servitude.

[77] A complication is that the track/railway owner may not know, without litigating the matter, whether the crossing is public or not.

[78] We understand that Network Rail provides information to authorised users of private crossings as to safety issues.

[79] On the extinction of public rights of way in general, and for further detail regarding extinction by agreement, acquiescence and destruction. See D J Cusine and R R M Paisley, *Servitudes and Rights of Way* (1st ed 1998) para 24.01- 24.13.

[80] Prescription and Limitation (Scotland) Act 1973, s 8. For discussion, see D J Cusine and R R M Paisley, *Servitudes and Rights of Way* (1st ed 1998) para 24.03-04.

reason, in Part 8 we discuss a new statutory order-making procedure which would allow the compulsory extinction or diversion of a public right of way over a level crossing.

ACCESS RIGHTS UNDER THE LAND REFORM (SCOTLAND) ACT 2003

Creation and extent

12.82   Part 1 of the Land Reform (Scotland) Act 2003 created "access rights". As noted in Part 6, an access right is not a public right of passage for the purposes of the Roads (Scotland) Act 1984. It would seem that such access rights are in fact wider in scope than a public right of passage. Section 1 of the 2003 Act provides:

> (1) Everyone has the statutory rights established by this Part of this Act.

> (2) Those rights (in this Part of this Act called "access rights") are—

> (a) the right to be, for any of the purposes set out in subsection (3) below, on land; and

> (b) the right to cross land….

12.83   As mentioned in Part 6, section 17 of the 2003 Act requires each of the local authorities in Scotland to draw up a plan for a system of paths (known as "core paths") sufficient for the purposes of giving the public reasonable access throughout their respective areas. It seems clear that a public right of access exists automatically over any way which is designated as a core path. Again as mentioned in Part 6, the effect of the inclusion of a piece of land in a core path plan is that access rights will apply in circumstances where that would not ordinarily be the case.

12.84   On this basis, if a way which crossed a railway on the level were to be included in a core path plan, it would seem that access rights would then exist over that crossing, notwithstanding the apparent exclusion of access rights by virtue of section 6 of the 2003 Act, as detailed below. However, we understand that there are no private level crossings in existence at present over which a core path exists.

Do access rights apply to private level crossings?

12.85   The main question for consideration in this area is whether access rights extend to private level crossings. If access rights apply to land on both sides of a railway, and there is a level crossing which is a private level crossing of some description, can a walker who is one side cross to the other? The policy of the 2003 Act is that, subject to the exclusions in section 6 of the Act, discussed below, members of the public have a general right to cross land, providing that right is exercised responsibly. On that basis, it might seem consistent with the policy of the 2003 Act that access rights should be exercisable over private crossings. However, thought must be given to how section 6 in fact applies. The discussion of this issue below is limited to section 1(2)(b) of the 2003 Act, that is, the right to cross land.

161

The Access Code

12.86   Section 2(1) of the 2003 Act provides that a person has access rights in terms of section 1 only insofar as those rights are exercised responsibly. In turn, section 10 places an obligation on Scottish Natural Heritage to draw up a code providing guidance as to when access rights are, and are not, deemed to be exercised responsibly.[81] According to section 2(2)(b), in determining whether access rights are being exercised responsibly, account is to be taken of whether a person has disregarded the guidance on responsible conduct set out in the Access Code. The Code lists the main places where access rights under the Act do not apply, including "railway infrastructure".[82] However, the expression is a general one, and it is not clear to us whether it is intended to include level crossings. It is important to note that the function of the Code is merely to provide guidance as to the *manner* in which access rights are to be exercised insofar as they exist under the Act. It is not intended to determine *where* in Scotland access rights apply.[83]

Section 6(1)(a)(i) of the 2003 Act

12.87   Section 6(1)(a)(i) of the 2003 Act excludes access rights from land on which there is "a building or other structure or works, plant or fixed machinery". Whilst there may appear to be an argument that a level crossing constitutes a structure, section 6(1)(a)(i) has to be read in this context in conjunction with section 6(2). This provides that anything designed to facilitate passage is not to be regarded as a structure. It would seem that there is at least a basis for argument that a level crossing is designed to facilitate passage, meaning that it would not be classed as a structure for the purposes of section 6(1)(a)(i) of the 2003 Act. It would appear that a stronger argument can perhaps be derived from the exclusion of access rights from land on which there are works. Section 60 of the Railways Clauses (Consolidation) (Scotland) Act 1845, to the extent that it is not excluded from a special Act, makes provision for the construction of statutory right of way crossings. These are described as [accommodation] "works". Moreover, it is to be noted that the Waverley Railway (Scotland) Act 2006, in providing for the construction of various railway lines, is said to provide for railway "works". If it is accepted that a railway line constitutes "works", it seems that, subject to the comments below on core paths, access rights must be said to be excluded from any land on which there is a railway line, regardless of whether there is a level crossing.

Section 6(1)(d) of the 2003 Act

12.88   It seems to us that the provision most likely to be relevant is section 6(1)(d). This excludes land "to which public access is, by or under any enactment other than this Act, prohibited, excluded or restricted". The Explanatory Notes to the 2003 Act say:

---

[81] The Scottish Outdoor Access Code was produced by Scottish Natural Heritage in terms of section 10, and approved by the Scottish Parliament on 1 July 2004.

[82] The Scottish Outdoor Access Code, para 2.11.

[83] See *Gloag v Perth and Kinross Council* 2007 SCLR 530.

Section 6(1)(d) provides that the regulation of public access by or under any other enactment is not diminished or replaced by access rights. There are, for example, other enactments which prohibit, exclude or restrict public access over military establishments and railways.[84]

12.89 It seems to us that the most relevant provision is section 55 of the British Transport Commission Act 1949, which we discussed in Part 11 in relation to rights of way in England and Wales, and which we also discuss in Part 13 in relation to criminal offences. that the 1949 Act is not a public general statute and we have had difficulty in determining its current amended text.[85] But the wording of section 55(1) appears to be as follows:

> Any person who shall trespass upon any of the lines of railway or sidings or in any tunnel or upon any railway embankment cutting or similar work now or hereafter belonging or leased to or worked by any of the Boards and any wholly owned subsidiary of any of the Boards and any successor of the British Railways Board (but not to a subsidiary of any such successor unless it is itself a successor) or who shall trespass upon any other lands of any of the Boards and any successor of the British Railways Board in dangerous proximity to any such lines of railway or other works or to any electrical apparatus used for or in connection with the working if the railway shall on summary conviction be liable to a penalty not exceeding level three on the standard scale.

12.90 Another provision which is relevant is Regulation 3 of the Railway Safety (Miscellaneous Provisions) Regulations 1997,[86] which provides that:

> So far as is reasonably practicable, a person in control of any infrastructure of a transport system to which this regulation applies shall ensure, where and to the extent necessary for safety, that unauthorised access to that infrastructure is prevented.

12.91 Regulation 2 provides that the permanent way is part of the infrastructure. This provision may engage the "prohibited, excluded or restricted" provision in the 2003 Act. But the proviso "where and to the extent necessary for safety" in regulation 3 is a basis for doubting whether level crossings in general were in contemplation when the Regulations were made, or only those deemed unacceptably dangerous. As outlined in Part 11, there are other statutory provisions relating to trespass on the railways which apply in Scotland as well as in England and Wales.

---

[84] See para 29 of the Explanatory Notes:
http://www.opsi.gov.uk/legislation/scotland/acts2003/en/aspen_20030002_en_1 (last visited 27 June 2010).

[85] The chances that a member of the public could do so, or could even discover the provision in the first place are slight.

[86] Railway Safety (Miscellaneous Provisions) Regulations 1997, SI 1997 No 553. These Regulations apply in England and Wales as well as in Scotland.

Section 6(1)(g) of the 2003 Act

12.92 Section 6(1)(g) excludes land on which "building, civil engineering or demolition works; or works being carried out by a statutory undertaker for the purposes of the undertaking, are being carried out".

12.93 The second part of this is limited to cases where the works are being done by a "statutory undertaker". The term is defined in section 32. The relevant part of section 32 reads:

> a person authorised by any enactment to carry on any railway, light railway, tramway, road transport, water transport, canal, inland navigation, dock, harbour, pier or lighthouse undertaking or any undertaking for the supply of hydraulic power.

12.94 Railways are expressly mentioned. Under section 8 of the Railways Act 1993, the Secretary of State has power to grant a licence authorising a person to be "the operator of such railway assets … as may be specified in the licence". A network licence was granted under section 8 to Railtrack plc, which as mentioned in Part 1, changed its name in March 2003 to Network Rail Infrastructure Limited.[87] From this it would seem that Network Rail Infrastructure Limited is a statutory undertaker for the purposes of the 2003 Act.

12.95 The first part of section 6(1)(g) is not limited by the reference to "statutory undertaker" and so is potentially applicable whether or not Network Rail is a statutory undertaker. However, we incline to read the expression "building, civil engineering or demolition works" as referring to temporary works, and notably construction work and demolition work, rather than routine ongoing operations.

The 20 special cases[88]

12.96 For completeness, we should mention that Network Rail has agreed to keep open for public use about 20 crossings in remote areas, being crossings that are, in the view of Network Rail, private crossings. This has been a limited response to pressure from access groups (as already mentioned, *de facto* public use happens in respect of other crossings that are said to be private crossings).

Extinction of access rights

12.97 The route of a core path may be changed (or the core path removed altogether) under section 20 of the 2003 Act. In general, the access rights granted by section 1 of the 2003 Act, although subject to certain qualifications, cannot be extinguished. Further primary legislation would probably be necessary in order to remove or diminish the current extent of the rights under section 1.

Provisional conclusions: access rights over private level crossings

12.98 It seems that in cases where there is a private level crossing on a working railway there are several provisions in the 2003 Act which exclude access rights. It is to

---

[87] See: http://www.railwaysarchive.co.uk/documents/DfT_NL002.pdf (last visited 27 June 2010).

[88] See http://www.ramblers.org.uk/scotland/ourwork_scotland/access/casestudies/networkrail (last visited 27 June 2010).

be noted that none of the provisions specifically refer to level crossings and the exclusion of access over private level crossings is perhaps wider than strictly necessary because access across a private crossing is arguably less dangerous than access over other parts of the railway line.

12.99 A proviso concerns railways which are in disuse. Here, the argument that access rights include the whole railway, are clearly stronger.

12.100 The question of whether access rights *should* extend to private crossings is perhaps more difficult. Our provisional view of the current law is that, in the absence of a core path, access rights do not apply in respect of private level crossings over the operational railway. Particularly in remote areas of Scotland, this may make access to the countryside difficult. It seems that in the drafting of the 2003 Act, the position of private level crossings was not specifically considered. There are conflicting public policy imperatives: on one hand, the need to preserve public access to the countryside; on the other, the need to ensure the safe and efficient operation of the railway system. It should be noted that individual level crossings may be opened for public access by designation as a core path. Our consultation leads us to believe that in a number of individual cases, this would be an appropriate and beneficial solution. Extending access rights to all private level crossings is, however, a different matter.

12.101 Moreover, to the extent that access rights may extend to a private crossing, the question arises as to what the consequence would be if the private crossing were to be closed. The natural consequence would be that access rights would no longer apply. However, we ask consultees:

12.102 **Should the Land Reform (Scotland) Act 2003 be amended to clarify whether access rights do or do not extend over private level crossings?**

12.103 **If so, which policy approach should be adopted?**

New level crossings in furtherance of public access rights?

12.104 In *British Transport Commission v Westmorland County Council*[89] Lord Radcliffe commented[90] that "the construction of railways ... drove steel[91] barriers over many hundreds of miles of the English countryside". The same is true of the Scottish countryside. The existence of these steel barriers may, in some places, be an impediment to the exercise of access rights conferred by the Land Reform (Scotland) Act 2003. The land on each side of the railway may be – typically is – subject to access rights, yet those exercising such rights may find themselves defeated by the lack of public crossings connecting the two areas. The distance between public crossings (whether crossings on the level or by bridge or underpass) can be very considerable, especially in certain remoter areas. The greater the distance between public crossings, the greater the temptation for those exercising access rights to cross the railway track at a place convenient to

---

[89] *British Transport Commission v Westmorland County Council* [1958] AC 126.

[90] *British Transport Commission v Westmorland County Council* [1958] AC 126, p 153.

[91] In many languages railways are called iron ways. It is true that rails were originally made of iron, but they have long been made of steel. Lord Radcliffe's comment, though imperfectly accurate for the early days of the railways, is accurate today.

themselves. This is especially so where the railway is unfenced. Our consultations have disclosed that this sort of irregular crossing of railways does indeed happen and in fact is quite common in certain places in the Highlands. The situation cannot be regarded as satisfactory. It is not satisfactory that people cross railways at unregulated places, and it is not satisfactory that there are seemingly too few public crossings to make the realisation of public access rights possible. It may therefore be arguable that new non-vehicular public crossings are needed in certain areas. It is true that the general policy today is against new level crossings, and we accept the soundness of that policy. But if new public crossings are in fact needed, it may be that cost considerations would exclude bridges and underpasses, leaving crossings on the level as the only practicable alternative.

12.105   The question thus arises as to whether the current law provides a satisfactory framework for the construction of new public non-vehicular crossings. The issue is not merely one of *enabling* the infrastructure manager to install such crossings, but also one of *requiring* such installation. In theory there is the possibility of a new crossing being established as part of the "core path" system under the Land Reform (Scotland) Act 2003, but the core path system was not set up with railways in mind and it may be doubted whether it provides a satisfactory basis. To test views, we ask:

12.106   **Should it be competent for the appropriate public authority to require railway operator to install new non-vehicular public level crossings in order to facilitate the exercise of access rights?**

12.107   **If so, should that authority be the local authority or the Scottish Ministers, or should the decision be a joint one?**

12.108   **Who should be responsible for the expense of new crossings?**

12.109   A closely-related issue is where there exists a private level crossing and, to promote access rights, it would be desirable for that crossing to be made available for public non-vehicular use. Such a change would not involve the physical creation of a new crossing. Rather, it would involve the extension of access rights to an existing crossing. This has already happened (at least *de facto*) in 20 cases where Network Rail has opened private level crossings[92] to the public. We ask:

12.110   **Should it be competent for the appropriate public authority to order that a private level crossing become subject to access rights?**

---

[92]   Or at least, crossings which in the view of Network Rail are private crossings. There are cases where disagreement exists as to whether a crossing is public or private, Network Rail taking the latter view.

PART 13
CRIMINAL OFFENCES

INTRODUCTION

13.1 This Part considers the role that the criminal law can play in preventing members of the public from using level crossings in a way which causes danger to themselves and rail users. Railways are crossed at public and private crossings by motorists, farmers, people operating agricultural machinery, cyclists, pedestrians, horse riders and others. Whilst criminal offences relating to the railways and roads can potentially be applied to conduct committed at level crossings, on the whole the existing criminal offences have not been designed with level crossings in mind. This Part seeks to assess how satisfactory the current criminal law is in addressing misconduct at level crossings and considers the creation of new offences specific to level crossing users.

13.2 It is important not to over-state the contribution that appropriate criminal offences can make to improving safety at level crossings. Criminal law sets standards of behaviour which it is expected that the public will meet. Failure to meet these standards can result in punishment, which should have a deterrent effect Certainly, the criminal law has a role to play, but other measures should also be considered. For example, prosecution and sentencing practices and guidance, changes to the design of level crossings, better signs and warnings, safety education campaigns, the inclusion of level crossing awareness in the training of new drivers, and the highlighting of level crossing safety issues in guidance such as the Highway Code may well improve behaviour and public attitudes and therefore, safety. We have not gathered evidence on the extent to which criminal offences act as an effective deterrent to level-crossing misuse. In the case of misuse by pedestrians, the greatest risk of injury or death is to the pedestrian, rather than train occupants, although train drivers and passengers can experience psychiatric injury as a result of an accident at a level crossing.

13.3 There is a perception that level crossing misuse is frequently under-charged and that this reduces the deterrent effect of prosecuting offenders. For example, prosecutions arising out of the British Transport Police's Operation Galley[1] indicate that the large majority of those prosecuted for offences at level crossings were charged with failing to comply with a road traffic sign. This is a minor offence, which can be dealt with by means of a fixed penalty notice. For many motorists acting in this way, a charge of driving without due care and attention or indeed dangerous driving would appear to be more appropriate. It may be that there is insufficient evidence to charge the more serious offences or that the less serious offences are easier and more cost effective to prosecute. Where officers observe the offence, or its commission is recorded on CCTV, the determination of the appropriate charge will depend on an assessment of the gravity of the motorist's conduct, rather than a lack of evidence of an element of the offence.

---

[1] Operation Galley is an initiative run by the British Transport Police, first in June 2009 and repeated in March 2010. The initiative seeks to tackle level crossing misuse by means of on-the-spot enforcement and public education. See "The Line", Issue 5, March 2010, the magazine of British Transport Police available at:
http://www.btp.police.uk/pdf/the%20line%20march%20web.pdf (last visited 27 June 2010).

13.4 We are also aware that concern has been raised about the level of sentences imposed by magistrates and sheriffs for misuse of level crossings. Also it may be that less serious offences (incurring less severe penalties) are being charged, perhaps because offenders are more likely to plead guilty to less serious offences.

13.5 Road traffic offences generally apply to drivers of vehicles only. However as mentioned above, the greatest risk of accidents at level crossings arises from behaviour of pedestrians and indeed the vast majority of such accidents cause injury or death to pedestrians rather than to occupants of trains.[2] Aside from the road traffic offences, the current criminal law which can apply to misuse of level crossings consists of a confusing collection of offences of varying degrees of severity, spread across bye-laws, public and private legislation, some of which has been superseded or amended on numerous occasions. For example, the offences relating to railways are the only provisions of the Malicious Damage Act 1861 still in force and the current wording of section 55 of the British Transport Commission Act 1949 is particularly difficult to ascertain.[3]

13.6 As we suggest later in this Part, we think there is a case for a new set of offences specifically designed to deal with misconduct of drivers, pedestrians and others using level crossings.

CONDUCT AT LEVEL CROSSINGS

13.7 The main cause of danger, or of actual collisions, is the conduct of those crossing the railway. The Rail Safety and Standards Board (RSSB) has attributed 95% of the risk of death or serious injury at level crossings to the conduct of motorists and pedestrians.[4] The risk mainly affects those crossing the railway, rather than train occupants. The risk caused by factors within the control of the rail industry is negligible.

Pedestrians

13.8 In 2009, 8 pedestrians and 5 occupants of road vehicles died at level crossings, compared with 5 pedestrians and 3 road vehicle occupants in 2008.[5] RSSB concludes that the risk of death or serious injury to pedestrians makes up 77% of the total risk to those crossing the railway at level crossings. A large proportion of this risk occurs at footpath crossings.[6]

---

[2] RSSB, *Road Rail Interface Special Topic Report,* April 2010, p 9.

[3] See Part 12, for full wording currently in force.

[4] Rail Safety and Standards Board (RSSB), *Road-Rail Interface Special Topic Report 2010,* p 9. Available at http://www.rssb.co.uk/SPR/REPORTS/Pages/SPRPublishedDocuments.aspx (last visited 27 June 2010).

[5] RSSB, *Annual Safety Performance Report 2009.* Available at: http://www.rssb.co.uk/SiteCollectionDocuments/pdf/reports/ASPR_2009_10_Full_Report.pdf (last visited 1 July 2010).

[6] See also the RSSB Road-Rail Interface Special Topic Report 2010 which contains more detailed analysis of key safety facts at level crossings for the 6 years 2004 to 2009. The Report indicates that for the 6 years covered by the report the vast majority of deaths at level crossings were attributable to suicides and suspected suicides.

Motorists

13.9 Collisions between train and road vehicles make up 20% of the total risk of death or serious injury at level crossings.[7] Fatalities and injuries amongst road vehicle occupants are consistently lower than amongst pedestrians. However, it is the collision between a train and a road vehicle which is the most likely cause of a catastrophic incident. The collision between a train and a car at Ufton Nervet level crossing in 2004 caused 7 deaths. The collision between a train and a low-loader transporter carrying a 120-ton electrical transformer at Hixon in 1968 caused 11 deaths.[8]

Types of conduct

13.10 RSSB has divided the conduct of level crossing users into three broad groups:

(1) Proper use: a user takes reasonable precautions and complies with all warning signs when crossing.

(2) Error misuse: users are mistaken as to the reasonable precautions they should take, including how they should comply with warning signs or barriers.

(3) Violation misuse: a user deliberately fails to take reasonable precautions, including failing to comply with warning signs, or deliberately uses a level crossing in a way which is dangerous.[9]

13.11 These three groups do not translate readily into legal categories but are helpful in distinguishing between misuse which results from error and that which results from the deliberate flouting of safety measures.

THE EXISTING CRIMINAL LAW

13.12 In this section we consider the adequacy of the existing criminal law. In doing so, we look at whether the offences cover the conduct we wish to prohibit, at whether the current law covers each different type of level crossing user, and also at whether the application of the law effectively prevents harm as intended.

13.13 Appendix B consists of a table setting out the existing criminal offences which can apply in relation to conduct at level crossings.[10]

The railway offences

13.14 The railway offences appear to have two main objectives. The first is to prohibit unauthorised access onto the railway. This objective is met by a variety of

---

[7] RSSB, *Overview of Safety Performance 2009.* RSSB, *2008 Annual Safety Performance Report,* p 155.

[8] Ministry of Transport, *Report of the Public Inquiry into the Accident at Hixon Level Crossing on January 6, 1968* (1968) Cmnd 3706, para 70, p 29.

[9] RSSB, *Level Crossings Factsheet,* p 2. Available at: http://www.rssb.co.uk/SiteCollectionDocuments/pdf/Level%20Crossing%20Factsheet%20-%202006.pdf (last visited 1 July 2010).

[10] As mentioned in Part 2, the criminal law in England and Wales is different from that in Scotland. Some offences apply to the whole of Great Britain. Others are specific to either England and Wales or Scotland. Appendix B sets out these differences in detail.

trespass offences. The second is to protect the railway and those travelling upon it from acts which might compromise safety.

The trespass offences

13.15 There are at least three trespass offences which apply throughout Great Britain. The principal one is that contained in section 55 of the British Transport Commission Act 1949. This section makes it an offence to trespass upon a railway where a notice at the nearest station warns against trespass. We understand that such a notice is placed at every station. The penalty for this offence is a fine up to £1,000 (level 3 on the standard scale).[11] The other offences – under section 16 of the Railway Regulation Act 1840 and section 23 of the Regulation of the Railways Act 1868 – depend on specific warnings or requests being given to the trespasser before the offence can be made out. We focus on the section 55 offence as we understand from the British Transport Police that this is the offence which is most frequently charged in cases of suspected trespass on the railways. In England and Wales, a fixed penalty may be imposed for an offence under section 55 of the 1949 Act, although we have no evidence that fixed penalties are imposed in practice.[12]

13.16 The offence works by turning the civil wrong of trespass into a criminal offence. First, the offender must be trespassing. Trespass is the act of unauthorised and unjustifiable entry upon land in the possession of another.[13] The notion of trespass is apt to encompass misuse at a private level crossing. Use of the crossing beyond that authorised by the right of way will be civil trespass. A person who is not authorised to use the crossing will always be a civil trespasser on the railway's land if he or she uses the crossing. If an authorised person uses the crossing in a way or at a time not authorised by the right of way, that too will be civil trespass. This will include using the crossing at a time when it is cleared for a train to pass.

13.17 The situation is different at a public level crossing. The public in general has a continuing right to use a highway/road. The question is not without some difficulty. Our view is that a person who uses a public highway/road in defiance of a sign prohibiting such use (such as a red traffic light on an ordinary road) does not necessarily become a trespasser, although they may be liable to a separate penalty for failing to comply with the sign. In *Harrison v Duke of Rutland*,[14] the Court of Appeal found that a demonstrator was a trespasser when using his right of way solely for the purpose of interfering with the landowner's interests. However, in *DPP v Jones (Margaret)*, the House of Lords held on the facts that demonstrators at Stonehenge had not committed the offence of holding a

---

[11] Criminal Justice Act 1982, s 37 as regards England and Wales; Criminal Procedure (Scotland) Act 1995, s 225 as regards Scotland.

[12] Penalties for Disorderly Behaviour (Amount of Penalty) Order 2002, SI 2002/1837.

[13] That is to say, in England and Wales, trespass is the act of unauthorised and unjustifiable entry upon land in the possession of another: Gray and Gray, *Elements of Land Law* (5th ed 2009) p 1260. In Scotland, trespass consists of temporary or transient intrusion into land owned or otherwise lawfully possessed by someone else; See Kenneth G C Reid, *The Law of Property in Scotland* (1st ed 1999) para 180; see also William M Gordon and Scott Wortley, *Scottish Land Law* (3rd ed 2009) Vol 1, p 399.

[14] [1893] 1 QB 142.

trespassory assembly,[15] when they had been passing and re-passing over the highway, albeit for the purpose of a demonstration prohibited by the police.[16] We therefore think that a member of the public who passes over a highway/road at a public level crossing when the line is cleared for a train may not be a trespasser.[17]

13.18   We conclude that the trespass offence in section 55 of the 1949 Act may apply at *private* level crossings but may not apply at public crossings. We take the view that this offence would benefit from reform and clarification. At *public* level crossings, however, there is a modern offence of failing to comply with a sign which may be more appropriate.[18]

13.19   A particular feature of the section 55 offence is its obscurity. The 1949 Act is a private Act, which makes it less accessible to the public than a public general Act. In addition the Act has been heavily amended by subsequent legislation. It took us some time to arrive at a text that we were content was accurate.[19] This level of obscurity is highly unsatisfactory and may be in breach of Articles 6(3)(a) and 7(1) of the European Convention on Human Rights.[20] This, combined with our conclusion that this offence does not apply to those using public level crossings, leads us to the view that there is need for a thorough review, and possibly the creation of new level crossing-specific offences.

Offences aimed at protecting the railway and those using it

13.20   The second objective of the railway offences is to protect the railway from acts which might affect the infrastructure and compromise the safety of rail users and staff. In England and Wales, the Offences Against the Person Act 1861 and the Malicious Damage Act 1861 provide a variety of offences which prohibit interference in the safe and proper running of the railways. The 1861 Acts do not apply in Scotland. While there are no equivalent statutory offences in Scotland, certain common law crimes would be relevant. One is the crime of malicious mischief which concerns destruction of, or damage to, *property*. The other crimes concern injury or danger to *persons*. The crime of culpable and reckless injury

---

[15]   Public Order Act 1986, s 14A and 14B.

[16]   [1999] 2 AC 240.

[17]   This may not always be the case as in certain circumstances a person may indeed be a trespasser. Where in England and Wales the highway was dedicated *after* the railway line was built, it might be that the dedication of the highway was limited in nature. Generally, restrictions can be imposed on the use of a public highway upon dedication, but not later: Stephen Sauvain QC, *Highway Law* (4th ed 2009) paras 2.23 to 2.31. But of course nearly all highways pre-date the railway.

[18]   Section 36 of the Road Traffic Act 1988..

[19]   For the full wording currently in force, see Part 12 above.

[20]   Article 6(3)(a) provides that everyone charged with a criminal offence has the right "to be informed promptly, in a language which he understands and in detail, of the nature and cause of the accusation against him." Article 7(1) provides that no one shall be held guilty of any criminal offence on account of any act or omission which did not constitute a criminal offence under national or international law at the time when it was committed. As Clayton and Tomlinson point out: "The criminal law must be sufficiently accessible and precise to enable an individual to know in advance whether his conduct is criminal". Richard Clayton and Hugh Tomlinson, *The Law of Human Rights* (2000) para 11.261.

occurs where someone unintentionally but recklessly causes injury to another person. Where no injury is actually caused by reckless behaviour, but that behaviour is objectively dangerous to others, the crime of recklessly causing danger is relevant.[21]

SUMMARY OFFENCES

Railway bye-laws

13.21 The Railways Act 2005 gives the railway operator the power to make bye-laws relating to the railways.[22] The bye-laws cover a wide variety of conduct but those most relevant to level crossings include:

(1) Bye-law 6(5), which makes it an offence to damage any part of the railway;

(2) Bye-law 9(3), which contains the offence of opening a barrier or gate except where there is a notice allowing its use;

(3) Bye-law 11(1), which provides that no person shall obstruct or interfere with, amongst other things, any equipment on the railway;

(4) Bye-law 11(2), which makes it an offence to put anything upon the railway which is capable of injuring, damaging or endangering any person or property;

(5) Bye-law 14(1), which makes it an offence for anyone to use a motor vehicle or bicycle on the railway in contravention of a traffic sign.

13.22 In addition, bye-law 12(1) allows a railway operator to issue reasonable safety instructions by placing a notice on the railway. Failure to comply with such a notice without good reason is an offence. The notice must be placed on or near the part of the railway to which the safety instructions relate. Bye-law 12(1) permits the railway operator to issue safety instructions in respect of all types of level crossing and all types of user. Breach of any of the railway bye-laws is a criminal offence punishable by a fine of up to £1,000 (level 3).[23]

Failure to shut a gate at a private crossing

13.23 Section 75 of the Railways Clauses Consolidation Act 1845 and section 68 of the Railways Clauses Consolidation (Scotland) Act 1845 make it an offence to fail to shut and fasten a gate or lower a barrier on a private level crossing in England

---

[21] Gordon, *Criminal Law* (3rd ed 2001) (edited by Michael Christie), para 29.58, refers to the latter crime as that of causing danger to the lieges by culpable recklessness. T H Jones and M G A Christie, *Criminal Law* (4th ed 2008) p 231, refer to it as reckless endangerment of the lieges.

[22] Railways Act 2005, s 46.

[23] Bye-law 24(1) provides that breach of a bye-law is an offence with a maximum penalty of a fine not exceeding level 3 on the standard scale. In relation to England and Wales, the Criminal Justice Act 1982, s 37 provides that the fine applying to an offence on level 3 of the Standard Scale is a fine not exceeding £1,000. In relation to Scotland, the Criminal Procedure (Scotland) Act 1995, s 225 provides for a fine of the same amount.

and Wales, and Scotland respectively.[24] The penalty is a fine of up to £1,000 (level 3).

Failure to comply with a sign at a private crossing

13.24 Section 55 of the Transport and Works Act 1992 makes it an offence to fail to comply with any requirement, restriction or prohibition shown on a sign on or near a private road or path near a place where the road or path crosses the railway. The penalty is a fine of up to £1,000 (level 3). The offence applies throughout Great Britain. Section 52 of the 1992 Act provides that the signs must be ones approved by the Secretary of State,[25] and that the Secretary of State can direct railway operators to place signs at level crossings near a private road or path. The section 55 offence is the offence most commonly prosecuted in relation to private level crossings.

SERIOUS RAILWAY OFFENCES

13.25 The serious railway offences contained in the Offences Against the Person Act 1861 and the Malicious Damage Act 1861 can be divided into those where the fault element is "an unlawful act or a wilful omission or neglect" and those where the fault element is "intent". As stated earlier, these offences apply to England and Wales only.

Offences punishable by a maximum of life imprisonment

13.26 Section 32 of the Offences Against the Person Act 1861 makes it an offence to interfere with the railway with the intention of endangering safety. Section 33 of the same Act contains an offence of interfering with a train with intent to endanger the safety of the people on the train. Those offences are punishable by a maximum term of imprisonment for life. Section 35 of the Malicious Damage Act 1861 makes it an offence to obstruct a train with intent. In Scotland, the crime of culpable and reckless injury is also punishable by a maximum term of imprisonment for life.

Offences punishable by a maximum of two years' imprisonment

13.27 There are two relevant offences in England and Wales, punishable by a maximum term of imprisonment of two years, namely those in section 34 of the Offences Against the Person Act 1861 and section 36 of the Malicious Damage Act 1861. Section 34 of the Offences Against the Person Act 1861 makes it an offence to endanger the safety of passengers and people being in or upon the railway (for example railway workers), and section 36 of the Malicious Damage Act 1861 makes it an offence to obstruct a train.

13.28 The test as to whether the safety of the railway and its users has in fact been

---

[24] These offences originally applied only to private crossings created by special Acts to which the Railways Clauses Consolidation Act 1845 and Railways Clauses Consolidation (Scotland) Act 1845 respectively applied automatically unless expressly excluded. However, the Accommodation Level Crossings Act 1995 (a private Act promoted by Railtrack), s 2 extended the application of the offence contained in the 1845 Acts to the mainline network.

[25] For example, under the Private Crossings (Signs and Barriers) Regulations 1996, SI 1996 No 1786.

endangered for the purposes of section 34 of the Offences Against the Person Act 1861 is an objective one. That is to say, the offence is committed if the accused's conduct, in the view of the magistrates or jury, endangers the safety of passengers on a train. The offence would include, where relevant, circumstances where the accused's conduct fell below an accepted safety standard in using the railway.[26]

13.29　The fault element for both offences has two alternative limbs: "by any unlawful act" or "by any wilful omission or neglect". In the context of "unlawful act manslaughter", the unlawful act must be a criminal one.[27] The courts have not yet considered this issue in the context of section 34 of the Offences Against the Person Act 1861 or section 36 of the Malicious Damage Act 1861. "Wilful misconduct" has been held to be assimilable to recklessness, albeit at a time when recklessness was defined by the courts as meaning either that the accused was aware of the risk and went ahead to commit the act (or omit to act) regardless, or that the accused acted (or omitted to act) not caring whether there was a risk.[28] More recently, the House of Lords in *R v G* held that the accused was only guilty of recklessness when he or she was aware of the risk but went ahead regardless.[29] Whether or not a person was aware of the risk will be assessed on the basis of the circumstances as he or she saw them. Any new offence resulting from our proposals would apply the test of recklessness set out by the House of Lords in *R v G* in England and Wales.

CONCLUSIONS

13.30　Whilst several of the offences outlined above can be applied to cases of misconduct at a level crossing, very few have been specifically designed to police or deter such behaviour. Those that have are lower level offences relating to the use of gates or complying with signs.

13.31　In England and Wales, the offence of endangering safety contained in section 34 of the Offences Against the Person Act 1861 is a more serious offence. The offence focuses on the effect of a person's conduct as regards safety rather than on an individual's conduct, and is antiquated in its formulation.

13.32　It is particularly noteworthy that amongst the railway offences there is no equivalent to the road traffic offence of causing death which could apply to level crossing users who are not motorists, as discussed below.

13.33　The offences in sections 32 and 33 of the Offences Against the Person Act 1861 both deal with the intentional creation of danger on the railway by placing items on the railway or by throwing or causing items to fall on a train or the railway. There is no requirement that actual harm results from the endangerment, whether harm was intended or not. The early road traffic legislation sought to punish the creation of danger, but left to the common law of murder and manslaughter (or culpable homicide in Scotland), and to legislation relating to the offences against

---

[26]　*R v Pearce* [1967] 1 QB 150, 50 App Rep 305, CA.

[27]　*R v Franklin* (1883) 15 Cox CC 163.

[28]　*R v Sheppard* [1981] AC 394 in the context of wilful neglect of a child.

[29]　*R v G* [2003] UKHL 50, [2004] 1 AC 1034. For further discussion see David Ormerod, *Smith and Hogan, Criminal Law* (12th ed, 2008) pp 161-162.

the person, punishment for causing death or injury on the roads.[30] There is now a series of offences of causing death through dangerous or careless conduct on public roads. We believe that there is a case for the creation of an analogous offence when death is caused by the dangerous use of a level crossing either intending or being reckless as to the risk.

Road traffic offences

13.34 The road traffic offences in so far as they happen to be relevant to level crossings, have evolved in the main to regulate who has permission to drive vehicles on public roads, the conduct of drivers, and the standard at which those vehicles must be driven. Road traffic offences do not, in general, regulate the conduct of pedestrians.

13.35 Unlike the rail offences, or indeed the general criminal law, the penalties attached to the road traffic offences contain two elements: a punitive element in the form of a fine or imprisonment, and a regulatory element which takes the form of an endorsement of a driving licence, disqualification from driving, or a requirement that the offender pass an extended driving test after disqualification before being granted a new driving licence.

Pedestrians failing to comply with a light signal at a level crossing

13.36 As we have said, almost all of the road traffic offences apply exclusively to motorists. It is, however, an offence for a pedestrian to fail to comply with a "red figure" stop sign placed at a level crossing when the sign is illuminated. Section 91 of the Road Traffic Offenders Act 1988 makes it an offence to fail to comply with most Regulations made under the Road Traffic Act 1988 or the Road Traffic Regulation Act 1984. For example, Regulation 52 of the Traffic Signs Regulations and General Directions 2002[31] specifies a "red figure" sign which, when illuminated, requires pedestrians not to use a level crossing. It is therefore an offence, punishable by a fine of up to £1,000 (level 3), for pedestrians not to comply with such a sign.

Drivers failing to comply with a traffic sign

13.37 Section 36 of the Road Traffic Act 1988 makes it an offence for drivers of motor vehicles to fail to comply with an authorised traffic sign.[32] The offence is committed when a driver fails to comply with a sign depicting a prohibition, restriction, or requirement.[33] This offence applies to traffic signs at level crossings. The penalty for this offence is a fine of up to £1,000 (level 3).[34] A fixed

---

[30] See the remarks of Lord Atkin in *DPP v Andrews* [1937] AC 576, 583.

[31] SI 2002 No 3113.

[32] As authorised by the Secretary of State for Transport, Secretary of State Scotland and the Secretary of State for Wales acting jointly, under the Road Traffic Act 1988, s 36(5).

[33] Road Traffic Act 1988, s 36(2).

[34] Road Traffic Act 1988, s 36(5) provides for an additional discretionary penalty of disqualification for failure to comply with those signs which are listed in the Traffic Signs Regulations and General Directions 2002 (SI 2002 No 3113), reg 10. Although Schedule 3 to the Regulations prescribes the format of level crossing signs, these signs are not included in Regulation 10.

penalty notice may be issued in respect of this offence.[35]

Careless driving and causing death by careless driving

13.38 Section 3 of the Road Traffic Act 1988 makes it an offence to drive a motor vehicle on a road or other public place without due care and attention, or without reasonable consideration for other road users. A person drives without due care and attention if the way he or she drives falls below what would be expected of a competent and careful driver.[36] We discuss the operation of this test in the context of dangerous driving below. The penalty for this offence is a fine of up to £5,000 (level 5), discretionary disqualification and obligatory endorsement of penalty points. Section 2B of the 1988 Act makes it an offence to cause death by careless driving for which the penalty is a maximum of five years' imprisonment, obligatory disqualification for a minimum period of 12 months and mandatory endorsement of penalty points.[37]

Dangerous driving and causing death by dangerous driving

13.39 Section 2 of the Road Traffic Act 1988 makes it an offence to drive a vehicle dangerously. Section 1 of the 1988 Act provides for the aggravated offence of causing the death of another person by dangerous driving. A person will be guilty of causing death by dangerous driving if he or she drives dangerously and causes the death of another person. There is no need to show the dangerous driving was the principal or substantial cause, only that it was *a* cause.[38] The punitive penalties for these offences are currently up to two years' imprisonment and/or a fine for dangerous driving and up to 14 years' imprisonment for causing death by dangerous driving. The regulatory penalties are mandatory disqualification for a minimum of 12 months for dangerous driving and a minimum of two years for causing death by dangerous driving. Both offences attract a mandatory endorsement of penalty points upon the driver's licence and a mandatory order that the driver pass an extended driving test before being granted a new driving licence.[39]

13.40 The meaning of dangerous driving is set out in section 2A of the 1988 Act. For driving to be dangerous three elements must be established:

(1) The way a driver drives must fall far below the standard of driving that would be expected of a competent and careful driver;[40]

(2) It must be obvious to a competent and careful driver that driving in that way is dangerous;[41] and

---

[35] Road Traffic Offenders Act 1988, sch 3.

[36] Road Traffic Act 1988, s 3ZA.

[37] Road Traffic Offenders Act 1988, Sch 2, Part 1.

[38] *R v Hennigan* (1971) 55 Cr App R 262.

[39] Road Traffic Offenders Act 1988, section 36.

[40] Road Traffic Act 1988, s 2A(1)(a).

[41] Road Traffic Act 1988, s 2A(1)(b).

(3) The danger must be a risk of injury to any person or serious damage to property.[42]

DRIVING FAR BELOW THE STANDARD OF A COMPETENT AND CAREFUL DRIVER

13.41 A person is only legally permitted to drive if he or she has acquired the skills of a competent and careful driver and successfully passed a driving test (or holds a provisional licence and drives under supervision). It is this standard of expertise against which his or her driving is judged. It is not just the accused's driving which can be taken into account when deciding whether his or her driving fell far below what would be expected of a competent driver; "any circumstance shown to have been within the knowledge of the accused"[43] should also be taken into account. It is not permissible to take into account any factor personal to the driver which would raise or lower the standard of driving against which the accused's driving is judged. This is because the standard of the competent and careful driver is an objective one to be applied to all drivers irrespective of whether they are specialist police drivers or have just passed their driving test.[44]

IT MUST BE OBVIOUS TO A COMPETENT AND CAREFUL DRIVER THAT DRIVING IN THAT WAY IS DANGEROUS

13.42 Even if a driver drives far below the standard of a competent and careful driver, his or her driving will not be dangerous unless it is obvious that the driving is far below the permitted standard. It is for the jury to decide what is or what is not dangerous driving.[45]

THERE MUST BE A RISK OF INJURY TO ANY PERSON OR SERIOUS DAMAGE TO PROPERTY

13.43 The driving cannot be dangerous unless there is a risk of injury to any person or serious damage to property. The risk of injury includes a risk of injury to the driver and the risk of serious damage to property includes serious damage to the driver's property.

REFORM

13.44 A level crossing creates a unique set of circumstances, which the existing criminal law, whether it be rail or road traffic, has not, for the most part, been explicitly designed to meet. As we have seen, there are two important elements contained within this unique set of circumstances. These are the variety of types of crossing and the diversity of people using them to cross the railway. If new level crossings offences were to be introduced, there would be an advantage in these offences being generic. Where appropriate these offences should also apply to anyone working on the railway who misuses a level crossing. Any new offences should address the main cause of death and injury at level crossings: the conduct of those using level crossings to cross the railway.

---

[42] Road Traffic Act 1998, s 2A(3).

[43] Road Traffic Act 1988, s 2A(3).

[44] *R v Bannister* [2009] EWCA 1571, [2010] RTR 4.

[45] Attorney General's Reference (No 4 of 2000) [2001] EWCA Crim 780, [2001] RTR 27 at [7].

13.45 The road traffic offences tend to cover those driving on roads and not pedestrians or other users such as horse riders. Section 192(1)(a) of the Road Traffic Act 1988 defines "road" in relation to England and Wales as meaning "any highway or any other road to which the public has access …". As regards Scotland, section 192(1)(b) of the 1988 Act defines "road" as meaning "any road within the meaning of the Roads (Scotland) Act 1984 and any other way to which the public has access…". These definitions mean that conduct on some private level crossings could be caught by the 1988 Act, where the way which crosses the railway is one to which the public takes access by the tolerance or permission of the owner of the right of way. However, it seems likely that conduct on only a very small minority of private crossings would be caught by the 1988 Act. There are unlikely to be many private level crossings where the owner of the right of way allows the public to take access over the crossing. In relation to crossings which would not be caught by the definition of "road" for the purposes of the 1988 Act, there appears to be a gap as regards the application of road traffic offences.

13.46 It would clearly be wrong to *exclude* conduct on a level crossing from regulation by road traffic offences. Such offences constitute a modern "code" which is regularly updated with a view to tackling misbehaviour on the road. As mentioned above, one of the advantages of road traffic offences is the availability of regulatory penalties.

13.47 **We therefore provisionally propose that the general road traffic offences should continue to regulate the conduct of drivers at level crossings over public highways/roads.**

A possible scheme of level crossing-specific offences

13.48 Notwithstanding our proposal that the current road traffic offences should remain applicable to conduct at level crossings, we propose that there should be a new set of offences specifically for level crossings. The new offences would be capable of applying to pedestrians and to private level crossings, both of which are not covered in the main by the existing road traffic offences. We propose a scheme comprising three tiers of offences, which would apply to all users of all level crossings. First, there would be a relatively minor regulatory offence of failing to comply with a sign at a level crossing. Second, there would be a middle-level offence of using a level crossing in a dangerous way - that is, creating the risk of serious injury or damage to property - what we call an offence of dangerous conduct). Third, there would be a serious offence of dangerous conduct which causes death at a level crossing, with penalties equivalent to causing death by dangerous driving.

Possible new minor offence of failure to comply with a sign

13.49 There are both railway and road traffic offences which in particular circumstances cover the failure to comply with signs or barriers at level crossings. The new offence we are suggesting would apply to all types of level crossing, and could be committed by all categories of level crossing user. The existing sign offences are strict liability offences for which the maximum penalty is a fine. We consider that the application of strict liability to these offences is legitimate. Compliance with such warnings is an essential element of the safety regime in a dangerous environment.

13.50 The benefits of having strict liability offences in relation to non-compliance with signs are already reflected in existing criminal law. We have identified five such offences, which apply respectively to:

(1) Motorists on public roads.[46]

(2) Motorists and cyclists.[47]

(3) Pedestrians failing to comply with a particular sign when illuminated.[48]

(4) All users but only of private crossings.[49]

(5) Lastly there is the offence contained in railway bye-law 12(1) of failing to comply with a reasonable safety instruction placed upon a notice.

13.51 The result is that all groups of users and types of level crossing are subject to at least one sign offence, and some types of user are subject to several.

13.52 If a new, broad offence on the lines we suggest were to be introduced, the key question would be: to which signs should the new offence relate? We think there would have to be a procedure to authorise classes of signs to which the offence would relate. This does not imply that there would have to be a new, universal scheme of signs and warnings for level crossings. Rather, existing systems of signs – such as road traffic signs and signs erected at private level crossings under section 52 of the Transport and Works Act 1992[50] – would suffice.

PENALTY

13.53 The maximum penalty for the existing offences is a fine of up to £1,000 (level 3). The question arises as to whether a higher penalty should be imposed for any new offence of failure to comply, in order to reflect the seriousness of the potential consequences if a near miss or collision should occur. There is a general requirement that, unless there are exceptional policy reasons, the penalty for strict liability offences should be relatively minor. This should be balanced against the greater risk of catastrophic incident at a level crossing when compared with a failure to comply with a traffic sign on a road other than at a level crossing. If the penalty were to be set at a higher level, consideration should also be given to whether offences could still be dealt with by way of fixed penalty notice.

Possible new middle-level offence of dangerous conduct at level crossings

13.54 The second tier offence would be an offence of intentionally or recklessly using a level crossing in a way which creates a danger of injury or serious damage to property. The offence would apply to all users of all types of level crossing as well

---

[46] Road Traffic Act 1988, s 36.

[47] Railway bye-law 14(1).

[48] Road Traffic Act 1988, s 91 in conjunction with the Traffic Signs Regulations and General Directions 2002 (SI 2002 No 3113), reg 52.

[49] Transport and Works Act 1992, s 55.

[50] See section 52 of the 1992 Act as read with the Private Crossings (Signs and Barriers) Regulations 1996, SI 1996 No 1786.

as those working on the railway.

13.55 To convict a person of using a level crossing in a dangerous way, it would be necessary to prove first that the accused's behaviour had breached an objective standard of conduct, and second, that the accused was aware his or her conduct risked creating a danger of injury or serious damage to property.

THE CONDUCT ELEMENT OR *ACTUS REUS*

13.56 The conduct element of the offence would be using a level crossing in a dangerous way. "Dangerous use" would be defined as using a level crossing in a way which creates a risk of injury or serious damage to property.

13.57 The test as to what constitutes dangerous use would be an objective one. As with the offences of endangering safety on the railway and dangerous driving, it would be for a jury to decide whether in a particular case the accused's use of a level crossing was dangerous. The conduct element in endangerment of safety on the railway and the dangerous driving offences works on the basis of setting a standard against which the accused's conduct is assessed. For dangerous driving, the standard is that of the competent and careful driver. If the accused's driving falls far below that standard then the accused's driving will be dangerous.

13.58 The two existing offences, endangering safety and dangerous driving, have different objective standards. The standard for the endangerment of safety offence is a relatively open one: if the accused's conduct lowers the safety standard then the conduct element is present.

13.59 We consider that there is not a useful equivalent to the competent and careful driver in the context of level crossings, and therefore we propose a relatively open standard. The standard of conduct required would be not to use a level crossing in a way which creates a danger of injury or serious damage to property.

THE FAULT ELEMENT OR *MENS REA*

13.60 The offence of dangerous conduct at level crossings would be a reasonably serious criminal offence, punishable by imprisonment. Strict liability would not be appropriate. We suggest that the appropriate fault element for this offence would be recklessness.[51] To require intent would be too limiting and inappropriate – very few of those using level crossings in a dangerous way *intend* their behaviour to create a danger of injury or serious damage to property. A person is reckless if he or she voluntarily acts in a way which creates a risk that the prohibited result will occur, and he or she is aware, on the basis of the circumstances known to him or her, of this risk.

13.61 In our context this means that a person will be recklessly using a level crossing in a dangerous way if he or she is aware that there is a risk that his or her conduct will result in a danger of injury or serious damage to property. Level crossings are unusual and complex environments. We have considered whether the requirement that a level crossing user is aware he or she is creating a risk would make it too difficult to convict a user who argues they were not aware of the risk they created because they were not familiar with the safety requirements at level

---

[51] *R v G* [2003] UKHL 50, 1 AC 1034.

180

crossings. There may be some danger of this in unusual circumstances. However unaware users are of railway safety standards, the safe use of a level crossing seems reasonably clear. There may be users, such as children, against whom the prosecution will not be able to prove that they were aware of the risk that their behaviour created, and in such circumstances they should be acquitted.

PENALTY

13.62   The maximum penalty for this offence would be equivalent to that for dangerous driving, currently two years imprisonment.

Possible new serious offence of causing death by dangerous use of a level crossing

13.63   The most serious offence that we propose would be committed where dangerous use of a level crossing causes death. The elements of the offence would be the same as the offence of dangerous conduct at a level crossing, but that conduct would have caused death. The maximum penalty would be the same as that prescribed for the offence of causing death by dangerous driving: imprisonment of 14 years.

13.64   Again, we favour an offence which requires the accused to intend or be aware of the risk of injury or serious damage to property. Alternatively, the offence could be made out if the accused's conduct was dangerous and that dangerous conduct caused death, irrespective of his or her knowledge of the risk.

Relationship between new offences and existing offences

13.65   If this scheme of new offences were to be adopted, it would operate in tandem with the existing road traffic offences. We have already provisionally proposed that road traffic offences should not be excluded from level crossings. We do not think it would be sensible to exclude the new scheme where the motoring offences could apply. This would lead to a danger that prosecutors may feel that they should charge both offences – a new level crossing offence and a road traffic offence – in the alternative; or, contrariwise, that an offender might escape liability if the wrong offence were chosen.

13.66   Unfortunately, it would not be possible to repeal most railway offences, because the majority of them apply to the entire railway. In the same way that we propose that the new level crossing offences should not displace the relevant road traffic offences, we do not think that the proposed new offences should displace the railway offences. To do so would be to invite pointless disputes as to the boundary between the new offences and the general railway offences.

13.67   The exception here might be the small number of level crossing specific offences: those under section 75 of the Railways Clauses Consolidation Act 1845, section 68 of the Railways Clauses Consolidation (Scotland) Act 1845, and section 55 of the Transport and Works Act 1992. We suggest that it may be possible to repeal those provisions.

Advantages and disadvantages of new offences

13.68   A proposed new scheme would provide a hierarchy of offences appropriate to level crossings. It would be much simpler than the current law. It would be clearer, drafted in modern language and free from distinctions between types of level crossings. The offences would apply to all level crossing users and on all types of level crossing. The provisions setting out the offences would also be readily accessible in a public general Act.

13.69 The principal disadvantage we can see is that the scheme would add three *further* offences to an already crowded field, and one or other of the new offences would overlap with many of those already existing. If the offences are too similar to dangerous driving and causing death by dangerous driving, confusion amongst the police and prosecutors could result, undermining their effectiveness as a coherent code. One way of avoiding such confusion would be to restrict the new offences to circumstances where the existing road traffic offences do not apply, for example, on private roads or when the user is not a driver.

13.70 **Do consultees think that any new offences should be limited to circumstances where existing road traffic offences do not apply?**

13.71 As mentioned at the beginning of this Part, the criminal law is not the only method of improving safety at level crossings, nor is the creation of new offences by itself likely to act as an effective deterrent against misuse. The impact of the offences will depend upon their enforcement. It may be that if the existing offences, particularly the more serious offences, were charged and prosecuted more frequently, the deterrent effect would be greater.[52]

13.72 In coming to a provisional proposal, we recognise that the arguments are finely balanced. However, we tend to prefer the reform option.

13.73 Accordingly, **we propose that there should be a new scheme of level crossing offences, comprising:**

(1) **An offence of failing to comply with an authorised sign at any kind of level crossing, punishable by a fine;**

(2) **An offence of dangerous use of any kind of level crossing, where the accused's behaviour had breached an objective standard of conduct (not to behave in such a way as to create a risk of injury or serious damage to property); and the accused was aware his or her conduct risked creating a danger of injury or serious damage to property. This offence would be punishable by a prison term similar to that for dangerous driving; or**

(3) **An offence of dangerous use of any kind of level crossing, where the accused's behaviour had breached an objective standard of conduct (with no requirement that the accused was aware of any risk). This offence would be punishable by a prison term similar to that for dangerous driving; and**

(4) **An offence of dangerous use of a level crossing, intentionally or recklessly causing death, punishable, as with causing death by dangerous driving, with a maximum prison term of 14 years; or**

---

[52] See the results of Operation Galley, mentioned above.

(5) An offence of dangerous use of a level crossing, causing death (with no requirement of intention or recklessness). This offence would be punishable by a maximum prison term of 14 years.

13.74 We would welcome the views of consultees on the proposed offences and penalties.

13.75 If consultees do not think that new offences should be created, we would welcome views on whether penalties for existing offences relevant to level crossing misuse should be increased.

13.76 What other steps do consultees think should be taken in order to reduce the incidence of offending at level crossings?

PART 14
SIGNS AND THE HIGHWAY CODE

INTRODUCTION

14.1 In this Part we outline the provisions regulating traffic signs at or near level crossings and the relevant rules of the Highway Code. We then consider the extent to which the current arrangements might benefit from review.

14.2 We are concerned here with the legal regime for traffic signs, lights and markings on roads on the approaches to and at level crossings. We are not concerned here with the provision of gates and barriers, which are part of the protective arrangements at level crossings.

A public footpath crosses a narrow gauge private hobby railway at an ungated level crossing in the South of England.

SIGNS, LIGHTS AND MARKINGS ON PUBLIC ROADS AT OR NEAR LEVEL CROSSINGS

14.3 The types of signs for use on public roads are governed by the Traffic Signs Regulations and General Directions 2002[1] made under the Road Traffic Regulation Act 1984 and the Road Traffic Act 1988. The Regulations and Directions apply to Scotland as well as to England and Wales. They include specific provisions prescribing the technical specifications for light signals to

[1] SI 2002 No 3113. The UK has signed, but not ratified, the Vienna Convention on Road Signs and Signals 1968. The UK acts, wherever possible, as if it were bound by the Convention. The Convention describes a system of road signs, signals, symbols and road markings which contracting parties are obliged to adopt. There are specific articles relating to signs at level crossings: arts 33-36 and in Annex 1, paras 25-29 inclusive. See http://www.unece.org/trans/conventn/signalse.pdf (last visited 27 June 2010).

control traffic and for warning pedestrians at level crossings.[2] The Regulations and Directions therefore cover all public level crossings, both vehicular and non-vehicular.

14.4   Section 65(1) of the 1984 Act gives traffic authorities[3] the *power* to place traffic signs on roads providing such signs are in conformity with the Regulations and General Directions made under the Act. "Road" is defined as meaning "any length of highway or of any other road to which the public has access" in relation to England and Wales and as "any way...over which there is a public right of passage" in relation to Scotland.[4]

14.5   In contrast with the 1984 Act, the Level Crossings Act 1983 makes provision regarding the *compulsory* placing of signs at level crossings by the *railway operator or the traffic authority*. The 1983 Act applies to public level crossings. However as mentioned earlier, in England and Wales (but not Scotland), it also applies to private level crossings to which the public has lawful access.

14.6   As mentioned earlier in the consultation paper, a level crossing order may impose duties on the operator of a level crossing or the local traffic authority, if necessary or expedient for the safety or convenience of level crossing users.

14.7   In terms of a level crossing order, the railway operator (in most cases, Network Rail) or the local traffic authority, or both, may be required to provide "at or near the crossing any protective equipment specified in the order and to maintain and operate that equipment".[5] "Protective equipment" is defined in section 1(11) of the Level Crossings Act 1983 as including lights and traffic signs (as well as barriers and other devices). The term "traffic sign" is defined as having the same meaning as in the Road Traffic Regulation Act 1984. Section 64(1) of the 1984 Act defines "traffic sign" as meaning "any object or device" for warning traffic as specified in regulations or otherwise authorised by the Secretary of State. Section 64(2) of the 1984 Act provides that "traffic signs shall be of the size, colour and type prescribed by regulations made as mentioned in subsection (1)(a)...". As we have seen, the size, colour and types of signs have been prescribed by the Secretary of State under the Traffic Signs Regulations and General Directions 2002. Therefore any signs which are required in terms of a level crossing order made under the 1983 Act must accord with the technical specifications prescribed by the Traffic Signs Regulations and General Directions 2002. In practice therefore, a railway operator or a local traffic authority which is subject to requirements in a level crossing order is bound to comply with the requirements of the Regulations and General Directions 2002.

14.8   Section 1 of the 1983 Act contains a wide power for the Secretary of State (in practice, the Office of Rail Regulation - ORR) to require that signs be provided not only at a crossing itself, but also on the approaches to it. The costs of design,

---

[2]   See in particular regs 39, 40 and 52.

[3]   The 1984 Act refers to "traffic authority" but this essentially means the relevant highway authority in England and Wales or the roads authority in Scotland. See the Road Traffic Regulation Act 1984, s 121A.

[4]   Road Traffic Regulation Act 1984, s 142(1). The definition as regards Scotland is the same as that in the Roads (Scotland) Act 1984.

[5]   Level Crossings Act 1983, s 1(2)(a).

installation and maintenance are borne by the railway operator and/or the relevant local traffic authority.

14.9 The *Railway Safety Principles and Guidance* issued by ORR provides guidance to the railway industry on specific aspects of railway construction including advice about signs at level crossings.[6] The guidance is not mandatory but sets out good practice aimed at assisting those with responsibility for the provision and maintenance of protective arrangements at level crossings.[7] The section dealing with level crossings is currently being reviewed by ORR following recent consultation on revised guidance. Guidance has also been produced for railway operators.[8]

SIGNS, LIGHTS AND MARKINGS ON PRIVATE ROADS AT OR NEAR LEVEL CROSSINGS

14.10 The majority of level crossings in Great Britain are not public crossings. In most cases level crossings were created at the time of the construction of the railway to "accommodate" the landowner whose land was bisected by the railway. The types of signs that may be used on or near these crossings are prescribed by the Private Crossings (Signs and Barriers) Regulations 1996,[9] which were made under section 52(1) of the Transport and Works Act 1992. The Regulations apply to Scotland as well as to England and Wales. Section 52 also gives the railway operator the power to place these signs at or near private level crossings. Provision is also made for the Secretary of State to require the railway operator to do so. It has been suggested to us that the system for making changes to the types of signs in use at level crossings might benefit from review.

THE HIGHWAY CODE

14.11 The Highway Code is also relevant to consideration of signs at level crossings. The Code is made under section 38 of the Road Traffic Act 1988 with a view to the promotion of road safety in Great Britain. The aim of the Code is to provide guidance for persons using roads.[10] The Code applies to pedestrians as well as motorists, cyclists and horse riders. Although failure to comply with the rules contained in the Code is not of itself a criminal offence, failure to comply with the rules may be used as evidence in proceedings for an offence under road traffic legislation.[11]

---

[6] These are available on ORR's website at http://www.rail-reg.gov.uk/server/show/nav.1647 (last visited 27 June 2010).

[7] Railway Safety Principles and Guidance, part 2, s E, pp 48-61. See http://www.rail-reg.gov.uk/upload/pdf/rspg-2e-levxngs.pdf (last visited 27 June 2010).

[8] By the Rail Safety and Standards Board: see RSSB, *Guidance on Level Crossings Interface Requirements* (GK/GN0692, Issue 1, February 2010). Available at: http://www.rgsonline.co.uk/Railway_Group_Standards/Control Command and Signalling/Guidance Notes/GKGN0692 Iss 1.pdf (last visited 27 June 2010).

[9] Private Crossings (Signs and Barriers) Regulations 1996, SI 1996 No 1786.

[10] Road Traffic Act 1988, s 38(8).

[11] Road Traffic Act 1988, s 38(7). The Code adopts the words "MUST" and "MUST NOT" as appropriate to denote legislative requirements and prohibitions.

14.12 Rules 291 to 299 of the Highway Code apply specifically to level crossings. Those rules provide guidance to drivers, motor cyclists, cyclists, horse riders, people with animals, and users of powered wheelchairs/mobility scooters in the use of level crossings. The Code also contains rules for drivers, horse riders and pedestrians using level crossings.[12] For example, rule 34 applies to pedestrians. It refers for its authority to regulation 52 of the Traffic Signs Regulations and General Directions 2002 (made under the Road Traffic Act 1988 and the Road Traffic Regulation Act 1984). Regulation 52 makes clear that there is a prohibition against pedestrians crossing a level crossing when red lights show. This prohibition is reinforced by the guidance in rule 34 of the Highway Code.

14.13 Criminal liability for failure to comply with regulation 52 of the Traffic Signs Regulations and General Directions 2002 is derived from section 91 of the Road Traffic Offenders Act 1988. That section provides a penalty for contravention of regulations made under the Road Traffic Act 1988 or the Road Traffic Regulation Act 1984, including the Regulations and General Directions 2002.

ISSUES RELATING TO SIGNS AND THE HIGHWAY CODE

14.14 We have been made aware of a number of complaints about signs and warnings at level crossings. We are also aware of calls for review of the current law on signs "to make them more effective, coherent, comprehensive and accessible".[13] We have also heard criticism of the guidance given in the Highway Code in relation to level crossings.

14.15 It is neither within our remit for this project, nor within our area of expertise, to advise on the design of signs or warnings, or the wording of guidance given to motorists or others. However, **we would be interested in views about whether the *legal structure* relating to the specification of signs is adequate, or is in need of a general review.**

14.16 Consultees may feel that the system of signs, warnings and guidance needs reviewing as a whole; or that a different approach is needed for signs, warnings and guidance in relation to level crossings. We therefore ask:

14.17 **Are the current legal structures providing for signs and warnings at level crossings, and for providing guidance in the form of the Highway Code to motorists or others, adequate?**

---

[12] Rules 291 to 299 apply to drivers and horse riders; rule 34 applies to pedestrians.

[13] Rail Accident Report – Investigation into safety at user worked level crossings, RAIB Report 13/2009, para 171. Available at:
http://www.raib.gov.uk/publications/investigation_reports/reports_2009/report13200 9.cfm (last visited 27 June 2010).

PART 15
SUMMARY OF PROPOSALS AND QUESTIONS

15.1 This Part brings together all of the provisional proposals made and questions asked in this consultation paper.

PART 1: INTRODUCTION

15.2 We would welcome the views of consultees on whether, for the purposes of our proposals, "railway" should be defined as a transport system where the tracks are segregated from other traffic.

15.3 We welcome consultees' views on the economic impact of the proposed reforms.

PART 2: SCOTLAND AND WALES: DEVOLUTION AND OTHER ISSUES

15.4 This Part does not contain any proposals or questions.

PART 3: DISABILITY AND ACCESSIBILITY

15.5 We would welcome any comments that consultees may have on disability and accessibility issues in respect of level crossings.

PART 4: CREATION OF LEVEL CROSSINGS

15.6 We would welcome the views of consultees on the current system of creating level crossings.

PART 5: THE CURRENT REGULATION OF LEVEL CROSSINGS

15.7 Depending on the outcome of consultation, we suggest that if the current system of regulation is to be retained, the relationships between special Acts, level crossing orders and HSWA 1974 duties, should be clarified for the future.

PART 6: CLOSURE OF LEVEL CROSSINGS

15.8 This Part does not contain any proposals or questions.

PART 7: THE CASE FOR REFORM

15.9 We provisionally propose that the regulatory regime for level crossings should aim to:

(1) ensure safety at level crossings;

(2) promote the efficient operation of railways and, where present, highways/roads, taking account of the need to strike a balance between the interests of rail, road and other users;

(3) allocate duties and responsibilities appropriately amongst the various actors; and

(4) provide appropriate means to define rights of way at level crossings in so far as feasible, and to extinguish them where necessary.

15.10 We welcome views on whether these objectives provide an appropriate guide for reform. Would any other objectives be appropriate?

15.11 We provisionally think that the current regulatory regime should be reformed as it does not sufficiently recognise the potentially competing interests affecting level crossings and does not adequately cater for all level crossings.

PART 8: SAFETY REGULATION AND CLOSURE: REFORM PROPOSALS

15.12 We provisionally propose that the regulation of safety at level crossings should be governed entirely by the general scheme of HSWA 1974.

15.13 However, if consultees consider that it would be preferable to retain the current system of regulating safety at level crossings, what changes should be made to improve the system?

15.14 We invite consultees to comment on our provisional proposal that ORR, as the safety regulator for the railways, should remain as the body with overall responsibility for safety regulation at level crossings.

15.15 If our preferred option of moving to a HSWA 1974-based system of regulating safety is accepted, we propose that regulations should be made by the Secretary of State under section 15 of HSWA 1974 in relation to level crossings.

15.16 If our preferred option of moving to a HSWA 1974-based system of regulating safety is accepted, we propose that ORR should be given the power to issue approved codes of practice under HSWA 1974 in relation to level crossings.

15.17 We ask consultees whether it would be desirable expressly to provide that a breach of section 3 of HSWA 1974 at a level crossing should be subject to enforcement by ORR, not HSE.

15.18 Would it be desirable for ORR and HSE to have concurrent jurisdiction for enforcement of breaches of the general duties under HSWA 1974 or "relevant statutory provisions" where the breach occurs partly at a level crossing; or should ORR's railway-specific jurisdiction oust that of HSE?

15.19 We invite consultees to comment on the problem that HSWA 1974 cannot apply to owners of rights of way over private level crossings who are not business users.

15.20 Do consultees think that a move to a HSWA 1974-based system would create problems in practice?

15.21 We ask consultees to consider whether there is a "convenience gap" in our proposal to replace reliance on special Acts and level crossing orders with a HSWA 1974-based system. If so, how should the gap be closed?

15.22 We ask consultees whether in practice it would be necessary to have a legal instrument that would:

(1) require rail operators to take safety-neutral steps to enhance the convenience of the users of the highway/road at a level crossing; and/or

(2) require highway/roads or traffic authorities to take safety-neutral steps to enhance the convenience of rail users, by enhancing the efficiency of the level crossing for rail use.

15.23 Is there a need for provision to enable convenience-related measures to be put in place at level crossings? If so, would it be preferable to:

(1) extend the power under section 15 of HSWA 1974 to make regulations, to include considerations of convenience; or

(2) create a new power to make separate convenience-related orders for particular level crossings?

15.24 We provisionally propose a new procedure for level crossing closure orders to allow for closure of both private and public level crossings.

15.25 Should there be a list of factors to be taken into account in considering an application for a level crossing closure order?

15.26 If so, we would welcome the views of consultees on the following list of factors:

(1) safety of users of the crossing (including information as to the incidence of accidents at the level crossing);

(2) costs involved in maintenance of the crossing compared with costs involved in closing or closing and replacing the crossing;

(3) the effect of closure as opposed to retention (in the case of public level crossings) on the efficiency of the rail and road networks;

(4) the effect (in the case of public level crossings) on the integrity of the network of non-vehicular public rights of way;

(5) the effect of closure compared to retention of the crossing on the local community;

(6) the effect on those holding private rights over the crossing;

(7) the usability of the level crossing or its potential alternatives for all level crossing users;

(8) the convenience of level crossing users; and

(9) the effect on the environment and local amenity.

15.27 Should the factors be set out in order of importance? If so, how should they be ordered?

15.28 We provisionally propose that the application for a closure order should be determined in England by the Secretary of State, in Wales by Welsh Ministers and in Scotland by the Scottish Ministers.

15.29 In relation to the question as to whether to stop up a highway or road, and whether to divert a highway or road either side of the railway, we suggest three

190

options:

    (1)   decision by the local highway/roads authority;

    (2)   decision by the Secretary of State/Scottish Ministers/Welsh Ministers but subject to consultation with interested parties and local bodies; or

    (3)   initial decision by the local highway/roads authority, subject to an appeal on the merits to the Secretary of State/Scottish Ministers/Welsh Ministers.

We provisionally favour the third option, but would invite comments from consultees.

15.30   We invite views from consultees on what time-limit for the use of compulsory purchase orders would be appropriate.

15.31   We invite views of consultees on whether planning consent should be deemed to be included in a level crossing closure order.

15.32   We provisionally propose that level crossing closure orders should be capable of including provision for the apportionment of the costs of closure and replacement between the statutory authorities concerned.

15.33   We invite consultees to comment on the apportionment of costs of closure and replacement of level crossings.

15.34   We provisionally propose that the procedure for level crossing closure orders should be subject to short time-limits at each stage, including consideration by the Secretary of State/Scottish Ministers/Welsh Ministers.

15.35   We ask consultees for their views on what time-limits there should be for the application process.

15.36   We invite views on what the time-limits should be for closure orders including the stopping up or diversion of a highway or road.

15.37   We provisionally propose that, after the expiry of the consultation period, the Secretary of State/Scottish Ministers/Welsh Ministers should decide whether, exceptionally, to hold a hearing before a person appointed by them. Otherwise, further consideration of competing views should be dealt with by the exchange of written representations.

15.38   Provisionally we do not consider that it is necessary to exclude the possibility of obtaining a TAW/S order where a level crossing closure order may be obtained, or the other way round, but we invite consultees' views.

15.39   We provisionally propose that level crossing closure orders should be statutory instruments and that they should be treated as general instruments.

15.40   We provisionally propose that under the new system for closure of level crossings, the function of making level crossing closure orders in relation to both public and private level crossings in Scotland should be transferred to the Scottish Ministers.

15.41   We therefore provisionally propose that under the new system for closure of level crossings, the function of making level crossing closure orders in relation to both public and private level crossings in Wales should be transferred to the Welsh Ministers.

15.42   We invite views of consultees on whether it would be useful to introduce a system of infrastructure agreements for level crossings.

15.43   We provisionally propose the expansion of the role of road-rail partnership groups, as they have proven to be successful in bringing together the various and often competing interests dealing with matters relating to level crossings.

15.44   Should there be statutory provision requiring the construction of new level crossings on existing railway lines in certain specified circumstances?

15.45   If so, should the decision-maker be able to override opposition to the construction of a new level crossing?

15.46   We would welcome the views of consultees on our proposal that the provisions in special Acts should be disapplied in so far as they deal with safety at level crossings to the extent that HSWA 1974 applies.

15.47   We would also welcome the views of consultees as to whether there should be a power for the Secretary of State to make orders to enable the repeal of provisions in special Acts in so far as the provisions relate to safety matters.

15.48   We provisionally propose that all existing level crossings orders should be revoked if the HSWA 1974-based system is adopted.

15.49   We provisionally consider that our proposals should apply to all level crossings on all types of railway.

15.50   However, we would welcome the views of consultees as to whether our provisional proposals should be adapted for heritage railways and private railways and if so, how.

PART 9: PLANNING: ENGLAND AND WALES

15.51   We would welcome examples or experiences of how consultation works in practice.

15.52   Do consultees think that the current practice of consultation relating to level crossings is adequate between local planning authorities, railway interests, developers and the public? If not, we would welcome specific examples.

15.53   Do consultees think that the current legal requirements for consultation where development affects a level crossing should be modified? If so, what modifications should be made?

15.54   We provisionally think that the current legal provision is sufficient to allow for developer contributions towards closure, replacement or improvement of level crossings. It may be that what is required is guidance, which would be beyond the scope of this project.

15.55 Do consultees think that section 106 obligations are appropriate legal mechanisms for obtaining developer contributions for upgrading or replacing level crossing infrastructure?

15.56 Will the situation be improved if the Community Infrastructure Levy is adopted by local planning authorities?

15.57 If not, what more is needed?

PART 10: PLANNING: SCOTLAND

15.58 We would welcome examples or experiences of how consultation works in practice.

15.59 Should amendments be made to the requirements under the 2008 Regulations for consultation with Network Rail Infrastructure Limited and other railway undertakers, where development is likely to affect a level crossing to a material degree?

15.60 Should there be a requirement for a transport plan to be produced in connection with an application for planning permission for a development in the vicinity of a level crossing which is likely to have a material effect on the traffic (in terms of volume and/or composition) that uses the level crossing?

15.61 Our provisional view is that any future procedure governing closure of level crossings should aim to involve planning authorities in the decision to close or replace a crossing (in particular where development is a factor necessitating closure).

15.62 Are there any legal obstacles to the use of agreements (in particular, planning agreements under section 75 of the Town and Country Planning (Scotland) Act 1997) to secure contributions from developers towards level crossing infrastructure? Are there any other improvements which could be made in this area?

PART 11: RIGHTS OF WAY AND ACCESS ISSUES: ENGLAND AND WALES

15.63 Do consultees think there should be a statutory prohibition on the future acquisition of private rights of way over the railway by prescription?

15.64 We provisionally propose that there should be a statutory list of factors which should be taken into account by courts when deciding whether changed or increased use at a private level crossing amounts to excessive use.

15.65 We provisionally propose the following factors:

   (1)   impact on safety of the railway and crossing users;

   (2)   the operational requirements of the railway, including how heavily used the railway line is;

   (3)   whether the use is of a substantially different character to the original use;

(4)   the frequency of use compared to the original frequency of use; and

(5)   whether the use will have such an impact upon the railway as to require expenditure on the part of the railway operator.

15.66   Do consultees think there should be such a statutory list of factors to be taken into consideration when construing the extent of a general right of way?

15.67   If consultees agree that there should be a list of factors, is the list above satisfactory or are there any other key factors which should be taken into account when assessing whether increased use of a private level crossing amounts to excessive use?

15.68   Do consultees think that it would be helpful for the law expressly to state that private rights over a level crossing can be extinguished by agreement between the rights holder(s) and the railway operator?

15.69   Do consultees agree that the law should be as laid down in *Midland Railway Company v Gribble*? If so, should this rule be given statutory effect, or is it sufficient that it remains a matter of case law?

15.70   Do consultees think there should there be a statutory prohibition on the future implied dedication of highways over the railway?

PART 12: RIGHTS OF WAY AND ACCESS ISSUES: SCOTLAND

15.71   Do consultees agree that it should be competent for the owner of the railway to grant a servitude of way?

15.72   Should it be possible for prescriptive use to create a servitude across a railway?

15.73   For Scotland, a suitable approach might be something on the following lines:

The use made of the statutory right of way over a crossing is not to be such as would:

(1)   be unreasonably detrimental to the safety of the railway users and crossing users;

(2)   interfere unreasonably with the operational requirements of the railway;

(3)   be substantially different in character (including frequency) as compared with the original use; and

(4)   give rise to unreasonable expenditure on the part of the railway infrastructure manager.

15.74   Would it be desirable to clarify the extent of use permitted under the Railways Clauses Consolidation (Scotland) Act 1845?

15.75   If this is the case, would such a list of factors be useful?

15.76   Alternatively, would alignment with the law of servitudes be helpful in determining the permissible extent of use of a statutory right of way crossing?

15.77   Should the law expressly state that the authorised user of a statutory right of way crossing can enter into a discharge agreement with the railway operator validly to extinguish the right to use the crossing, as happens in practice at present?

15.78   If so, are any qualifications or exceptions necessary?

15.79   In consultees' experience, are there any practical difficulties involved in the current process of extinguishing a right of way over a level crossing?

15.80   Should the *Robertson* rule (assuming that it correctly states the law) be replaced by the *Gribble* rule, for existing crossings as well as for new ones?

15.81   If so (and assuming that that would in fact result in a change in the law) would you agree that the owner of the track would in principle be liable to compensate those who suffered loss as a result? If so, do you have views about how such compensation should be calculated?

15.82   Would it be useful for there to be express legislative provision as to the extinction of statutory crossing rights by negative prescription? If so, what should the law provide?

15.83   Should the jurisdiction of the Lands Tribunal for Scotland be extended to include statutory rights of way over level crossings created under section 60 of the Railways Clauses Consolidation (Scotland) Act 1845?

15.84   Is legislation needed to clarify the power of a track/railway owner to make a voluntary grant of public rights of way?

15.85   Should the public use of a private level crossing be capable of giving rise to a public right of way through the operation of prescription?

15.86   Should the Land Reform (Scotland) Act 2003 be amended to clarify whether access rights do or do not extend over private level crossings?

15.87   If so, which policy approach should be adopted?

15.88   Should it be competent for the appropriate public authority to require the railway operator to install new non-vehicular public level crossings in order to facilitate the exercise of access rights?

15.89   If so, should that authority be the local authority or the Scottish Ministers, or should the decision be a joint one?

15.90   Who should be responsible for the expense of new crossings?

15.91   Should it be competent for the appropriate public authority to order that a private level crossing become subject to access rights?

PART 13: CRIMINAL OFFENCES

15.92   We provisionally propose that the general road traffic offences should continue to regulate the conduct of drivers at level crossings over public highways/roads.

15.93   Do consultees think that any new offences should be limited to circumstances where existing road traffic offences do not apply?

15.94   We propose that there should be a new scheme of level crossing offences, comprising:

(1)   An offence of failing to comply with an authorised sign at any kind of level crossing, punishable by a fine;

(2)   An offence of dangerous use of any kind of level crossing, where the accused's behaviour had breached an objective standard of conduct (not to behave in such a way as to create a risk of injury or serious damage to property); and the accused was aware his or her conduct risked creating a danger of injury or serious damage to property. This offence would be punishable by a prison term similar to that for dangerous driving; or

(3)   An offence of dangerous use of any kind of level crossing, where the accused's behaviour had breached an objective standard of conduct (with no requirement that the accused was aware of any risk). This offence would be punishable by a prison term similar to that for dangerous driving; and

(4)   An offence of dangerous use of a level crossing, intentionally or recklessly causing death, punishable, as with causing death by dangerous driving, with a maximum prison term of 14 years; or

(5)   An offence of dangerous use of a level crossing, causing death (with no requirement of intention or recklessness). This offence would be punishable by a maximum prison term of 14 years.

15.95   We would welcome the views of consultees on the proposed offences and penalties.

15.96   If consultees do not think that new offences should be created, we would welcome views on whether penalties for existing offences relevant to level crossing misuse should be increased.

15.97   What other steps do consultees think should be taken in order to reduce the incidence of offending at level crossings?

PART 14: SIGNS AND THE HIGHWAY CODE

15.98   We would be interested in views about whether the *legal structure* relating to the specification of signs is adequate, or is in need of a general review.

15.99   Are the current legal structures providing for signs and warnings at level crossings, and for providing guidance in the form of the Highway Code to motorists or others, adequate?

APPENDIX A
MAIN LEGISLATIVE PROVISIONS

A.1   We do not warrant that this table is comprehensive as to the legislation and key provisions.

LEGISLATION	KEY PROVISIONS
Highway (Railway Crossings) Act 1839	Section 1
Railway Regulation Act 1840	Section 16
Railway Regulation Act 1842	Sections 9 and 10
Railways Clauses Consolidation Act 1845	Sections 1, 46-50, 53, 55, 56, 61, 62, 68 and 73-75
Railways Clauses Consolidation (Scotland) Act 1845	Sections 1, 39, 40, 52, 60, 65 and 68
Malicious Damage Act 1861	Sections 35 and 36
Offences Against the Person Act 1861	Sections 32-35
Railways Clauses Act 1863	Sections 5-7
Regulation of Railways Act 1868	Section 23
Regulation of Railways Act 1871	
Regulation of Railways Act 1873	
Railway and Canal Traffic Act 1888	Section 16
Regulation of Railways Act 1889	
Road and Rail Traffic Act 1933	Section 42
British Transport Commission Act 1949	Sections 55 and 57
British Transport Commission Act 1957	Section 66
Countryside (Scotland) Act 1967	Section 30, 34, 35 and 47
Transport Act 1968	Sections 123 and 124

LEGISLATION	KEY PROVISIONS
Prescription and Limitation (Scotland) Act 1973	Sections 3 and 8
Health and Safety at Work etc Act 1974	Sections 1-10, 15, 16, 18-26, 53 and 82, and schedule 1.
Highways Act 1980	Section 6, 14, 18, 31, 34, 41, 62, 116, 118A, 119A, 120(3A), 121(1), 121(2) with section 28, and 255
Level Crossings Act 1983	Section 1
Roads (Scotland) Act 1984	Sections 1, 2, 48, 68, 151, 152(2) and 152(3)
Road Traffic Regulation Act 1984	Sections 64, 65(1), 121A(5) and 142(1)
Road Traffic Act 1988	Sections 1, 2, 2A, 2B, 3, 3ZA, 36, 38, 39, 65, 77, 91 and 192(1)
Road Traffic Offenders Act 1988	Sections 36, 91 and 98, schedule 2 part 1 and schedule 3
Town and Country Planning Act 1990	Sections 70, 76A, 90(2A), 106, 106A, 205, 216, 247 and 257
New Roads and Street Works Act 1991	Section 93
Road Traffic Act 1991	Section 1
Town and Country Planning (General Development Procedure) (Scotland) Order 1992(SI 1992 No 224)	Article 15
Town and Country Planning (General Permitted Development) (Scotland) Order 1992 (SI 1992 No 223)	Article 3 and schedule 1, part 13, class 34
Transport and Works Act 1992	Sections 1, 3, 5(6), 6, 9, 11(4), 13, 47, 48, 52, 54, 55 and 67(1), and schedule 1
Railways Act 1993	Sections 8 and 117
Accommodation Level Crossings Act 1995	Section 2

LEGISLATION	KEY PROVISIONS
Disability Discrimination Act 1995	Sections 1(1), 19-21, 21B, 21D, 21E and 49A
Town and Country Planning (General Development Procedure) Order 1995 (SI 1995 No 419)	Articles 3 and 10(e), and schedule 2, part 17, class A
Town and Country Planning (General Permitted Development) Order 1995 (SI 1995 No 418)	Article 10, and schedule 2, part 11 and schedule 2, part 17
Private Crossings (Signs and Barriers) Regulations 1996(SI 1996 No 1786)	Sections 52, 54 and 55
Level Crossings Regulations 1997 (SI 1997 No 487)	Regulation 3
Railway Safety (Miscellaneous Provisions) Regulations 1997 (SI 1997 No 553)	Regulations 2 and 3
Town and Country Planning (Scotland) Act 1997	Sections 1, 7, 9, 17, 25(1), 26A(1), 28, 37, 38(1), 41, 46, 47, 57(A), 75, 107, 108, 189, 202, 207 and 208
Transport Act 2000	Sections 108, 109, 113A and 113B.
Traffic Signs Regulations and General Directions 2002 (SI 2002 No 3113)	Regulations 10, 39, 40 and 52, and schedule 3
Land Reform (Scotland) Act 2003	Sections 1, 2, 5, 6, 10, 17(1), 20 and 32
Railway and Transport Safety Act 2003	Sections 3 and 16
Title Conditions (Scotland) Act 2003	Sections 90 and 122(1)
Planning and Compulsory Purchase Act 2004	Sections 3 and 38(6)
Railways Act 2005	Sections 2 and 46, and schedule 2, section 2, schedule 2 section 7, schedule 2 section 9, and schedule 3
Health and Safety (Enforcing Authority for Railways and Other Guided Transport Systems) Regulations 2006 (SI 2006 No 557)	Regulations 3 and 4(4)

LEGISLATION	KEY PROVISIONS
Planning etc (Scotland) Act 2006	Section 23
Railways and Other Guided Transport Systems (Safety) Regulations 2006 (SI 2006 No 599)	
Road Safety Act 2006	Sections 30 and 50(2)
Transport and Works (Applications and Objections Procedure) (England and Wales) Rules 2006 (SI 2006 No 1466)	Rules 9, 12, 14, 15 and 23
Transport and Works (Model Clauses for Railways and Tramways) Order 2006 (SI 2006 No 1954)	Clauses 2 and 13, and schedule 2
Transport and Works (Applications and Objections Procedure) (Scotland) Rules 2007 (SSI 2007 No 570)	
Transport and Works (Scotland) Act 2007	Sections 1, 2, 7, 9, 11, 13 and 23, and schedule 1
Planning Act 2008	Sections 14(1)(k), 33(2)(c), 118(9), 205, 206-223, 211, 216, 221 and 222
Town and Country Planning (Development Management Procedure) (Scotland) Regulations 2008 (SSI 2008 No 432)	Regulation 25 read with schedule 5, paragraph 9
Community Infrastructure Levy Regulations 2010 (SI 2010 No 948)	Section 216(d)-(f)
Equality Act 2010	Sections 20 and 149

APPENDIX B
TABLE OF CRIMINAL OFFENCES

B.1   The following table lists the main criminal offences relevant to level crossings.

OFFENCE	CONTRARY TO	PENALTY	GEOGRAPHICAL APPLICATION
Obstruction of a railway employee in the execution of his or her duty, or trespass upon the railway and refusal to leave when requested	Railway Regulation Act 1840, section 16	In Scotland, fine up to level 1 (£200); in England and Wales, fine up to level 3 (£1000)	GB
Failure to shut or fasten a gate or lower a barrier on a private level crossing	Railways Clauses Consolidation Act 1845, section 75	Fine up to level 3 (£1000)	England and Wales
Failure to shut or fasten a gate or lower a barrier on a private level crossing	Railways Clauses (Scotland) Consolidation Act 1845, section 68	Fine up to level 3 (£1000)	Scotland
Unlawfully and maliciously obstructing any railway, displacing rails, diverting points, hiding or removing signals, or anything to destroy engines or rolling stock	Malicious Damage Act 1861, section 35	Imprisonment up to life	England and Wales
Obstructing engines or carriages on railways	Malicious Damage Act 1861, section 36	On indictment, imprisonment up to two years and/or a fine; on summary, imprisonment up to six months and/or a fine of up to level 5 (£5000)	England and Wales
Unlawfully and maliciously obstructing any railway, displacing rails, diverting points, hiding or removing signals, or anything to endanger the safety of passengers or persons on the railway	Offences Against the Person Act 1861, section 32	Imprisonment up to life	England and Wales
Unlawfully or maliciously throwing any missile at a train to injure or endanger the safety of anyone on a train with intent to cause danger to passengers or persons on the railway	Offences Against the Person Act 1861, section 33	Imprisonment up to life	England and Wales
Endangering the safety of any person upon the railway	Offences Against the Person Act 1861, section 34	On indictment, imprisonment up to two years and/or a fine; on summary, imprisonment up to six months and/or a fine	England and Wales

OFFENCE	CONTRARY TO	PENALTY	GEOGRAPHICAL APPLICATION
Crossing the railway at an unauthorised point after being given a warning	Regulation of Railways Act 1868, section 23	Fine up to level 1 (£200)	GB
Trespass upon a railway and surrounding land provided a public warning is displayed at the nearest station	British Transport Commission Act 1949, section 55 (This is a private Act)	Fine up to level 3 (£1000)	GB
Throwing a missile at a train or railway equipment if the missile is likely to damage property or injure people	British Transport Commission Act 1949, section 56 (This is a private Act)	Fine up to level 3 (£1000)	GB
Causing death by dangerous driving on a road or other public place	Road Traffic Act 1988, section 1	Imprisonment up to 14 years; disqualification from driving for a minimum period of two years and mandatory endorsement of licence with 3-11 penalty points; mandatory order for disqualification from driving until offender passes an extended driving test	GB
Dangerous driving on a road or other public place	Road Traffic Act 1988, section 2	On indictment, imprisonment up to two years and/or a fine; on summary, imprisonment up to six months and/or a statutory maximum fine; on indictment or on summary, disqualification from driving for a minimum period of 12 months, mandatory endorsement of licence with 3-11 penalty points, and mandatory order for disqualification from driving until offender passes an extended driving test	GB
Causing death by careless driving on a road or other public place	Road Traffic Act 1988, section 2B	On indictment, imprisonment up to five years and/or a fine; on summary, imprisonment not exceeding 12 months (E&W) or 6 months (Scotland) and/or a fine; on indictment or on summary, obligatory disqualification from driving for a minimum period of 12 months and mandatory endorsement of licence with 3-11 penalty points	GB

OFFENCE	CONTRARY TO	PENALTY	GEOGRAPHICAL APPLICATION
Careless driving on a road or other public place	Road Traffic Act 1988, section 3	Fine up to level 5 (£5000); discretionary disqualification from driving; mandatory endorsement of licence with 3-9 penalty points	GB
Placing anything on a road or interfering with a vehicle or traffic equipment in such circumstances where it is dangerous to do so	Road Traffic Act 1988, section 22A	On indictment, imprisonment up to seven years and/or a fine; on summary, imprisonment up to six months and/or statutory maximum fine	England and Wales only (section 22A(6) of the 1988 Act)
Dangerous cycling on a road or other public place	Road Traffic Act 1988, section 28	Fine up to level 4 (£2,500)	GB
Careless cycling on a road or other public place	Road Traffic Act 1988, section 29	Fine up to level 3 (£1000)	GB
Driver of motor vehicle's failure to comply with an authorised traffic sign depicting a prohibition, restriction or requirement	Road Traffic Act 1988, section 36	Fine up to level 3 (£1000); discretionary disqualification from driving and mandatory endorsement of licence for failure to comply with those signs which are listed in regulation 10 of the Traffic Signs Regulations and General Directions 2002 (SI 2002 No 3113)	GB
Failure to comply with most regulations made under the Road Traffic Act 1988 or the Road Traffic Regulation Act 1984 - for example, failure to comply with regulation 52 of the Traffic Signs Regulations and General Directions 2002 (SI 2002 No 3113) which specifies a "red figure" sign that, when illuminated, requires pedestrians not to use a level crossing	Road Traffic Offenders Act 1988, section 91	Fine up to level 3 (£1000)	GB
Failure to comply with any requirements, restrictions or prohibitions shown on a sign on or near a private road or path near a place where the road or path crosses the railway	Transport and Works Act 1992, section 55	Fine up to level 3 (£1000)	GB

OFFENCE	CONTRARY TO	PENALTY	GEOGRAPHICAL APPLICATION
The railway operator has the power to make bye-laws relating to the railways	Railways Act 2005, section 46	Breach of a railway bye-law is a criminal offence, punishable by a fine up to level 3 (£1000)	GB
Malicious mischief: intentional or reckless destruction of or damage to property belonging to another person without that person's permission or consent	Scottish common law (This crime would be broadly equivalent to an offence under the Malicious Damage Act 1861)	At discretion of the court	Scotland
Reckless injury to persons and recklessly causing danger to persons	Scottish common law (This crime would be broadly equivalent to an offence under the Offences Against the Person Act 1861)	At discretion of the court	Scotland

APPENDIX C
GLOSSARY

AUTOMATIC FULL-BARRIER CROSSINGS

C.1 Full-barrier level crossings have barriers which when closed block the entire width of the highway/road. The main protection is provided by a combination of road traffic light signals, audible warning devices and the barriers. The lights and sirens are activated at a set time before the operation of the barriers. The operation of the barriers is initiated automatically as the train approaches, and the barriers are subsequently raised automatically when the train has passed.[1]

AUTOMATIC HALF BARRIER CROSSING (AHB)

C.2 A level crossing at which access is prevented by means of two half-barriers placed across the highway/road so that they block the flow of road traffic onto the crossing, but leaving an escape route for motorists who are already on the crossing when the barriers come down. The barriers automatically come down across the highway/road as a train approaches, and the barriers are subsequently raised automatically when the train has passed.[2] At this type of crossing, protection is also afforded by road traffic light signals and audible warning devices.

AUTOMATIC OPEN CROSSING, LOCALLY MONITORED (AOCL)

C.3 A level crossing without any form of barrier protection. Warnings to road vehicles and pedestrians are by road traffic light signals and audible warning devices only. The warning sequence is initiated automatically by the approach of a train, which will normally have to stop short of the crossing until the driver is sure that the warning devices are operating and the crossing is clear.[3] Train speeds are limited to 55 mph or less. If a second train is approaching, the lights continue to flash after the passage of the first train, an additional signal lights up, and the tone of the audible warning changes.

AUTOMATIC OPEN CROSSING, REMOTELY MONITORED (AOCR)

C.4 A level crossing which is very similar to an AOCL, except the crossing is not monitored by the train driver. At such crossings telephones connected to the railway signal box are available to enable users to check whether it is clear to cross.[4]

---

[1] http://www.networkrail.co.uk/aspx/5269.aspx (last visited 27 June 2010).

[2] http://www.networkrail.co.uk/aspx/5269.aspx (last visited 27 June 2010).

[3] http://www.networkrail.co.uk/aspx/5269.aspx (last visited 27 June 2010).

[4] Stanley Hall and Peter van der Mark, *Level Crossings* (2008) pp 57, 60.

NETWORK RAIL

C.5 Network Rail is a not-for-profit private company limited by guarantee although run according to the requirements of a public limited company. It is responsible for and owns the infrastructure (track, signals, bridges and stations) for the mainline network in Great Britain. Its stated purpose is to provide a safe, reliable and efficient railway for Britain.[5] It is funded by way of a network grant from the Department for Transport and Transport Scotland and access charges paid to it by train and freight operating companies, though in part train and freight operating companies are also funded from central government grants.[6] Its members represent the interests of the rail industry and the general public.

OFFICE OF RAIL REGULATION (ORR)

C.6 ORR was established under the Railways and Transport Safety Act 2003. It is the independent economic and safety regulator for railways. ORR is a non-ministerial government department, although it is held accountable through, and represented by, Department for Transport Ministers in Parliament. ORR has powers in the following general areas of regulation: railway safety; the occupational health and safety of railway employees; consumer protection; the licensing of operators; the granting of railway access rights; the ratification of network and service modifications referred to it by the Secretary of State, Scottish or Welsh Ministers; competition law; the approval of codes and rules for the rail industry; and the determination of certain disputes.[7] In relation to health and safety, ORR has both a policy and an enforcement role. Section 1(1) of the Level Crossings Act 1983 allows the Secretary of State to make an order "for the protection of those using the crossing"; in practice, these orders are made by officers of the ORR on behalf of the Secretary of State.

C.7 ORR has general duties to provide information, advice and assistance to the Secretary of State, Welsh and Scottish Ministers and the Office of Fair Trading.[8]

RAIL ACCIDENT INVESTIGATION BRANCH (RAIB)

C.8 The RAIB was established by the Railway and Transport Safety Act 2003.[9] The RAIB carries out the investigation of rail accidents and incidents involving a derailment or collision of rolling stock which result in the death of at least one person, serious injury to five or more persons, or extensive damage to rolling stock, the infrastructure or the environment. Although the RAIB forms part of the Department for Transport, it remains functionally independent. RAIB investigations are focused solely on safety improvement; the RAIB cannot apportion blame nor prosecute.

---

[5] Network Rail, *Our legal and financial structure* http://www.networkrail.co.uk/aspx/713.aspx (last visited 27 June 2010).

[6] Network Rail, *How we are regulated* http://www.networkrail.co.uk/aspx/717.aspx (last visited 27 June 2010).

[7] Office of Rail Regulation, *About ORR* http://www.rail-reg.gov.uk/server/show/nav.75 (last visited 27 June 2010).

[8] See, for example, Railways Act 1993, s 69(2) and (3). See also generally Halsbury's Law of England, vol 39(1A) (reissue) para 53.

[9] Railway and Transport Safety Act 2003, s 3.

C.9 RAIB recommendations aimed at industry parties are addressed to ORR for consideration and/or action. ORR in turn directs the RAIB's recommendations to the relevant industry party. ORR is required to provide full details of the consideration given to any recommendation within 12 months of the publication of the RAIB report in which the recommendation is contained.[10]

RAIL OPERATORS

C.10 The rail operator is the body which owns, operates and is responsible for maintaining the railway and its associated infrastructure. Rail operators mainly have duties in relation to the safety and maintenance of level crossings. They are often also the initiative-taker, in the sense of having a power to request that some other body exercise a power, for example, in relation to orders to stop up or divert a rail crossing under the Highways Act 1980.

RAIL SAFETY AND STANDARDS BOARD (RSSB)

C.11 RSSB is a not-for-profit private company limited by guarantee, whose members are drawn from the railway industry.[11] It was established in 2003. Its stated primary objective is:

> ...to lead and facilitate the Railway Industry's work to achieve continuous improvement in the health and safety performance of the railways in Great Britain and thus to facilitate the reduction of risk to passengers, employees and the affected public so far as is reasonably practicable, so aiding compliance by providers of railway services with their obligations under health and safety law.[12]

C.12 RSSB's key functions include the monitoring of risk, the collection and reporting of data relating to safety, and the provision of advice to the railway industry about safety, risk management and technical issues. It also manages a research and development programme (which concentrates on industry-wide and strategic matters) on behalf of the rail industry and the Government.[13]

RAILWAY SAFETY DIRECTORATE (HM RAILWAY INSPECTORATE)

C.13 Her Majesty's Railway Inspectorate was established in 1840 as a result of the Railway Regulation Act 1840. Since its establishment, it has existed under the auspices of various bodies, including the Health and Safety Commission/Executive (HSC/HSE) from 1990 to 2006. When the Railways Act 2005 transferred the HSE's railway safety functions to ORR, HM Railway Inspectorate (HMRI) was also transferred from the HSE to ORR.

---

[10] The roles and responsibilities of the RAIB and ORR are set out in the Railways (Accident Investigation and Reporting) Regulations 2005, SI 2005 No 1992.

[11] See Rail Safety Standards Board, *About Us*
http://www.rssb.co.uk/AboutUs/Pages/default.aspx (last visited 27 June 2010).

[12] *Constitution Agreement relating to the Rail Safety and Standards Board Limited* (1 April 2003) para 2.1. Available at:
http://www.rssb.co.uk/AboutUs/Pages/ConstitutionDocument.aspx (last visited 27 June 2010).

[13] See Rail Safety Standards Board, *A Guide to RSSB*
http://www.rssb.co.uk/AboutUs/Pages/a_guide.aspx (last visited 27 June 2010).

C.14   In May 2009, "HM Railway Inspectorate" ceased to exist when the Railway Safety Directorate was created within ORR. HMRI now forms part of that Directorate, although the individual inspectors are known as HM Inspectors of Railways.

C.15   The overall aim of the Railway Safety Directorate is to ensure that duty-holders in the railway industry manage health and safety risks effectively and thus comply with their statutory duties. The Directorate achieves this by conducting inspections and audits and by providing advice and guidance on how to comply with the law. In respect of enforcement, the Directorate can issue enforcement notices and, in England and Wales, prosecute duty holders.

TRAIN OPERATING COMPANIES (TOCS) AND FREIGHT OPERATING COMPANIES (FOCS)

C.16   Train operating companies and freight operating companies are those private companies that provide passenger and goods-carrying services on the railway. They are subject to the requirements of the Railways and Other Guided Transport Systems (Safety) Regulations 2006 (SI 2006 No 599) ("ROGS"). Although these companies are subject to general railway safety requirements (for example, the duty to obey railway signals), they do not have any specific powers or duties in relation to level crossings.

The Scottish Law Commission at work on the project: Professor George Gretton of the SLC (centre in yellow vest), Andrew Harvey HMRI (right) and David Whitmarsh HMRI (left) examine the automatic half-barrier level crossing (AHB) at Cornton on the Stirling to Perth line as a High Speed Train (HST) passes.

Photographer: Susan Sutherland, Project Manager, Scottish Law Commission.